AN INDEPENDENT STUDY GUIDE TO

Reading Latin

PETER V. JONES & KEITH C. SIDWELL

AN INDEPENDENT STUDY GUIDE TO

Reading Latin

CAMBRIDGE UNIVERSITY PRESS
Cambridge, New York, Melbourne, Madrid, Cape Town, Singapore, São Paulo, Delhi

Cambridge University Press
The Edinburgh Building, Cambridge CB2 8RU, UK

Published in the United States of America by Cambridge University Press, New York

www.cambridge.org
Information on this title: www.cambridge.org/9780521653732

First published 1979
Eighth printing 2008

Printed in the United Kingdom at the University Press, Cambridge

A catalogue record of this publication is available from the British Library

British Library of Congress Cataloguing in Publication data

Jones, P. V. (Peter V.)
    An independent study guide to reading Latin / Peter V. Jones & Keith C. Sidwell.
        p.   cm.
    ISBN 0 521 65373 8 (paperback)
        1. Latin language – Self-instruction. 2. Latin language – Readers.
        I. Sidwell, Keith C.   II. Title.
    PA2094.5.J66 2000   478'.68421–dc21 00–1025956

ISBN 978-0-521-65373-2 paperback

CONTENTS

PREFACE

This *Study Guide* provides translations, answers and reading hints for Peter Jones and Keith Sidwell's *Reading Latin* (*Text* and *Grammar, Vocabulary and Exercises*, Cambridge University Press, 1986). It is designed for two sorts of reader: those who are learning Latin rapidly and intensively, and those who are learning Latin on their own or with only limited access to a teacher.

There are two important features.

First, we believe it is important that there should be times when learners are out there on their own. Then again, teachers working with the book need some material which they know students cannot simply lift from this answer book. So the 'Reading/Test exercises' at the end of each grammatical section have *not* been translated. These test only what should have already been learned, and will provide compelling evidence of whether it has been or not. We recommend that those who are learning by themselves try to find someone who will correct these exercises. The exercises marked 'optional' have not been provided with a key either. These reinforce what should have been learned from the regular exercises. If teachers need to set them, then they also need to know that the answers are not easily available to students. Again, those who are learning alone will find it advisable to have a teacher check their answers to these exercises, if they have found it necessary to embark on them in order to reinforce earlier work.

Second, the translations of the *Text* intentionally vary in style, from the absolutely literal with English words in Latin word-order (in Sections 1 and 4) to the moderately colloquial. The purpose of these extremes is to force constant attention on the *Latin*. The literal, Latin-order translations, almost gibberish in English, achieve this one way ('What on earth does *that* mean? I'd better look at the Latin for clarification'); the moderately colloquial another way ('How on earth does the Latin mean *that?*').

Users of the course will find an index of *topics* dealt with in the *Text* volume listed section by section in *The World of Rome: An Introduction to Roman Culture*, Cambridge University Press 1997, ed. Peter Jones and Keith Sidwell, Appendix 3, pp. 347–52. This can be used in association with the other indexes to find information about Roman history, culture and literature. Those interested in pursuing the study of later Latin will find that *Reading Medieval Latin*, Keith Sidwell, Cambridge University Press 1995, is designed to give help to students who have reached the end of Section 5 of *Reading Latin*.

We express here our gratitude to Ken Dowden, Lorna Kellett, Sally Knights, Alison Lewis, Sarah Parnaby, Phillip Parr, Helen Price, David Tristram and Hilary Walters of the Joint Association of Classical Teachers' Latin Committee. They gave us permission to plunder their privately produced *Study Guide*. This did not deal with the *Text* or *Deliciae Latinae*, but gave the answers to most of the exercises in the *Grammar* etc., and offered other advice.

We are also grateful to Mark Humphries (National University of Ireland, Maynooth, Ireland), Cedric Littlewood (University of Victoria, Canada), Carmel McCallum-Barry (University College Cork, Ireland), David Miller (University of Bristol, UK) and David Woods (University College Cork, Ireland) for their help with testing this *Study Guide*.

Finally, we are more grateful than ever to our copy-editor Susan Moore, who did her usual superb job licking a chaotic manuscript into shape.

Peter Jones
28 Akenside Terrace
Newcastle upon Tyne NE2 1TN
UK

Professor Keith Sidwell
Department of Ancient Classics
University College Cork
Cork
Ireland

September 1999

GENERAL INTRODUCTION

PRELIMINARIES

THE COURSE

Peter V. Jones and Keith C. Sidwell, *Reading Latin* (Cambridge University Press 1986), comes in two volumes:

> *Text* = the (small) book, which contains a Latin text in six Sections (hereafter referred to as *Text*).
>
> *Grammar, Vocabulary and Exercises* = the (big) book which contains the Grammar, Vocabulary and Exercises, from now on called *GVE*. Note that the page numbers are at the foot of the page in *GVE*.

You need *both* volumes.

How Reading Latin *works*

Each Section of the Latin *Text* has a parallel Section in *GVE*, supplying new vocabulary, learning vocabulary, grammatical explanations and exercises, and *Deliciae Latinae*.

> **First** you read the *Text* with the help of the Vocabulary in *GVE*;
>
> **Then** you learn the Learning Vocabulary in *GVE*;
>
> **Finally** you work through the Grammar and Exercises in *GVE*.

The *Deliciae Latinae* sections are for amusement and are optional (though strongly recommended).

This Guide

This *Guide* supplies help under three headings:

NOTES to help you as you read the *Text* for the first time (these give help over and above the Vocabulary in *GVE*).

TRANSLATION of the *Text* and reading passages in *GVE* so that you can check that you have got them right.

ANSWERS to the *Exercises*.

TRANSLATIONS (where necessary) of the material in *Deliciae Latinae*.

But please note the following vital exceptions:

- We do *not* provide answers for those exercises marked *Optional* in *GVE*.
- After Section IA, we do *not* provide translations *either* of the Latin-into-English Reading/Test exercises *or* of the Latin-into-English part of the English–Latin exercises in *GVE*.

Your aims in using this course

- If you want to learn to read original Latin helped along, say, by a translation, translate all the reading passages in the *Text* and do all the exercises *not* marked *. This is the *minimum* you will need to achieve your aim.
- If you want to gain a detailed mastery of the language and perhaps take an examination, do all the exercises *including* those marked *.
- Whatever your answer, you should also try the English-into-Latin exercises (marked **). These are quite demanding, but are very good for the brain and will help your understanding of the language considerably.

Conventions

1. *V* and *U* are written *V* as capital, but *u* in lower case. So we write *QVIS* in capitals but *quis* in lower case (see p. xiv of *GVE*).
2. The *Text* and *GVE* mark the long vowels with ‾ (ma-

cron). The macron is there mainly to help your pronun-
ciation. Do not mark these macra when you write Latin.
Grammatical sections also print a stress accent (e.g. *ámas*).
See **GVE** p. xv for an explanation of the rules of stress.

3. The following abbreviations are used:

   masc. *or* m. = masculine; fem. *or* f. = feminine; neut. *or*
   n. = neuter; sing. *or* s. = singular; pl. = plural; nom. =
   nominative; acc. = accusative; gen. = genitive; dat. =
   dative; abl. = ablative; subj. = subject; obj. = object.

For the full list of abbreviations used in **GVE**, see **GVE** p. xiii.

SIMPLIFIED GRAMMATICAL INTRODUCTION

Grammar systematically describes how a language works. It uses
technical terms to do so. If you have previously learnt languages
in a formal way, you will already know many of these terms.
If, however, you are unfamiliar with grammatical terms, you will
need some help with them.

1. There is an alphabetical *Glossary of English–Latin Grammar*
   in **GVE** pp. xvii–xxiii, but it is designed for reference
   purposes, and you will find simpler explanations of specific
   points as you meet them during the course.
2. If you have a tutor, or if you know someone who knows
   Latin or another language in a grammatical way, you may
   find it helpful to ask them to explain any problems as they
   arise.
3. This *Simplified Introduction* is designed to lead you towards
   an initial understanding of the way Latin works and what
   lies ahead. Regard it as a supplement to the *Glossary* in
   GVE. It is intentionally light in tone. If you already know
   how languages work, skip it.

A. THE VITAL PARTS OF SPEECH

A NOUN names somebody or something, whether con-
crete or abstract – *table, chair, speed, thought, Nigel.*

A PRONOUN stands for a noun: not Tom but *he*, not Jessica but *she*, not table but *it*. So, e.g. *I, me, you, they* and so on.

An ADJECTIVE tells you about ('qualifies') a noun – a *smart* table, a *comfy* chair, *terrific* speed, *instant* thought, a *brilliant* boy, a *brainy* girl.

A VERB expresses an action – I *jump*, she *runs*, he *thinks*, we *find*; or a state – I *am*, it *is*, they *remain*.

For the three other main parts of speech, which present no difficulties in Latin, see *adverb*, *conjunction*, and *preposition* in the *Glossary*.

B. CASE IN ENGLISH

Consider the following sentence:

Nasty Brutus kills nice Caesar.

Now do the analysis:

Nouns? *Brutus* and *Caesar.*
Adjectives? *Nasty* and *nice.*
Verb? *Kills.*

Now: we call the do-er of the action the *subject*, the person on the receiving end the *object*. Thus 'Paul loves Philippa' – Paul subject, Philippa object (the object of Paul's love).

So do a further analysis:

Who is the subject? Brutus.
And the object? Caesar.

Now check you understand subjects (doing the action) and objects (on the receiving end) by defining subject and object in the following sentences:

1. Romulus founded Rome.
2. Scipio defeated Hannibal.
3. We see the men.
4. The cat eats the food.
5. I like toffee-apples.

Answers: *subjects* Romulus, Scipio, we, the cat, I; *objects* Rome, Hannibal, men, food, toffee-apples.

How do we know that Brutus is nasty, Caesar nice?
Answer: because Brutus comes next to 'nasty', Caesar next to 'nice'.

Correct. How do we know Brutus is killing Caesar and not vice versa?
Answer: because Brutus comes first in the sentence.

Correct. Would 'Nasty Caesar kills nice Brutus' mean something quite different?
Answer: it would indeed.

And how do we know?
Answer: because of the word-order.

Conclusion?
Word-*order* controls meaning in English.

C. CASE IN LATIN

Try this:

> The Latin for 'kills' is *necat*.
> The Latin for 'Brutus' (subject) is *Brutus*.
> The Latin for 'Caesar' (subject) is *Caesar*.
> The Latin for 'Brutus' (object) is *Brutum*.
> The Latin for 'Caesar' (object) is *Caesarem*.

(**NB** these different forms are called C A S E S.)

Now check you are quite sure what a subject and an object are.

Now write the Latin for:

1. 'Brutus kills Caesar.'
2. 'Caesar kills Brutus.'

We confidently predict that you have written:

1. *Brutus necat Caesarem.*
2. *Caesar necat Brutum.*

Question: if you had written those identical Latin words but in a different order, e.g.

1. *Caesarem necat Brutus.*
2. *Brutum necat Caesar.*

would the meaning have been altered?

No.

Why not?

Because *Brutus* and *Caesar* announce 'subject' *wherever* they occur in the sentence; and *Brutum* and *Caesarem* announce 'object' *wherever* they occur in the sentence.

So you can put the words of those two sentences in any *order* you like and, as long as you do not change the *forms*, they will still mean the same thing. Here, then, is a challenge. If, by putting the words in a different order, you can make the words *Brutus necat Caesarem* mean anything other than 'Brutus kills Caesar', let us know. Single-handed, you will have destroyed the Latin language.

Conclusion?

Word-*form* controls meaning in Latin, not word-*order*, as in English.

One final step. Those adjectives.

> 'Nasty' (subject) in Latin is *horribilis*.
> 'Nice' (subject) is *benignus*.
> 'Nasty' (object) in Latin is *horribilem*.
> 'Nice' (object) is *benignum*.

Now add these to the two sentences, according to taste.

You might come up with:

> *horribilis Caesar necat benignum Brutum.*
> 'Nasty Caesar kills nice Brutus.'

But again, you could put those words in any order, and the sentence would still mean the same.

Try for example:

> *necat benignum horribilis Caesar Brutum.*

In English word-order, that comes out:

'Kills nice nasty Caesar Brutus'.

This observation has little to recommend it. To a Roman, however, it would be crystal-clear, because word *order* is irrelevant: the *form* of each word announces its function (subject or object) with absolute clarity.

Thus at *necat* a Roman would register 'x kills y.'
At *benignum* a Roman would register 'x kills nice y.'
At *horribilis* 'Nasty x kills nice y.'
At *Brutum* 'Nasty x kills nice Brutus.'
At *Caesar* 'Nasty Caesar kills nice Brutus.'

A correction. We said above that English 'does not have cases'. But we say 'She loves him', not 'She loves he', so we do have a small case system.

ADVICE

If you find A–C above difficult to understand, do not despair. You may find the early stages of Latin difficult, but one learns by doing. Peter Jones' *Learn Latin* (Duckworth 1997), based on a newspaper series, is a brief, light-hearted introduction to absolute basics and may prove useful in getting you over the first hurdle.

D. INFLECTION

What we have been dealing with above is *inflections*.

'Inflection' means the way words change to express different meanings. Consider *king* (one of them), *kings* (lots of them), *king's* (belonging to the king), *kings'* (belonging to the kings); or *he*, *him*, *his* (singular), *they*, *them*, *theirs* (plural). English is not a heavily inflected language. *Latin is very heavily inflected indeed.* Latin nouns, pronouns, adjectives and verbs (as we have seen) change their shape all the time to express different meanings. This is *the* major difference between Latin and English.

Terms

The way a Latin noun or adjective changes shape is called a 'declension' (such words 'decline'). Decline *Brutus* and you start *Brutus Brutum...*

The way a Latin verb changes shape is called a 'conjugation' (such words 'conjugate').

Example

English conjugates the verb 'to kill' as follows: *I kill, you kill, he/she/it kills; we kill, you kill, they kill. Kill* hardly changes: we just add the pronouns *I* etc. to change the person.

Latin conjugates 'to kill' as follows: *neco, necas, necat; necamus, necatis, necant.* Every word here is different. But how are they different?

Get out the magnifying-glass and look more closely. Every word here has a base or STEM *nec-* 'kill' on to which different ENDINGS (indicating the person) are attached. Here stands revealed LATIN'S GREAT SECRET – it is all about UNCHANGING STEMS and CHANGING ENDINGS.

Latin nouns and adjectives as well as verbs all work in this way, as we have seen – *Brut-us, Brut-um, horribil-is, horribil-em,* etc.: same stem, different endings.

SEMI-FINAL SUGGESTIONS

If you are studying the course with the help of a tutor, even if infrequently, you will be able to discuss points with him/her and perhaps get written work corrected. If you are working entirely on your own, however, you may find some problems difficult to solve.

- Find someone who knows Latin and who can discuss the difficulty with you.
- Try to study the course together with someone else, even if he/she is a beginner too; talking things through may help to solve difficulties.

- If you really cannot solve a problem, try reading ahead and coming back to the difficult passage in a day or so.
- Always make sure that you have read the grammar sections thoroughly and used all the vocabulary help given.
- Try the *Total Vocabularies* at the back of **GVE** (beginning p. 557) and look up points you find difficult in the *Index* (p. 602). You may find references to alternative explanations there which are more helpful.
- Always reread earlier texts when you feel new material getting on top of you. It will boost confidence ('Why did I find it difficult?') and give some pleasurable revision at the same time.

If you live in the UK, the Joint Association of Classical Teachers maintains an up-to-date list of Latin tutors who are willing to help you in person, over the telephone or by post. For this Postal Tutors' List, contact:

The Secretary, J A C T, Institute of Classical Studies, Senate House, Malet Street, London WC1E 7HU.

If you live in Ireland (Republic), write to the Classical Association of Ireland, c/o The Department of Classics, University College Dublin, Dublin 4, and ask for the name of a contact in your area.

AND FINALLY...

Section 1 of *Reading Latin* is based on a play by Plautus, *Aulularia* ('The Pot of Gold'). Although the text is heavily adapted, you may find it useful to read the play in translation to get a general idea of the story. There is one available in the Penguin Classics series.

Do not try to do too much at once. When learning any language it is best to work on the principle of 'little and often' (especially 'often').

Section One
Plautus' Aulularia

INTRODUCTION: *familia Euclionis*
(*Text pp. 2–3*)

PREAMBLE

1. The English translation of the whole of Section 1 is word-for-word, in the Latin word-order. Where English uses more words than Latin, hyphens are used, e.g. *amat*, 'he-loves', *serui*, 'of-the-slave'. If the strange word-order makes the English ambiguous, the Latin will solve the problem.
2. Latin does not have a word for 'the' or 'a'.
3. In English, verbs in a question do not take the same form as verbs in a statement. Compare 'you are' and 'are you?' and 'you carry' and 'do you carry?' This is not the case in Latin, which uses exactly the same form of the verb in statements and questions. In this Section we have translated all Latin verbs as statements, e.g. *quid est?* 'What it-is?'
4. Explanations of the translation are given [in square brackets].
5. Latin *Text* line numbers are given in the translation thus, [**5**].

NOTES FOR INTRODUCTION

Page 2

If you have read the *General Introduction* (pp. 5–7) of this volume, you will be looking keenly for subjects and objects. You will find plenty of subjects in this Section, but no objects (objects come in Section 1A). What you will find is the verb 'to be'. This does not control an object but a *complement*.

Consider: 'Euclio is an old man.' 'Euclio' subject, 'is' verb, 'an old man' – what is 'an old man'? 'An old man' *describes* 'Euclio'. 'An old man' is the *complement* to Euclio with the verb 'to be'. 'Euclio' is subject, in the nominative case. 'An old man', the complement, is therefore in the nominative case as well, to show he is the same person as Euclio. 'An old man', as we say, 'agrees' with Euclio.

Rule: the verb 'to be' takes the nominative case before and after (usually the subject before, the complement after, in English).

1   *quis es tu*: *quis* means 'who?', *es* means 'you are' and *tu* means '*you*', very emphatically. Latin adds *tu* only when it wants to emphasise the '*you*'. *es* on its own means 'you are', unemphasised. Compare *ego sum Euclio* and *ego sum Phaedra*, where *ego* 'I' is very emphatic, '*I* am ...', with *senex sum* 'I am an old man'.

           senex sum: note that Latin word-order is not the same as English. In particular, the Latin verb often comes late in the sentence compared with English, e.g. *senex sum* 'an-old-man I-am', i.e. 'I am an old man'. *senex* is the complement.

3   *filia Euclionis sum*: observe that *Euclio* becomes *Euclionis* when it means 'of Euclio'. *filia Euclionis* is the complement.

4   *Staphyla sum*: *Staphyla* is the complement.

5   *familia Euclionis*: the complement.

Page 3

1   *pater Phaedrae*: note that *Phaedra* becomes *Phaedrae* when it means 'of Phaedra', cf. *Euclio*, *Euclionis* above.

2   *filia Euclionis*: the complement.

3   *serua Euclionis est*: the subject is 'she', understood, and in-

cluded in, *est. serua* is the complement: thus 'she is the slave-woman of Euclio'.

4   *senex auarus*: complement. Latin says 'an old man greedy', English 'a greedy old man'. In Latin, adjectives often follow their nouns.

5   *cum filia*: in cases like this, sense requires that we translate 'with *his* daughter' rather than 'with the/a daughter'.

    est: when *est* begins a sentence, it usually means 'there is'; cf. l. 7 *sunt* 'there are'.

    et: *et* means 'and' when it joins two things together. Here it means 'too', 'also'.

TRANSLATION OF INTRODUCTION

Introduction: The-household of-Euclio.

Who you-are *you*? *I* I-am Euclio. An-old-man I-am.
Who you-are *you*? *I* I-am Phaedra. The-daughter of-Euclio I-am.
[4] Who you-are *you*? Staphyla I-am, the-slave-woman of-Euclio.
Who you-are [pl.]? The-household of-Euclio we-are.

The-play's characters
Euclio: Euclio the-old-man he-is, father of-Phaedra.
Phaedra: Phaedra the-daughter of-Euclio she-is.
Staphyla: the-slave-woman of-Euclio she-is.

Euclio an-old-man he-is. Euclio an-old-man greedy he-is. Euclio in the-house he-lives [5] with his-daughter. The-daughter of-Euclio Phaedra she-is. There-is also a-slave-woman in the-house. The slave-woman's name it-is Staphyla.

    Euclio's household in the-house it-lives. There-are in the-household of-Euclio the-head-of-the-family, and Phaedra the-daughter of-Euclio, and Staphyla the-slave-woman. All in the-house they-live.

Now learn the Learning Vocabulary at *GVE* p. 1.

EXERCISES FOR INTRODUCTION

Page 4

Morphology

1   you (s.)* are = *es*; there are = *sunt*; he is = *est*; there is = *est*; you
    (pl.)* are = *estis*; they are = *sunt*; it is = *est*; I am = *sum*; she is = *est*.

Note: * (s.) means singular, (pl.) means plural.

2   *sum* = I am, *sumus* = we are; *sunt* = they are, *est* = he is; *estis* = you
    (pl.) are, *es* = you (s.) are; *est* = he/she/it is *or* there is, *sunt* = they
    are *or* there are; *sumus* = we are, *sum* = I am; *es* = you (s.) are,
    estis = you (pl.) are.

Reading

(a)   It's the household.
(b)   The slave-girl is Staphyla.
(c)   For the pot is full of gold.
(d)   The cook is a slave.
(e)   Phaedra is the daughter.
(f)   In the house (there) are Euclio, Phaedra and the slave-girl.
(g)   The old man is a miser.
(h)   Near the river there is a small field.

**English–Latin

(a)   There are, in the household Euclio, Phaedra, [and] Staphyla.
      est in familia serua.

(b)   Euclio and Phaedra are in the house.
      serua in aedibus est.

(c)   I am Euclio.
      es seruus/serua.

(d)   Euclio's daughter is Phaedra.
      serua Euclionis Staphyla est.

(e)   Who are you? (s.)
      Euclio sum.

(f)   Who are you? (pl.)
      Euclio et Phaedra sumus.

I A (Text pp. 3–6)

NOTES FOR I A

Page 4

14   *seruus intrat . . . stat et clamat*: 'slave' is the stated subject of
      the first sentence with a third-person verb *intrat* 'he enters'
      (i.e. 'the slave enters'). No new subject is introduced in the
      second sentence. So we can assume the third-person verbs
      stat et clamat have *seruus* as their subject.

15   *seruam uocat*: *serua* indicates the subject of the sentence (the
      slave-woman is doing something); *seruam*, as here, indicates
      that the slave-woman is the object of the sentence, i.e. she
      is not doing anything, but is on the *receiving end* of the
      verb, 'he calls the slave-woman'. In English, subjects tend
      to come first in a sentence (here 'he'), then the verb
      ('calls'), then the object ('slave-woman'). Latin word-order
      is much more flexible (see *General Introduction* and **GVE 6**
      pp. 9–11).

16   *te*: 'you', object; *tu* is the subject form.

17   *me*: 'me', object; *ego* is the subject form.

22   *non aperis*: lit. 'not you open', where English says 'you do
      not open'. Observe that Latin has omitted 'it', referring to
      the door *ianua*.

31   *Daue*: 'O Davus', the so-called vocative case. See **GVE 9**
      p. 13.

      otiosi: compare l. 25, *tu . . . otiosus es*. The form *otiosi* refers
      to more than one person.

Page 5

36   *enim*: 'for', 'because'. This word never comes first in Latin,
      but always does in English.

45   *plenae*: 'full'. The form *plenae* is plural; compare *plena* l. 42,
      singular.

coquorum et tibicinarum: the forms meaning '*of* cooks and pipe-girls', cf. the subject forms *coqui, tibicinae* in l. 46.

46   *cuncti*: 'all', masculine, plural. Compare *cuncta* feminine, singular 'the whole', l. 43.

51–52   *nullum . . . nullam*: note that *nullum* is masculine, *nullam* feminine. See **GVE 14** pp. 22–3. Note that Latin omits 'and' from this list.

56   *coronamque*: *que* attached to the end of a noun is the same as *et* in front of it, i.e. *coronamque = et coronam*. Observe how we indicate this in the translation ('garland/and').

Page 6

67   *saluum . . . saluus*: *saluum* is neuter, *saluus* masculine, cf. **Text** p. 5, ll. 51–2.

TRANSLATION OF 1A

The-play's characters
[10] Demaenetus: Demaenetus an-old-man he-is, Euclio's grandfather.
Slave: the-slave's name it-is Davus.
Slave-woman: the-slave-woman's name it-is Pamphila.
Cook and pipe-girl.

> (*The-slave onto the-stage he-enters. Before the-door of-Demaenetus he-stands and he-shouts. Why* [15] *he-shouts? He-shouts because the-slave-woman he-calls*)

SLAVE
     Hey, Pamphila! *I* Davus you I-call.
SLAVE-WOMAN
     Who me he/she-calls? Who he/she-shouts?
SL.   *I* Davus you I-call.
SL.-W.   What it-is? Why me you-call?
     [20] (*The-slave to the-door he-approaches, but the-door shut it-is. The-slave therefore the-door he-knocks-at*)
SL.   Hey *you*, slave-woman! *I* the-door I-knock-at, but *you* not you-open: the-door closed it-is.

SL.-W. (*the-door she-opens*) Why you-shout? *I* here and there I-run-about, *you* however [25] you-shout. *I* busy I-am, *you* however idle you-are. A-slave not you-are, but a-rascal.

SL. *I* idle not I-am, Pamphila. For today Demaenetus, master my, his-daughter in marriage he-gives: the-marriage-rites of-his-daughter they-are [i.e. it's the marriage].

[30] (*Demaenetus, the-master of-the-slave and of-the-slave-woman, onto the-stage he-enters*)

DEMAENETUS

Why you-shout, Davus and Pamphila? Why you-stand [i.e. about, doing nothing]? Why idle you-are? For today the-marriage-rites of-daughter my they-are. Why not into the-house you-enter and the-marriage-rites you-prepare?

(*Into the-house there-enter the-slave and the-slave-woman, and the-marriage-rites they-prepare. Onto the-stage there-enter the-cook* [35] *and the-pipe-girl. Demaenetus the-cook and the-pipe-girl he-sees*)

DEM. Hey *you*, who you-are? *I* for/because [first word] you not I-recognise.

COOK AND PIPE-GIRL

The-cook and the-pipe-girl we-are. To the-marriage-rites of-daughter your we-come.

DEM. Why not into house my you-enter and the-marriage-rites you-prepare?

[40] (*The-cook and the-pipe-girl into the-house of-Demaenetus they-enter*)

(*Demaenetus a-garland and ointment he-carries. A-pot also he-carries. The-pot of-gold full it-is*)

DEM. Alas! Today the-marriage-rites of-daughter my I-prepare. The-whole household it-hurries. Here and there there-run-about boys and girls, *I* cooks and pipe-girls [45] I-call. Now the-house full it-is [lit. 'are' because *aedes* is pl.] of-cooks and of-pipe-girls, and all cooks and pipe-girls thieves they-are. Alas! A-man lost I-am, more-precisely, most-lost of-men. For a-pot I-have of-gold full. Look! The-pot I-carry. (*The-old-man the-pot he-reveals*) Now the-pot under my-clothes I-secrete. For very-much I-am-afraid. Gold [50] for/because [first word] gives-off-a-smell; and thieves

gold they-sniff-out. Gold however not it-gives-off-a-
smell, if under the-earth it-lies-hidden. If the-gold under
the-earth it-lies-hidden, no cook no pipe-girl no thief I-
fear. The-pot therefore secretly under the-earth I-secrete.
Anyone me he/she-sees?
(*Demaenetus he-looks-around. No-one is-present. Demaenetus
therefore no-one he-sees*)
[55] Good. Alone I-am. But first to the-Lar I-approach and
the-ointment garland/and I-give, and I-pray.
(*To the-Lar he-approaches. The-ointment he-gives and the-
garland. Then to-the-Lar he-prays*)
O Lar, guardian of-my household, you I-beg and I-
beseech. *I* you always I-garland, always to-you ointment I-
give, always sacrifice and [60] respect. *You* in-return good
Luck you-give. Now to you the-pot of-gold full I-carry.
Under my-clothes however the-pot I-secrete. The-
household about the-pot it-is-ignorant. But today there-
are the-marriage-rites of-my-daughter. Full it-is [lit. 'are']
the-house of-cooks and of-pipe-girls. More-precisely, of-
thieves full it-is. The-gold it-gives-off-a-smell. *I* therefore
thieves I-fear. O Lar, you I-beg and I-beseech. [65] The-
pot protect!
(*The-old-man to the-hearth he-approaches. Near the-hearth a-
hole there-is. In the-hole the-pot he-secretes*)
Look. Safe the-gold it-is, safe also *I*. Now for/because [first
word] *you* the-pot you-have, Lar.

Now learn the Learning Vocabulary at *GVE* p. 7.

EXERCISES FOR I A

Page 9

Morphology

1   *celo, celas, celat, celamus, celatis, celant; timeo, times, timet, timemus, timetis,
timent; porto, portas, portat, portamus, portatis, portant; habeo, habes, habet,
habemus, habetis, habent.*

Note: we do not answer the *optional* sections.

2   *clamas* you (s.) shout, *clamatis*; *habent* they have, *habet*; *intrat* he enters, *intrant*; *uoco* I call, *uocamus*; *sumus* we are, *sum*; *portamus* we carry, *porto*; *times* you (s.) fear, *timetis*; *habetis* you (pl.) have, *habes*; *est* he is, *sunt*; *timet* he fears, *timent*; *uocant* they call, *uocat*; *celatis* you (pl.) hide, *celas*; *timemus* we fear, *timeo*; *habeo* I have, *habemus*; *sunt* they are, *est*.

3   you (pl.) have = *habetis*; I do hide = *celo*; we are carrying = *portamus*; they call = *uocant*; you (s.) are afraid of = *times*; she is dwelling = *habitat*; there are = *sunt*; it has = *habet*; there enters = *intrat*; she is = *est*.

Page 13

Exercises

1   *coquus, coquum, coqui, coquo, coquo, coqui, coquos, coquorum, coquis, coquis; aula, aulam, aulae, aulae, aula, aulae, aulas, aularum, aulis, aulis.*

Note: we do not answer the *optional* sections.

2   *seruarum* = gen. pl.; *coquo* = dat./abl. sing.; *coronam* = acc. sing.; *seruos* = acc. pl.; *scaenae* = gen./dat. sing. *or* nom. pl.; *filiā* = abl. sing. (NB *filia* = nom. sing.); *coquus* = nom. sing.; *serui* = gen. sing. *or* nom. pl.; *coquum* = acc. sing.; *filiae* = gen./dat. sing. *or* nom. pl.; *scaenas* = acc. pl.; *seruo* = dat./abl. sing.; *coquorum* = gen. pl.; *aula* = nom. sing. (NB *aulā* = abl. sing.); *seruis* = dat./abl. pl.

3(a)   I am a slave.   *sumus serui.*
 (b)   I carry a pot.   *aulas portamus.*
 (c)   They have garlands.   *coronam habet.*
 (d)   The slave-girl fears the slave.   *seruae timent seruos.*
 (e)   You call the slave-girls.   *seruam uocas.*
 (f)   The slave-girls carry the pots.   *serua aulam portat.*
 (g)   We hide the pots.   *celo aulam.*
 (h)   The cooks hide the slave-girls.   *seruam celat coquus.*
 (i)   The household has a garland.   *familiae coronas habent.*
 (j)   The slave calls the slave-girl.   *uocant serui seruas.*

If you have made any mistakes, first check the endings of the nouns to see if they are **nominative** (subject) or **accusative** (object).

Page 14

Exercise

onto the stage = *in scaenam* (acc. because movement towards); in the
pot = *in aulā* (abl. because position); onto the garlands = *in coronas*; into
the pots = *in aulas*; in the household = *in familiā*; towards the slave-
woman = *ad seruam*; in the slaves = *in seruis*; towards the daughter = *ad
filiam*.

Pages 15–17

Reading exercise

1(a)   The slave enters [onto] the stage. He [the slave] carries garlands.
 (b)   The cooks are in the house. They [the cooks] call the slave-
        women.
 (c)   A slave-woman is in Euclio's household. She [the slave-woman]
        is Staphyla.
 (d)   Onto the stage enters Demaenetus. He [Demaenetus] has a pot
        full of gold.
 (e)   The cook and the slave-woman are shouting. For they [the cook
        and the slave-woman] fear the slave.

*2(a)   *aulam* (obj.) *seruus* (subj.)
        'The slave -s the pot' (Latin verb -*t*, e.g. *portat*).

 (b)   *serua* (subj.) *coronam* (obj.), *aulam* (obj.) *seruus* (subj.)
        'The slave-woman -s the garland, the slave the pot' (-*t*, e.g.
        habet).

 (c)   *seruas* (obj.) *serui* (subj.)
        'The slaves – the slave-women' (-*nt*, e.g. *uocant*).

 (d)   *familia* (subj.) *coquos* (obj.)
        'The household -s the cooks' (-*t*, e.g. *timet*).

 (e)   *Lar* (subj.) *seruos* (obj.)
        'The Lar -s the slaves' (-*t*, e.g. *uocat*).

 (f)   *aurum* (subj.?obj.?) *ego* (subj. – therefore *aurum* obj.)
        'I – the gold' (-*o*, e.g. *habeo*).

 (g)   *Euclio* (subj.) *familiam* (obj.)
        'Euclio -s the household' (-*t*, e.g. *timet*).

(h) *aulas* (obj.) *auri-plenas* (obj., with *aulas*) *et coronas* (obj.) *seruae* (subj.)
'The slave-women – the pots full of gold and the garlands' (*-nt*, e.g. *portant*).

*3(a) And now the sun (subj.) had stretched out (verb) all the hills (obj.),
And now [= the sun] was dropped (verb) <u>into</u> (prep.) <u>the western bay</u>;
At last he (subj.) rose (verb) and twitched (verb) his mantle blue (obj.):
Tomorrow <u>to</u> (prep.) <u>fresh woods and pastures new</u>.

(b) Still green [= altar] <u>with</u> (prep.) <u>bays</u> each ancient Altar (subj.) stands (verb),
<u>Above</u> (prep.) the reach of sacrilegious hands;
[= Altar] Secure <u>from</u> (prep.) <u>Flames</u>, <u>from</u> (prep.) <u>Envy's fiercer rage, Destructive War</u>, and all-involving <u>Age</u>.
See (verb) <u>from</u> (prep.) <u>each clime</u> the learn'd (subj.) their incense (obj.) bring (verb)!

4 Demaenetus sees the cooks and pipe-girls. They are coming to his daughter's wedding. They enter the house of Demaenetus and prepare the wedding. Now the house of Demaenetus is full of cooks and pipe-girls. But Demaenetus is afraid. For he has a pot full of gold. For if the pot full of gold is in Demaenetus' house, Demaenetus is very afraid of thieves. Demaenetus hides the pot. Now the gold is safe. Now Demaenetus is safe. Now the pot is safe. For the Lar has the pot full of gold. Now the pot lies hidden near the Lar under the ground. Therefore Demaenetus now approaches the Lar and prays. 'O Lar, I, Demaenetus, call on you. O protector of my household, I bring to you my pot full of gold. My daughter's wedding is today. But I fear thieves. For my house is full of thieves. I beg and beseech you, protect* Demaenetus's pot full of gold.'

*Here imperative of *seruo*; in another context it could be abl. sing. of *serua*, 'slave-woman'.

**English–Latin*

(a) The cook carries Demaenetus' pot.
seruus coronas coquorum habet.

(b) You are shouting but I am carrying the pots.
serua timet. ego igitur coquum uoco.

(c) Why is the stage full of slaves?
cur aedes plenae sunt coquorum?

(d) I, the Lar, call you. Why do you fear me?
ego Phaedra intro. cur aulam celatis?

(e) If he has gold, Demaenetus is afraid.
si aulam celant, serui timent.

(f) It is garlands and pots the slaves are carrying.
coquum et seruam uocat Demaenetus.

I B *(Text pp. 6–8)*

NOTES FOR IB

Page 7

76 *Euclio . . . senex*: 'Euclio is not a good old man'. The position of *bonus* is emphatic, cf. 79–80 *filiam habet* <u>*bonam*</u>.

83 *nullam . . . filia*: 'daughter' is the subject, 'dowry' the object.

100 *me miserum*: 'Me unhappy!' 'Misery me!' Exclamations are often expressed through the accusative case.

Page 8

111–12 *curas . . . multas*: 'many cares'.

125–6 *plenae . . . aedes*: 'rich men's houses [subject] are full [complement] of many thieves'.

TRANSLATION OF IB

(*Euclio on the-stage he-sleeps. While he-sleeps, the-Lar onto the-stage he-enters and the-story* [**70**] *he-explains*)

LAR

Spectators, *I* I-am the-Lar of-the-household. The-god I-am of-the-household of-Euclio. Look, Euclio's house.

There-is in the-house of-Euclio treasure great. The-
treasure it-is of-Demaenetus, the-grandfather of-Euclio.
But the-treasure in a-pot it-is and beneath the-earth it-
lies-hidden. *I* for/because [first word] the-pot secretly in
the-house [75] I-protect. Euclio about the-treasure he-is-
ignorant. Why the-treasure secretly so-far I-protect? The-
story I-explain. Euclio not good he-is an-old-man, but
greedy and wicked. Euclio therefore not I-love. Besides,
Euclio me not he-looks-after. To-me never he-prays.
Ointment never he-gives, no garlands, no respect. But
Euclio a-daughter he-has [80] good. For there-looks-after
me Phaedra, Euclio's daughter, and much respect, much
ointment, many garlands she-gives. Phaedra therefore,
good daughter of-Euclio, very-much I love. But Euclio
poor he-is. No therefore dowry there-has the-daughter.
For the-old-man about the-pot of-his-grandfather he-is-
ignorant. Now however, because Phaedra good she-is,
the-pot of-gold [85] full to-Euclio I-give. For Euclio in a-
dream I-visit and the-pot I-reveal. Look, spectators.
(*Euclio he-sleeps. The-Lar the-vision of-his-grandfather onto the-
stage he-leads. Euclio he-is-astonished*)

EUCLIO

I-sleep or I-am-awake? Gods great! The-vision I-see of-
grandfather my, Demaenetus. Hullo, Demaenetus! Alas!
How-much changed [90] from that [former self] ... from
the-dead evidently into the-house he-enters. Look! A-pot
Demaenetus he-carries. Why a-pot you-carry, Demaenetus? Look! There-looks-round Demanetus and himself-
with he-mutters. Now to the-altar of-the-Lar he-hurries.
What you-do, Demaenetus? A-hole he-makes and in the-
hole the-pot he-places. Amazing by-Hercules it-is. What
however in the-pot there-is? Gods [95] great! The-pot of-
gold full it-is.

DEMAENETUS' VISION

Good. Now gold my safe it-is.

EUC.   Not I-believe, Demaenetus. No in the-house gold there-
is. The-dream false it-is. Poor *I* I-am and poor I-remain.
        [100] Alas, me unhappy. *I* I-am most-done-for of-men.
Poor I-am, but the-gods false dreams they-reveal. Grand-

father my in the-dream I-see. My-grandfather a-pot of-gold full he-carries. The-pot beneath the-earth secretly he-places next-to the-Lar. Not however I-believe. The-dream false it-is. Why the-Lar me not he-cares-for? Why me he-deceives?

[105] (*Euclio to the-Lar he-approaches. Suddenly however the-hole he-sees. Euclio quickly much earth from the-hole he-moves. At-length the-pot it-appears*)

EUC. What you-have, O Lar? What under your-feet you-keep? What's-this? A-pot I-see. Clearly the-dream true it-is. (*Euclio the-pot from the-hole he-moves. Inside he-looks and the-gold he-sees. He-is-amazed*)

[110] Hoorah! Yippee! Gold I-possess! Not I-am poor, but rich! But however by-Hercules a-man rich cares always he-has many. Thieves into his-house secretly they-enter. O me unhappy! Now thieves I-fear, because much money I-possess. Alas! How the-Lar me he-annoys. Today for/ because [*first word*] to-me much money, many at-the-same-time [115] cares he-gives; today therefore most-done-for of-men I-am.

What then? Ha! Good a-plan I-have. Anyone me he/she-sees? (*Euclio the-gold beneath his-clothes he-secretes and he-looks-around. No-one he-sees. At-length to the-Lar he-approaches*) To you, Lar, the-pot of-gold full I-carry. *You* the-pot protect and hide!

[120] (*Euclio the-pot in the-hole again he-places; then much earth over the-pot he-heaps-up*)

Good. The-gold safe it-is. But worried I-am. Why how-ever worried I-am? Worried I-am because treasure great many cares it-gives, and me greatly it-worries. For into rich men's houses thieves many [125] they-enter; full therefore of-thieves many they-are rich men's houses. O me unhappy!

Now learn the Learning Vocabulary at *GVE* p. 19.

Note: it is definitely worthwhile to start keeping your own vocabulary note-book.

Keep a careful note of the stem, genitive singular, declension and gender of nouns; and the conjugation of verbs.

You may care to 'sort' them in columns, nouns by declension, verbs by conjugation, and see the patterns emerging.

EXERCISES FOR 1B

Page 22

Exercises

1   *honor, honorem, honoris, honori, honore, honores, honores, honorum, honoribus, honoribus; fur, furem, furis, furi, fure, fures, fures, furum, furibus, furibus.*

Note: we do not answer *optional* exercises.

2   *Euclionis* – gen. sing., *furem* – acc. sing., *aedium* – gen. pl., *honores* – nom. *or* acc. pl., *Lar* – nom. sing., *senum* – gen. pl., *aedīs* – acc. pl. (NB see page 20), *honorem* – acc. sing., *fur* – nom. sing., *Laris* – gen. sing.

3(a)   Then the thief sees the old man's treasure.
       deinde thesauros senum fures uident.

 (b)   The Lar does not have honour.
       Lares honores non habent.

 (c)   Therefore the god does not look after the old man.
       igitur senes di non curant.

 (d)   But why are you praying, old men?
       quare tamen supplicas, senex?

 (e)   At last the old man has the ointment.
       unguenta senes tandem possident.

 (f)   The old man now lives in the house.
       in aedibus senes nunc habitant.

 (g)   A thief always likes a pot full of gold.
       fures aulas auri plenas semper amant.

 (h)   But a thief does not have respect.
       honores tamen non habent fures.

(i) Why do you not enter [into] the house, old man?
quare in aedis non intratis, senes?

(j) The old man secretly loves the slave-woman.
seruas clam amant senes.

Page 24

Exercises

Note: you may care to do Exercise 3 first.

2 Genitive plurals: *honorum* from *honor* 3rd decl. masc.; *furum* from *fur*
3rd decl. masc.; *unguentorum* from *unguentum* 2nd decl. neut.; *senum*
from *senex* 3rd decl. masc.

3 Plural nouns: *ingenia* from *ingenium* 2nd decl. neut. – talents; *unguentis*
from *unguentum* 2nd decl. neut. – ointments; *somnia* from *somnium*
2nd decl. neut. – dreams; *pericula* from *periculum* 2nd decl. neut. –
dangers.

Pages 25–6

Exercises

1 *multas curas*; *multum aurum*; *multi* or *multos fures* (nom. *or* acc. pl.);
multum senem; *multi honoris*; *multam aedem*; *multorum seruorum*; *multorum senum*; *multas aedis* (acc. pl.); *multae coronae* (gen./dat. sing. *or*
nom. pl.).

2
multus	masc. nom. sing.:	*senex, seruus*
multi	masc./neut. gen. sing. *or* masc. nom. pl.:	*Laris, senes,* *serui*
multis	masc./fem./neut. dat./abl. pl.:	*honoribus,* *senibus*
multas	fem. acc. pl.:	*aedīs, familias*
multae	fem. gen./dat. sing. *or* nom. pl.:	*seruae, aedi*
multa	fem. nom. sing. *or* neut. nom./acc. pl.:	*unguenta, cura*

3 many slave-girls *multae seruae*; of much respect *multi honoris*; of
many garlands *multarum coronarum*; much gold *multum aurum*; many
an old man *multum senem*; of many thieves *multorum furum*; many
old men *multos senes*.

If you have made any mistakes in the last three exercises, check the
gender and **declension** of the noun.

4(a)   Many thieves are in the house.
 (b)   Many old men have many cares.
 (c)   Many slave-girls are full of cares.
 (d)   Euclio has much gold [and] many pots full of gold.
 (e)   The old man has many slaves.

5(a)   No power is long-lived.
 (b)   Life is neither a good nor a bad thing.
 (c)   Nobility is the only and unparalleled goodness.
 (d)   Life is long if it is full.
 (e)   Fortune is blind.

Pages 27–9
[Optional exercises *omitted*]

Reading exercises

*1   English and Latin

(a)   In the long (adj., 'streets') echoing (adj., 'streets') streets the
       laughing (adj. 'dancers') dancers (subj.) throng (verb).

(b)   And the long (adj., 'carpets') carpets (subj.) rose (verb) along the
       gusty (adj., 'floor') floor.

(c)   I (subj.) bring (verb) you with reverent (adj., 'hands') hands
       The books (obj.) of my numberless (adj., 'dreams') dreams.

(d)   'Tis (verb) no sin (subj.) love's fruit (obj.) to steal
       But the sweet (adj., 'theft') theft (obj.) to reveal.

(e)   His fair (adj., 'Front') large (adj., 'Front') Front (subj.) and Eye
       (subj.) sublime (adj., 'Eye') declar'd (verb)
       Absolute (adj., 'Rule') Rule (obj.).

(f)   Gazing he (subj.) spoke (verb), and kindling at the view
       His (adj., 'arms') eager (adj., 'arms') arms (obj.) around the god-
       dess threw (verb).
       Glad (adj., 'earth') earth (subj.) perceives (verb), and from her
       bosom pours (verb)
       Unbidden (adj., 'herbs') herbs (obj.) and voluntary (adj., 'flowers')
       flowers (obj.).

2(a)   *clamant* is plural; *serui, senex, seruae* are all subjects.
       The slaves, the old man and the slave girls are shouting.

(b) *dat* is singular; *multum honorem* is the object, *Phaedra* is the subject.
Therefore Phaedra gives much respect.

(c) *possidet* is singular; *Lar* is the subject, *aedīs* is the object.
Now the Lar possesses the house.

(d) *amant* is plural; *di* is the subject, *multum honorem* is the object.
The gods like much respect.

(e) *dat* is singular; *aurum* is the subject (NB neuter noun), *multas curas* is the object.
Gold gives many worries.

(f) *habitant* is plural; *serui* is the subject.
Slaves also live in the house.

(g) *est* is singular; *aurum* is the subject.
There is much gold in the pot.

(h) *timent* is plural; *fures* is subject *or* object, *senes* is subject *or* object, *multi* must be subject.
Either: However, many thieves fear old men.
Or (better sense): However, many old men fear thieves.

(i) *intrant* is plural; *senex* and *seruus* are both subject.
Why are the old man and the slave entering [onto] the stage?

(j) *explicat* is singular; *Lar* is the subject, *curas* is the object.
At last the Lar explains the old man's worries.

3(a) The old man (obj.) the slave (subj.) (Latin verb *-t*).
(b) The house (obj.) the god (subj.) (*-t*).
(c) Respects (obj.) the Lar (subj.) (*-t*).
(d) The thief (subj.) the gold (obj.) (*-t*).
(e) Euclio's (gen.) daughter (obj.) the gods (subj.) (*-nt*).
(f) The daughters (subj.) of the old men (gen.) honours (obj.) (*-nt*).
(g) The temple (obj.) the god (subj.) (*-t*).
(h) Ointments (obj.) the gods (subj.) (*-nt*).
(i) The Lar (obj.) Phaedra (subj.), Phaedra (obj.) the Lar (subj.) (*-t*).
(j) Slaves (obj.) Phaedra (subj.) and slave women (obj.) (*-t*).

*4(a) Pots (fem. obj. pl.) for/because (first word) he/she/it has many (fem. obj. pl., with 'pots') Euclio (subj.) the old man (subj., describing Euclio).
'For Euclio the old man has many pots.'

(b) The house (fem. obj. pl.) of thieves (gen.) full (fem. obj. pl. – with 'house') many (masc. subj. pl.) they fear old men (masc. subj. pl., goes with 'many').
'Many old men fear a house full of thieves.'

(c) Treasure (obj.) of Euclio (gen.) secretly he/she/it sees the slave-woman (subj.).
'The slave-woman secretly sees the treasure of Euclio.'

(d) No (masc. subj. s.) there/he/she/it is in the house slave (masc. subj. s., goes with 'no').
'There is no slave in the house.'

(e) Phaedra (fem. obj. s.), daughter (fem. obj. s., so refers to Phaedra) of Euclio (gen.) and Staphyla (fem. obj. s.), daughters (fem. subj. pl. *or* of the daughter gen.) of Euclio (gen.) the slave-woman (fem. obj. s., so refers to Staphyla), Lar (subj.) he/she/it loves (s., so *filiae* cannot be pl. 'daughters' subj. but 'of the daughter' gen.).
'The Lar loves Phaedra, daughter of Euclio, and Staphyla, slave-woman of the daughter of Euclio.'

(f) Next Euclio (subj.) the pot (obj.), because thieves (subj.? obj.? pl.) greatly he/she/it fears (therefore 'thieves' must be obj.), he/she/it hides.
'Euclio hides the pot because he greatly fears thieves.'

(g) Me (obj.) therefore Phaedra (subj.) he/she/it loves, Phaedra (obj.) I (subj.).
'Phaedra loves me, I [love] Phaedra.'

(h) For gold (neut. subj? obj.? s.) Euclio (subj., therefore 'gold' probably obj.) much (neut. obj. s. with 'gold'?) he/she/it has, garlands (fem. obj. pl.) many (fem. obj. pl.), much (probably masc./neut. obj. s.) ointment (neut. obj. s., with 'much').
'Euclio has much gold, many garlands, much ointment.'

(i) The old man (subj.) however thieves (prob. obj.), because much (subj.? obj.? masc.? neut? s.) he/she/it has gold (neut. obj. s., surely), greatly he/she/it fears.
'The old man however greatly fears thieves because he has much gold.'

(j) Much (subj.? obj.? masc.? neut.?) slaves (subj. pl.) *or* of the slave (gen. s.) ointment (subj.? obj.? neut., so probably goes with

'much') to the Lar, many (fem. obj. pl.) garlands (fem. obj. pl.)
they carry (so could be 'the slaves carry', or 'they carry much
ointment of the slave' – surely the first).
'The slaves carry much ointment (so obj.) to the Lar [and] many
garlands.'

Reading exercise / Test exercise

From here on, the Latin–English Reading/Test exercises will not
be translated for you. It is, of course, *essential* that you try them.
They encapsulate everything you should have learned. They will
act as a sure check on your progress. The water-wings are off. You
are on your own now.

**English–Latin*

(a)   The Lar therefore does not like Euclio, because he does not pay
      him respect.
      di igitur Phaedram, mi fili, curant quod Larem curat.

(b)   The old man, however, has many worries, because he has much
      gold.
      serui autem coronas portant multas, quod honorem dant multum.

(c)   The house of Euclio is full of thieves, because the old man has a pot
      full of gold.
      deorum aedis auri est plena, quod aulas auri plenas dant diuitum filiae.

(d)   I have much perfume, many garlands, [and] much respect.
      tu multam curam, thesaurum multum habes.

(e)   I do not like you, Demaenetus.
      aurum, mi fili, non porto.

(f)   The slaves are shouting, the slave-women are supplicating, and the
      old man is afraid.
      orat filia, clamant senes, timent seruae.

DELICIAE LATINAE: IB

Page 32

Exercise

con-uoco I call together.
in-habito I dwell in.

in-uoco I call upon.
prae-uideo I see ahead.
com-porto I carry together, collect, gather.
prae-sum I am at the head of.
post-habeo I regard x as behind (i.e. less important than) Y.

Page 33

Exercise

supplicate, supplication, explicate, explication, importation, date, habitation, vision, possession.

Use an English dictionary to check the meanings.

Word exercises

1. familiar, familial, family; coronation; scene, scenery; timid; deity, deify; multitude, multi-purpose, multiply; video, revision, evident.

2. *pecunia, honor, amo, thesaurus, porto, clamo, filia, aedes, unguentum, fur, seruus, nullus.*

NB *-u-* between vowels becomes *-v-* in English.

Everyday Latin

ante before
post after *post mortem* 'after death'; *post scriptum* 'after it has been written'
uox populi, uox dei 'the voice of the people [is] the voice of God'
agnus dei 'the lamb of God [which taketh away the sins of the world]'
ignoramus (of course), because this means '*we* do not know' (a *verb*, not a *noun*)
datum, agendum, medium

Page 34

Real Latin

Vulgate

'And God said, "I am the God of your father, the God of Abraham, the God of Isaac, and the God of Jacob."' (Exodus 3.6)
'I am who I am.' (Exodus 3.14)

I C *(Text pp. 8–10)*

NOTES FOR IC

Page 9

133   *egone mala?*: *-ne* attached to a word indicates that the sentence will be a question, here lit. 'I evil?' 'Am I evil?' In
the translation we indicate *-ne* by attaching a question-
mark, 'I?'

134   *secum*: *se* 'himself', *cum* 'with'. This is represented in our
translation as 'himself-with'. Cf. ll. 141, 150.

145   *o me miseram*: 'O unhappy me', feminine; cf. *Text* p. 7, l.
100.

157   *cultrum fures habent*: the object 'knife' comes first in Latin,
the subject 'thieves' second.

169   *aurum . . . senex*: object *aurum* first, then subject *senex*.

Page 10

172   *ut . . . multas*: *thesaurus meus* subject, *curas multas* object.

TRANSLATION OF IC

(Euclio from the-house onto the-stage he-enters he-shouts/and)

EUCLIO
Get-out from the-house! Get-out at-once! Why not you-
get-out, slave-woman my?

STAPHYLA
(From the-house she-gets-out and onto the-stage she-enters)
What it-is, my master? **[130]** What you-are-doing? Why
me from the-house you-drive-out? Slave-woman yours I-
am. Why me you-beat, master?

EUC.   Shut-up! You I-beat because evil you-are, Staphyla.

STA.   *I*? Evil? Why evil I-am? Unhappy I-am, but not evil,
master. *(Herself-with she ponders)* But *you* mad you-are!

EUC.   **[135]** Shut-up! Get-out at-once! Go-away further still . . .

further still ... Stop! Stand-still! Wait! (*Euclio himself-with he-ponders*) I'm-lost! I'm-done-for! How evil my slave-woman she-is! For eyes in the-back-of-her-head she-has. How treasure my me unhappy always it-troubles! How the-treasure many worries it-gives! (*He-shouts again*) Wait there! You I-warn, Staphyla!

S T A. [**140**] Here I-wait *I*, my master. *You* however to-where you-go?

E U C. *I* into house my I-return (*himself-with he-ponders*) and treasure my secretly I-see. For thieves always into the-house of-men rich they-enter...

(*Euclio from the-stage he-goes-away and into the-house he-returns*)

S T A. [**145**] O me unhappy! Master my mad he-is. Through the-night never he-sleeps, but he-stays-awake; through the-day, me from the-house always he-drives-out. What in mind he-has? Why the-old-man so mad he-is?

(*Euclio at-last from the-house he-gets-out and onto the-stage he-returns*)

E U C. [**150**] (*Himself-with he-ponders*) Gods me they-protect! Treasure my safe it-is! (*He-shouts*) Now, Staphyla, listen and attention pay/give! *I* you I-warn. Go-away inside and the-door shut. For *I* now to the-praetor I-go-away – poor for/because [first word] I-am. If you-see a-cobweb, the-cobweb protect. My for/because [first word] cobweb it-is. If a-neighbour he-comes-up and fire he-asks-for, the-fire at once put-out. If [**155**] neighbours they-come-up and water they-ask-for, reply 'Water never in the-house I-have.' If a-neighbour he-comes-up and a-knife he-asks-for, at once reply 'The-knife thieves they-have.' If Good Luck to the-house she-comes, stop [her]!

S T A. Good Luck never to your house she-comes-up, master.

E U C. [**160**] Shut-up, slave-woman, and go-away at-once inside.

S T A. I-am-silent and at-once I-go-away. (*Staphyla she-goes-away and herself-with she-mutters*) Oh me unhappy! How Phaedra, the-daughter of-Euclio, me she-worries! For pregnant she-is Phaedra by Lyconides, the-neighbour of-Euclio. The-old-man however he-does-not-know, and *I* I-am-silent, nor plan I-have.

[**165**] (*She-goes-out from the-stage Staphyla*)

EUC. Now to the-praetor I-go-away, too-much by-Hercules unwillingly. For the-praetor today money among the-men he-divides. If to the-forum not I-go, neighbours my 'Well!' they-say *'we* to the-forum we-go, Euclio to the-forum not he-goes, but at-home he-stays. Gold therefore at-home the-old-man he-has!' For [**170**] now I-hide the-treasure carefully, but neighbours my always they-come-up, they-stand-around, 'How you-are, Euclio?' they-say, 'What you-are-up-to?' Me unhappy! How worries treasure my it-gives many [= many worries]!

Now learn the Learning Vocabulary at G*VE* pp. 36–7.

EXERCISES FOR I C

Page 37

Exercises

1   *time, timete; roga, rogate; tace, tacete; cogita, cogitate; mone, monete; cura, curate; posside, possidete.*

2   give a garland!; carry water!; stay in the house!; be quiet!; guard the treasure!; warn [your] daughter!

3   *uidete!; roga Euclionem!; tacete!; celate aulam!*

Page 38

Exercises

1   *i* go (sing.), *ite; eunt* they go, *it; itis* you (pl.) go, *is; eo* I go, *imus; it* he/she/it goes, *eunt; imus* we go, *eo; exitis* you (pl.) go out, *exis; abimus* we go away, *abeo; abitis* you (pl.) go away, *abis; redeunt* they return, *redit; reditis* you (pl.) return, *redis; ite* go (pl.), *i; redeo* I return, *redimus; exeunt* they go out, *exit.*

2   *abimus, redeunt, abi, aditis, exit, eo, redite, is.*

Page 39

Exercises

1   *meo, tuo,* abl. sing.; *meas, tuas,* acc. pl.; *mei, tui,* gen. sing.; *meā, tuā,* abl. sing.; *meorum, tuorum,* gen. pl.; *meo, tuo,* dat./abl. sing.; *meae, tuae,*

gen./dat. sing., nom. pl.; *meum, tuum,* acc. sing.; *meus, tuus,* nom. sing.

2   *misero,* dat. sing.; *misera,* abl. sing.; *miser,* nom. sing.; *miseram,* acc. sing.; *miseris,* dat./abl. pl.; *miseri,* gen. sing. *or* nom. pl.; *miserarum,* gen. pl.; *miseris,* dat./abl. pl.; *miserorum,* gen. pl.

Page 40

Exercises

1(a)   Neither slave-girls nor slaves stay in my master's house.
manet in dominorum meorum aedibus neque serua neque seruus.

NB *aedes* (when it means house) is plural.

(b)   The wicked old man's wicked slave-girl is annoying my master.
malorum senum malae seruae dominos meos uexant.

(c)   Your neighbour sees my neighbour.
tui uicini uicinos meos uident.

(d)   The poor old man's slave never stays in the house.
senum miserorum serui in aedibus numquam manent.

(e)   The poor slave-girls never approach or pray to my Lar.
serua misera ad Lares meos numquam adit neque supplicat.

(f)   The wicked master immediately thrashes his slave-girls, poor things.
domini mali seruam statim uerberant, miseram.

*2(a)   *malus* – nom. masc. sing. = *senex.*   *multum* – acc. masc. sing. = *honorem.*
The wicked old man does therefore not have much respect.

(b)   *meā* – abl. fem. sing. = *aulā.*   *tuus* – nom. masc. sing. = *ignis.*
Your fire is in my pot.

(c)   *meis* – dat./abl. pl. = *aedibus.*   *multi* – nom. masc. pl. = *patres.*
In my house however live many fathers.

(d)   *malos* – acc. masc. pl. = *senes.*   *meus* – nom. masc. sing. = *Lar.*
For my Lar does not like wicked old men.

(e)   *meus* – nom. masc. sing. = *pater.*   *tuum* – acc. masc. sing. = *ignem.*
Does my father keep your fire safe?

3(a)   Money alone reigns.
  (b)   The truth never dies.
  (c)   A greedy man is always in need.
  (d)   Death does not frighten a wise man off.
  (e)   Death in a rout is disgraceful, but death in victory is glorious.

Page 41

Exercise

ex aqua, in oculum, ab igne, ad dominos, ab aedibus, in scaenam.

Pages 41–2

Reading exercises

**1(a)   The neighbour (masc. obj. sing.) the old man (subj.) unhappy
         (masc. subj. sing., going with 'old man').
         'The unhappy old man -s (Latin verb -*t*) the neighbour.'

  (b)   The master (masc. subj. sing.) for/because (first word) my (masc.
         subj. sing., agreeing with 'master') your (masc.? neut.? subj.? obj.?
         sing.) fire (masc. obj. sing., so 'your' goes with it).
         'For my master -s (-*t*) your fire.'

  (c)   Neither I (subj.) my (masc.? neut.? subj.? obj.? sing.) neither you
         (subj.) your (masc.? neut.? subj.? obj.? sing.) slave (masc. obj.
         sing., so goes with 'my' and 'your').
         'Neither I my slave, nor you your(s) – (-*s*).'

  (d)   Then me (obj.) the slaves (masc. subj. pl.) *or* of the slave (masc.
         gen. sing.) evil (masc. subj. pl. or masc. gen. sing.) – slaves must
         be subj., as no other subj. in sentence.
         'Then the evil slaves – (-*nt*) me.'

  (e)   The slaves (masc. obj. pl.) evil (masc. obj. pl.) neighbour (masc.
         subj. sing.) my (masc. subj. sing.).
         'My neighbour -s (-*t*) the evil slaves.'

  (f)   The pot (fem. obj. sing.), my (masc. voc. sing.) master (masc.
         voc. sing.), the slave-woman (fem. subj. sing.) evil (fem. subj.
         sing.).
         'The evil slave-woman, my master, -s (-*t*) the pot.'

  (g)   The thief (masc. obj. sing.) unhappy (masc. obj. sing.) I (subj.)
         also.
         'I also – (-*o*) the unhappy thief.'

(h) The fire (masc. obj. sing.) you (subj.), I (subj.) the water (fem. obj. sing.).
'You the fire, I – (-*o*) the water.'

(i) Eyes (masc. obj. pl.) my (masc. obj. pl.) slave (fem. subj. sing.) your (fem. subj. sing.) always.
'Your slave always -s (-*t*) my eyes.'

(j) Why the gold (neut. subj.? obj.? sing.) and the ointment (neut. subj.? obj.? sing.) and the garlands (fem. obj. pl., so probably 'gold' and 'ointment' are obj. too) Euclio (masc. subj. sing.) un-happy (masc. subj. sing.) never.
'Why does unhappy Euclio never – (-*t*) the gold and ointment and garlands?'

*2(a) Close up (verb, imperative) the casement (obj.), draw (verb, im-perative) the blind (obj.),
   Shut out (verb, imperative) that (adj.) stealing (adj.) moon (obj.),
She (subj.) wears (verb) too much the guise (obj.) she (subj.) wore (verb)
   Before our (adj.) lutes (subj.) were strewn (verb)
With years-deep (adj.) dust (noun, 'with'), and names (subj.) we (subj.) read (verb)
   On a white (adj.) stone (noun, 'on') were hewn (verb).

(b) Hail (verb, imperative), native (adj.) language (noun, voc.), that by sinews (noun, 'by') weak (adj.)
Didst move (verb) my first endeavouring (all adjs.) tongue (obj.) to speak,
And mad'st (verb) imperfect (adj.) words (obj.) with childish (adj.) trips ('with') (noun),
Half unpronounced (adj.), slide (verb) through my infant (adj.) lips (noun, 'through').

(c) Know (imperative) then thyself (obj.), presume (imperative) not God (obj.) to scan;
The proper (adj.) study (subj.) of mankind (gen.) is (verb) man (complement).

Pages 42–3

Reading exercise / Test exercise
Omitted.

**English–Latin

From now on, only the English–Latin will be translated in these exercises.

(a) *seruae, exite et ignem rogate!*
(b) *tu autem, mi Euclio, quare seruam miseram amas?*
(c) *ut malus senex seruos uerberat miseros!*
(d) *o me miserum! ut miser senex sum!*
(e) *miserum senem misera filia amat.*
(f) *malae seruae oculi filiae miserae curam non uident.*

DELICIAE LATINAE: IC

Page 43

Exercise

1. *cogit-o, ex-cogit-o, in-st-o, re-in-st-o, re-uerber-o* (NB *v* in English becomes *-u-* in Latin), *ex-port-o, re-uoc-o, ab-rog-o, re-seru-o, ex-plico.*

2. mansion, admonition.

Word exercises

1. Use an English dictionary to check your answers.

2. ignite, ignition; binoculars, oculist; mansion; malevolent, malice; salvation.

Everyday Latin

noto is first conjugation.

Real Latin

Vulgate

'Honour thy father and thy mother.' (Exodus 20.12)
'Ye are the salt of the earth ... ye are the light of the world.' (Matthew 5.13)

Sayings of Cato

Love your parents.
Look after what you are given.

Keep your modesty intact.
Look after your household.
Keep your oath.
Love your wife.
Supplicate the god.

Epitaph

The unbeautiful tomb of a beautiful woman ...

I D *(Text pp. 10–12)*

NOTES FOR I D

Page 10

179   *amat*: someone is loving – but who? He or she? We cannot
       tell till the subject is stated – Lyconides. Contrast l. 180.

185   *te optimam habeo*: i.e. 'I regard you *as* the best'. See also ll.
       186, 188–9. Where *habeo* is constructed with two accusa-
       tives, it is likely to mean 'regard x as y', cf. **GVE 17B**
       p. 25.

186   *egone ... tune ...?*: for *-ne*, see these notes on **Text** p. 9,
       l. 133.

188   *ut tu ... ita ego*: so far *ut* has meant 'how!' But it has other
       meanings, and in this sentence it means 'as'. How do you
       know? Because it is eventually picked up by *ita* 'so'. From
       now on, therefore, hold *ut* as 'how!' or 'as' until it is
       resolved.

194   *uxores uiros*: *uxores* subject, *uiros* object.

198   *uirum diuitem pauperem ... faciunt*: 'they make a rich man
       poor'. Where *facio* 'I make' is constructed with two accu-
       satives, it will usually mean 'I make x [into] y.' Cf. on l.
       185 above.

199   *ut ... ita*: See on 188 above.

Page 11

203   *satis pecuniae aurique*: Latin says 'enough *of* x' (genitive); English 'enough x'. So also with *nimis* 'too much [of]' l. 204.

207   *quam uis uxorem*: lit. 'whom do you wish [as] wife?' Compare l. 185 above.

209   *satis*: here used to mean 'quite', qualifying *pulchra*.

211–13 *Euclio ... non malus est*: 'Euclio is not an evil man' is the main clause, interrupted by *quamquam ... habet*.

TRANSLATION OF 1D

The-drama's characters
Megadorus, neighbour of-Euclio and brother of-Eunomia: a-man rich.
Eunomia, sister of-Megadorus.
[**175**] (Lyconides son of-Eunomia he-is)
There-is a-neighbour of-Euclio. The-name of-the-neighbour Megadorus it-is. Megadorus a-sister he-has. The-name of-the-sister Eunomia it-is. Megadorus therefore brother of-Eunomia he-is, Eunomia [is] sister of-Megadorus. Eunomia a-son she-has. The-name of-the-son Lyconides it-is. He/she-loves Lyconides Phaedra [= Lyconides loves Phaedra], Euclio's [**180**] daughter. Lyconides Phaedra he-loves, Phaedra Lyconides.

(*Eunomia Megadorus from the-house onto the-stage she-leads*)

MEGADORUS
     Best woman, give to-me hand your.

EUNOMIA
     What you-say, my brother? Who he/she-is best? The-woman for/because [first word] best not I-see. Tell to-me.

MEG.   [**185**] *You* best you-are, sister my: you best I-regard-as.

EUN.   *I*? best? *You*? me thus best you-regard-as?

MEG.   So I-say.

EUN. As *you* me the-best you-regard-as woman, so *I* you brother I-regard-as the-best. Pay/give therefore to-me your-attention.

MEG. [190] Attention my yours it-is. Order, sister best, and advise: *I* I-listen. What you-want? Why me from the-house you lead? Say to-me.

EUN. My brother, now to-you I-say. A-wife not you-have.

MEG. Thus it-is. But what you-mean?

EUN. If wife not you-have, not you-have children. But wives men [195] always they-look-after they-protect/and [= wives always look after men ...] and beautiful children memorials beautiful of-men they-are. Why a-wife to-home not at-once you-lead?

MEG. I-am-lost, I-am-done-for! Shut-up, sister. What you-say? What you-want? *I* rich I-am; wives a-man rich poor at-once they-make.

EUN. As *you* brother you-are the-best, so *I* woman I-am the-best, sister/and [200] the-best your. You thus I-order I-advise/and: lead to-home a-wife!

MEG. But whom in mind you-have?

EUN. A-wife rich.

MEG. But rich I-am enough, and enough of-money of-gold/and I-have. Furthermore wives rich at-home too-much of-money of-gold/and they-ask-for. Not I-like [205] of-wives rich the-shouts, commands, ivory-adorned waggons, garments, purple. But ...

EUN. Tell to-me, I-ask, whom you-want wife? [= whom do you want as your wife?]

MEG. (*himself-with he-reflects, then* ...) A-girl neighbouring, Phaedra by-name, daughter of-Euclio, enough beautiful she-is ...

EUN. [210] Whom you-say? The-daughter? of-Euclio? As, however, beautiful she-is, so she-is poor. For the-father of-Phaedra money he-has none. Euclio, however, although an-old-man he-is nor enough of-money of-gold/and he-has, not evil he-is.

MEG. If rich wives they-are a-dowry/and great they-have, after the-wedding [**215**] great it-is wives' extravagance. They-stand-about fuller, embroiderer, goldsmith, wool-worker, shopkeepers makers-of-bridal-veils [i.e. all these people stand about]; they-stand-about makers-of-sleeves, they-stand-about retailers linen-weavers, shoemakers; sellers-of-breast-bands they-hang-about, they-hang-about at-the-same-time girdle-makers. Money you-give, they-go-away. Then they-hang-about collectors-of-offerings in the-house, weavers concerned-with-making-ornamental-hems, chest-makers. Money you-give, they-go-away. [**220**] Unendurable it-is the-expense of-wives, if a-dowry large they-have. But if a-wife a-dowry not she-has, in the-power of-her-husband she-is.

EUN. Rightly you-say, brother. Why not to-the-home of-Euclio you-approach?

MEG. I-approach. Look, Euclio now I-see. From the-forum he-returns.

EUN. Farewell, my brother.

[**225**] (*There-departs from the-scene the-sister of-Megadorus*)

MEG. And *you* farewell, sister my.

Now learn the Learning Vocabulary at *GVE* p. 46.

EXERCISES FOR 1D

Page 48

Exercises

1   *dicit*; *ducunt*; *audimus*; *dicimus*; *auditis*; *dic!*; *audite!*; *ducite!*; *dicis*; *audit*; *audiunt*.

2   *curo* 1 = I look after; *celat* 1 = he/she hides; *habetis* 2 = you (pl.) have; *ducunt* 3 = they lead; *rogas* 1 = you ask; *possidemus* 2 = we possess; *audio* 4 = I hear.

3   you (pl.) say, *dicis*; they hear, *audit*; we make prayers to, *supplico*; you (s.) hear, *auditis*; I say, *dicimus*; we lead, *duco*; we hear, *audio*; they shout, *clamat*; you (s.) are silent, *tacetis*.

Page 50

Exercises

1   *magnum miserum pulchrum; magni miseri pulchri; magno misero pulchro; magna misera pulchra; magnorum miserorum pulchrorum.*

2   *pulchrarum miserarum; pulchris miseris; pulchro misero; pulchrae miserae; pulchrae miserae; pulchro misero; pulchras miseras; pulchrum miserum; pulchra misera; pulchrae miserae; pulchris miseris; pulchri miseri; pulchros miseros.*

[Optional exercise *omitted*]

Page 51

Exercise

1   (a) *cuius*, (b) *quas*, (c) *quid*, (d) *quod*, (e) *quem*, (f) *cuius*, (g) *quam*, (h) *qui*.

Pages 52–3

Exercises

*1(a)   *multam* – acc. fem. sing. = *pecuniam*.
        Excellent wives do not possess a lot of money.

  (b)   *multi* – nom. masc. pl. = *filii*.
        Many sons love my sisters.

  (c)   *optimi* – nom. masc. pl. = *senes*.
        Excellent old men do not annoy wretched slaves.

  (d)   *pulchras* – acc. fem. pl. = *sorores*.
        Wicked brothers beat their beautiful sisters.

  (e)   *multi* – nom. masc. pl. = *senes*.
        Many old men take beautiful women home.

2   into the house; in the pot; towards the Lar; from the fires; into the water; out of the pots; in the house; in the water; from the master; out of the eyes.

*3   *in aedibus; ad puellam; ad fratres; ab uxore; in scaenam; in aedibus*†; *ex aqua; ab ignibus.*

†Misprint, repeat of the first question.

4   Too many garlands; enough slaves; too much water; enough names; too many sisters; enough fire.

5(a)   What man do I hear?
  (b)   Whose name are you now saying?
  (c)   There is always enough gold in Euclio's house.
  (d)   Euclio's unhappy daughter has too many cares.
  (e)   As for you, however, which woman are you taking home?

6(a)   Who is a good man?
  (b)   Who is not terrified of poverty?
  (c)   Who hides his love well?
  (d)   What is a happy life? Freedom from worry and continual peace.
  (e)   What is death? Either the end or a transition.
  (f)   Unrestrained anger produces madness.
  (g)   Fortune rules our life, not wisdom.

Page 53

Reading

*1(a)   *facit*: At last the man is making me his son.
  (b)   *habet*: Euclio considers his neighbour rich.
  (c)   You could choose any person of the verb because the subject is not specified, e.g.:
          faciunt: They make Euclio poor.
  (d)   *facit*: Megadorus makes Euclio's daughter his wife.
  (e)   *habeo*: I however consider rich men unfortunate.
  (f)   *facit*: The master makes wicked slaves unhappy.

*2   Apollo (subj.) bows and from (prep.) Mount Ida's (gen.) Height
          Swift (adj.) to (prep.) the Field precipitates his (adj.) Flight (obj.);
          Thence, from (prep.) the War, the breathless (adj.) hero (obj.) bore,
          Veil'd (adj.) in (prep.) a Cloud, to (prep.) silver (adj.) Simois' (gen.) shore:
          There bath'd his (adj.) honourable (adj.) wounds (obj.), and drest
          His (adj.) manly (adj.) Members (obj.) in (prep.) th' immortal (adj.) Vest,
          And with (prep.) Perfumes of Sweet (adj.) Ambrosial (adj.) Dews (gen.),
          Restores his (adj.) Freshness (obj.) and his (adj.) Form (obj.) renews.

Then Sleep (subj.) and Death (subj.), two (adj.) twins of winged
(adj.) Race (gen.),
Of matchless (adj.) Swiftness (gen.), but of silent (adj.) Pace
(gen.),
Received Sarpedon (obj.), at (prep.) the Gods' (gen.) command,
And in (prep.) a moment reach'd the Lycian (adj.) land (obj.);
The Corps (obj.) amidst (prep.) his (adj.) weeping (adj.) Friends
they (subj.) laid,
Where endless (adj.) Honours (subj.) wait the Sacred (adj.) Shade
(obj.).

Pages 54–5

Reading exercise / Test exercise

Omitted.

**English–Latin*

Latin–English omitted.

(a)   *ut Phaedra optima filia est, ita Euclio pater optimus.*
(b)   *pulchras feminas uxores malas habeo.*
(c)   *quis frater uicini est mei?*
(d)   *optimi uiri pulchras uxores in matrimonium ducunt.*
(e)   *puellae in aquam eunt.*
(f)   *nimis diues pecuniae habet, nimis curae.*

DELICIAE LATINAE: I D

Page 55

Word exercises

1.   Check the meanings in an English dictionary.

2.   nominative, nominate, nomenclature; domicile, domestic; pecuni-
     ary, impecunious; feminine; valedictory; satisfaction.

Everyday Latin

ex libris 'from the books [of . . .]'. Inside a book to show to whom it
belongs.

ex cathedra 'from the papal seat': an 'infallible' pronouncement by the Pope (hence, any authoritative statement).
Diues The rich man who did not give help to the poor Lazarus.
ad infinitum 'to infinity'. *in-* = 'not' (*finio* = 'I end').
in uino ueritas 'truth [is found] in wine' (i.e. people tell the truth when they drink wine).
ad nauseam 'to the point of vomiting'.
deus ex machina 'a god from the crane'. The crane was used in ancient Greek theatre to bring gods on stage, usually to resolve a dilemma intractable for the mortals involved in the plot. Hence it is used of the cause of resolution for any miraculous or surprising event.
ad astra 'to the stars'.

Page 56

Word-building

Induction, induce, inducement, reduction, reduce, abduction, abduct, conduction, conduct, conductor, seduce.
Audition, audit, auditory, audience.
Prediction, diction, malediction, benediction, contradiction.

Real Latin

Martial

It's Thais that Quintus loves. 'Which Thais?' One-eyed Thais. It's only one eye Thais doesn't have. He's short of *two*. (3.8)

Africanus has 100,000,000 sesterces, but still hunts legacies. Fortune gives too much to many, but enough to no one. (12.10)

Vulgate

The Lord is my shepherd (lit. 'The Lord directs me').

Ordinary of the Mass

In the name of the Father and of the Son and of the Holy Spirit.

I E *(Text pp. 12–14)*

NOTES FOR IE

Page 12

233   *quare . . . dicit*: lit. 'Why does he say me [to be] the best neighbour?' i.e. 'why does he call me the best neighbour?'

Page 13

249   *non dubium est*: 'it is not doubtful' – 'it', because *dubium* is neuter. *non dubius est* would mean 'he is not doubtful', *non dubia est* 'she is not doubtful'.

249–50 *o scelus . . . o pecuniam meam*: Both these accusatives express an exclamation, cf. these notes on **Text** p. 7, l. 100.

257   *ut tu me*: hold *ut* till solved; hold *tu . . . me* till we find a verb. *ita* solves *ut* ('as . . . so'); *ego te* looks as if it balances *tu me*; *cognoui* provides the verb for both clauses 'As you [know] me, so I know you.'

257–8 *filiam . . . posco*: 'I demand your daughter *as* my wife', cf. 259 *cuius filiam uxorem uis* ('*as* your wife') and these notes on **Text** p. 12, l. 233.

261–2 *irridesne . . . miserum*: *homo diues*, nominative, is the same person as 'you' in the verb *irrides* 'you, a rich man'; *hominem . . . miserum* is the object.

270   *si . . . bonamque*: 'if I have a beautiful and good girl as my wife'.

Page 14

277   *optimum est*: 'it's the best thing', cf. these notes on **Text** p. 13, l. 249.

278   *ut*: here means simply 'as', not picked up by *ita*.

280   *et*: 'also', cf. these notes on **Text** p. 3, l. 5.

287   *uxorem . . . filiam meam*: 'my daughter *as* his wife'.

288   *et tu et Megadorus*: note *et* . . . *et* can mean 'both . . . and'.
        This should have appeared in **GVE 32** p. 51 and in the
        total learning vocabulary.

289   *nimis*: 'too', qualifying *subitum* ('too sudden').

TRANSLATION OF 1E

(*He-departs from the-forum onto the-stage Euclio*)

EUCLIO

(*Himself-with he-reflects*) Now to-home I-return. For *I* I-am
here, mind my at-home it-is.

MEGADORUS

[**230**] Hail, Euclio, neighbour best.

EUC.   (*Megadorus he-sees*) And *you*, Megadorus. (*Himself-with he-
       reflects*) What he-wants Megadorus? What plan he-has?
       Why a-man rich a-poor-man ingratiatingly he-greets?
       Why me a-neighbour the-best he-says? I-am-lost! Gold
       my he-wants!

MEG.   [**235**] *You* thoroughly you-are-well?

EUC.   Certainly I-am-well, but not I-am-well from-the-point-
       of-view-of money. Not enough of-money I-have, and
       poverty my hardly I-endure.

MEG.   But why *you* poverty your hardly you-endure? If the-mind
       content it-is, enough you-have.

EUC.   [**240**] I-am-lost! I-am-done-for! The-scheme of-Megadorus
       obvious it-is: treasure my without-doubt he-wants.

MEG.   What *you* you-say?

EUC.   Nothing. Poverty me it-troubles and worries it-gives many.
       Poverty therefore hardly I-endure. For a-daughter I-have
       beautiful, but [**245**] poor I-am and a-dowry not I-have.

MEG.   Quiet! Good have spirit, Euclio, and pay/give to-me
       attention. A-plan for/because [first word] I-have.

EUC.   What plan you-have? What you-want? (*Himself-with he-
       reflects*) Scheme wicked! O villain! Not in-doubt it-is.
       Money he-wants my! To-my-house at-once [**250**] I-
       return. O money my!

(*He-departs from the-stage into the-house Euclio*)

MEG. To-where you-go-off? What you-want? Say to-me.

EUC. To-my-house I-go-off...

(*Euclio he-departs. Soon onto the-stage he-returns*)

[255] The-gods me protect, safe it-is the-money. I-return to you, Megadorus. Say to-me, what now you-want?

MEG. As *you* me, so *I* you I-know. Listen therefore. Daughter your wife I-demand [= I demand your daughter *as* ...]. Promise!

EUC. What you-say? Whose daughter wife you-want?

MEG. [260] Yours.

EUC. Why daughter you-demand my? You-laugh-at? me, a-man rich a-man poor and unhappy [= Are you, a rich man, laughing at me, a poor ...]?

MEG. Not at-you I-laugh. The-plan best it-is.

EUC. *You* you-are a-man rich, *I*, however, poor; my rank yours not [265] it-is. *You* you-are as-if an-ox, *I* as-if a-donkey. If the ox thus he orders 'Donkey, carry the load', and the donkey the-load not he-carries, but in the-mud he-lies, what the-ox he-does? The-donkey not he-gives-a-second-glance-to, but he-laughs-at. Donkeys to oxen not easily they-cross-over. Furthermore, a-dowry not I-have. Plan therefore your not good it-is.

MEG. [270] If [*as*] wife a-girl beautiful I-have good/and, enough of-a-dowry I-have, and mind my content it-is enough. Enough wealthy I-am. What need of-money there-is? Promise!

EUC. I-promise to-you daughter my, but no dowry. No for/ because [first word] I-have money.

MEG. [275] Thus it-is as you-want. Why not marriage-rites at-once we-make, as we-wish? Why not cooks we-call? What you-say?

EUC. By Hercules, best it-is. Go, Megadorus, do the-marriage-rites, and daughter my to-your-home lead, as you-wish — but without dowry — and cooks call. *I* for/because [first word] money not I-have. Farewell.

MEG. [280] I-go. Farewell also *you*.

(*He-goes-out from the-stage Megadorus*)

EUC. Gods immortal! Money truly has–influence. Not in–doubt it–is: money my he–wants Megadorus. Hey *you*, Staphyla! You I–want! Where you–are, villain? You–come–out? from the–house? You–hear? me? Why in the–house you–wait?

[285] (*From the–house onto the–stage there–enters Staphyla*) Today Megadorus cooks he–calls and marriage–rites he–makes. For today [as] wife to–his–home he–leads daughter my.

STAPH.
What you–say? What you–want both you and Megadorus? O girl unhappy! Sudden it–is too–much. Stupid it–is the–scheme!

EUC. [290] Shut–up and go–away: do everything, villain, carry everything! *I* to the–forum I–depart.
(*He–goes–out Euclio*)

STAPH.
Now the–schemes crimes/and of–Lyconides lie–exposed! Now the–destruction of–the–daughter of–Euclio it–is–present. For today pregnant to–his–house he–leads a–wife Megadorus, nor plan I–have *I*. I–am–lost!

Now learn the Learning Vocabulary at GVE p. 58.

EXERCISES FOR IE

Page 60

Exercises

1 *facis, audite, ferunt, fer/duc, uult, facimus, fert, ite, uis, posce, facio, cape dotem.*

2 *facimus* we make, 1st pers. pl., *facio*; *fert* he brings, 3rd pers. sing., *ferunt*; *uult* he wishes, 3rd pers. sing., *uolunt*; *ferunt* they bring, 3rd pers. pl., *fert*; *dic* say!, sing. imperative, *dicite*; *ferte* bring!, pl. imperative, *fer*; *uolumus* we wish, 1st pers. pl., *uolo*; *est* he is, 3rd pers. sing., *sunt*; *eunt* they go, 3rd pers. pl., *it*; *facis* you make, 2nd pers. sing., *facitis*; *ducite* lead!, pl. imperative, *duc*; *ite* go!, pl. imperative, *i*; *capite* capture!, pl. imperative, *cape.*

Page 61

Exercises

1   *onus* nom./acc. sing. *multum, oneris* gen. sing. *multi, onere* abl. sing. *multo, onera* nom./acc. pl. *multa, oneribus* dat./abl. pl. *multis.*

Note: in the following answer * = agreement.

2   *pulchro*: masc./neut., dat./abl. sing.: *oneris* (neut. gen. sing.); **scelere* (neut. abl. sing.); *domini* (masc. gen. sing./nom. pl.); *facinus* (neut. nom./acc. sing.); *dei* (masc. gen. sing.); *di* (masc. nom. pl.).
    pulchra: fem. nom. sing. *or* neut. nom./acc. pl.: **femina* (fem. nom. sing.); **facinora* (neut. nom./acc. pl.); **scelera* (neut. nom./acc. pl.); *seruae* (fem. gen./dat. sing./nom. pl.); *senex* (masc. nom. sing.).
    pulchrum: neut. nom./acc. sing. *or* masc. acc. sing.: **opus* (neut. nom./ acc. sing.); **seruum* (masc. acc. sing.); *feminam* (fem. acc. sing.); *senes* (masc. nom./acc. pl.); **Larem* (masc. acc. sing.); **scelus* (neut. nom./ acc. sing.); *facinoris* (neut. gen. sing.).
    pulchrorum: neut./masc. gen. pl.: **nominum* (neut. gen. pl.); *seruarum* (fem. gen. pl.); **deorum* (masc. gen. pl.); **senum* (masc. gen. pl.); **scelerum* (neut. gen. pl.).

Pages 61–2

Exercise

(a)   *est bona puella.* She's a good girl.
      estne bona puella? Is she a good girl?

(b)   *imus ad aedis Euclionis.* We are going to Euclio's house.
      imusne ad aedis Euclionis? Are we going to Euclio's house?

(c)   *fert bene onus serua.* The slave-woman carries the load well.
      fertne bene onus serua? Does the slave-woman carry the load well?

(d)   *optimum consilium habent.* They have the best plan.
      optimumne consilium habent? Do they have the best plan?

(e)   *Euclio filiam statim promittit.* Euclio promises his daughter at once.
      Euclione filiam statim promittit? Does Euclio promise his daughter at once?

(f)   *Megadorus satis pecuniae habet.* Megadorus has enough money.
      Megadorusne satis pecuniae habet? Does Megadorus have enough money?

(g) *soror fratrem bene audit.* The sister listens to her brother well.
     sororne fratrem bene audit? Does the sister listen to her brother well?

(h) *scaenam uidetis.* You see the stage.
     scaenamne uidetis? Do you see the stage?

(i) *Euclio honorem numquam dat.* Euclio never gives respect.
     Euclione honorem numquam dat? Does Euclio never give respect?

(j) *uxores nimis auri semper habent.* Wives always have too much gold.
     uxoresne nimis auri semper habent? Do wives always have too much gold?

Page 62

Exercises

1 into the house, out of the dowry, in mind, towards the men, from the water, out of the fires, at home, out of danger, into death, towards the waters, into danger.

2(a) Where is Megadorus? What plan does he have?
 (b) Does the rich man want a beautiful wife? What's the problem?
 (c) I therefore consider you to be good men.†
 (d) The slaves do too much villainy and too many wicked deeds in the house.
 (e) What burden are you carrying? Where are you going to?

†*uos*, occurring in some texts, is not learned till 1F; the exercise should have *te*.

3(a) Hasten slowly. [I.e. more haste, less speed!]
 (b) Goodness alone makes life happy.
 (c) The wise man does nothing unwillingly.
 (d) An author praises his work.
 (e) There is no moderation in the mob.
 (f) Pleasure is neither a good nor an evil.

Page 63

Reading exercises

*1(a) Masc. refers to Megadorus.
       Megadorus marries Euclio's daughter without a dowry. He is therefore an excellent man.

(b) Neut. refers to the fact given in the 1st sentence.
At home today, Megadorus neither prepares the marriage-rites nor summons cooks. That is bad.

(c) Fem. refers to Eunomia.
Eunomia is the sister of Megadorus. She is a good woman.

(d) Neut. refers to the fact given in the 1st sentence.
Eunomia has a brother. There is no doubt.

(e) Masc. refers to Euclio.
Euclio loves his daughter. He is not a bad man.

(f) Neut. refers to the fact given in the 1st sentence.
Euclio is afraid. That is not doubtful.

(g) Neut. refers to the fact given in the 1st sentence.
Staphyla hears Euclio's plan. That is a bad thing.

(h) Fem. refers to Staphyla.
Staphyla returns into the house. For she is full of care.

*2 But anxious (adj.) Cares (subj.) the pensive (adj.) Nymph (obj.) oppress'd (verb),
And secret (adj.) Passions (subj.) labour'd (verb) in her Breast.
Not youthful (adj.) Kings (subj.) in Battle seiz'd (adj.) alive (adj.),
Not scornful (adj.) Virgins (subj.) who their (adj.) Charms (obj.) survive (verb),
Not ardent (adj.) Lovers (subj.) robbed (adj.) of all (adj.) their (adj.) Bliss,
Not ancient (adj.) Ladies (subj.) when refused (adj.) a Kiss,
Not Tyrants (subj.) fierce (adj.) that unrepenting (adj.) die (verb),
Not Cynthia (subj.) when her (adj.) Mantle's (subj.) pinned (verb) awry,
E'er felt (verb) such Rage (obj.), Resentment (obj.) and Despair (obj.),
As thou, sad (adj.) Virgin! for thy ravish'd (adj.) Hair.

Page 64

Reading exercise / Test exercise
Omitted.

**English–Latin

Latin–English omitted.

(a) *irridetne Euclionem, homo diues pauperem?*
(b) *non dubium est. senex puellam filiam habet.*
(c) *i in aedis, serua. fer onera.*
(d) *quid noui? pecuniamne uis? non dubium est.*
(e) *quid uolunt? domumne eunt? onerane ferunt? boni sunt.*
(f) *bonum animum habe, domine. nam factum optimum est.*

DELICIAE LATINAE: IE

Page 65

Exercise

transmit, transmission; emit, emission; faction, affect, infect, infection, prefect; translate, translation, relate, relative, tralaticious, prolative; product, production.

Word exercise

1. See an English dictionary for meanings: nuptial > *nuptiae*; animate > *animus*; hominid > *homo*; voluntary > *uolo*; onus > *onus* (!); fact > *facio*.

2. Consult an English dictionary.

3. Consult an English dictionary.

Page 66

Real Latin

Martial

Tongilianus possesses a nose [i.e. a nose for a bad smell]. I know. I don't deny it.
But now there's nothing but a nose [for a bad thing] Tongilianus has. (12.88)

Our [friend] Caecilianus, O Titus, does not dine without wild boar. A handsome table-companion it is Caecilianus has! (7.59)

Vulgate

Save me, O Lord (lit. 'Make me safe'). (Ps. 59)
Father, if thou wilt, take this cup from me. (Luke 22.42)

Ordinary of the Mass

We praise thee, we bless thee, we adore thee, we glorify thee, we give thee thanks for the sake of thy great glory; Lord God, heavenly king, God the Father almighty.

I F *(Text pp. 14–17)*

NOTES FOR IF

Page 14

298–9   *nuptias . . . cenam ingentem*: *nuptias* is the object of *facere* ('to make marriage-rituals'), *cenam ingentem* of *coquere* ('to cook a huge dinner'). Verbs meaning 'to –' in Latin (called infinitives) frequently control their own objects, as here. Infinitives are introduced by words like *uolo* 'I want *to*', *opus est* 'there is need *to*', *difficile est* 'it is difficult *to*', etc.

Page 15

302   *ita*: precedes *ut* in this instance.

321   *difficile est*: 'it is difficult'. *difficile* is neuter. So also *facile*, ll. 323, 330.

324   *tecum*: *te* = 'you', *cum* = 'with', so 'with you'('you-with' in the translation).

Page 16

330   *mecum*: *me* = 'me', *cum* = 'with', so 'with me' ('me-with' in the translation).

344   *secum*: *se* = 'himself', cf. l. 324 above.

TRANSLATION OF IF

[**295**] (*All the-cooks they-enter. The-names of-the-cooks Pythodicus, Anthrax, Congrio they-are. Pythodicus leader of-the-cooks he-is.*)

PYTHODICUS
    Come, cooks! Enter onto the-stage, villains! Listen! Master my marriage-rites today to-make he-wants. Your therefore job it-is a-dinner huge to-cook.

CONGRIO
    [300] Whose daughter to-lead/marry he-wants?

PY.   The-daughter of-his-neighbour Euclio, Phaedra.

ANTHRAX
    Gods immortal, you-know? the-man? A-stone not so it-is dry as Euclio.

PY.   What say-you?

AN.   [305] From the-fire if smoke outside it-goes-out, he-shouts 'My money it-has-disappeared! Take me to the-praetor!' When to-sleep he-wishes, a-bag huge on his-mouth he-places, while he-sleeps.

PY.   Why?

AN.   Breath to-lose not he-wishes. If he-washes, water to-pour-away not [310] he-wishes. And at the-barber's nail-clippings to-lose not he-wants, but all he-collects and to-his-house he-carries.

PY.   Now shut-up and listen, cooks all. What *you* to-do you-wish? Whose house to-go-into you-wish, villains? What *you* you-want, Congrio?

CON.   I-wish *I* the-house of-a-man rich to-go-into ...

ALL COOKS
    [315] *We* all the-house of-Megadorus, a-man rich, to-go-into we-wish, not the-house of-Euclio, a-man poor and sad.

PY.   How Euclio you he-worries! Now shut-up you all. (*To Anthrax*) You go-off into the-house of-Megadorus; (*to Congrio*) you, to-the-house of-Euclio.

CON.   How it-worries me Euclio's poverty! For Euclio, we-know, greedy and [320] sad he-is. In his-house nothing except emptiness and cobwebs huge there-are. Nothing he-has Euclio, nothing he-gives. Difficult it-is therefore at Euclio's dinner to-cook.

PY.   Stupid? you-are, Congrio? Easy for/because it-is at Euclio's dinner to-cook. For no disturbance there-is. If anything you-want, from house your you-with [325] carry: for

nothing he-has Euclio! But Megadorus rich he-is. At
Megadorus' there-is a-great disturbance, great pots silver,
many clothes, much gold. If anything slaves they-lose,
they-shout at-once 'Cooks they-take-away all goods!
Thieves they-are cooks all! Seize the-cooks cocky! Flog
the-rascals!' But at [330] Euclio's easy it-is nothing to-
take-away: nothing for/because he-has! Come me-with,
of-crimes the-source!

CON.   I-come.

CON.   Aaaargh! Citizens all, give way! I-am-lost, I-am-done-for *I*
unhappy!

EUC.   O rascal evil! Come-back, cook! To-where [335] you-flee
you, of-crimes the-source? Why?

CON.   I-flee *I* because me to-flog you-wish. Why you-shout?

EUC.   Because a-knife huge you-have, rascal!

CON.   But *I* a-cook I-am. *We* all cooks we-are. All therefore
knives huge we-have.

EUC.   [340] *You* all rascals you-are. What business there-is in
house my? I-want to-know everything.

CON.   Shut-up therefore. A-huge we-cook dinner. The-marriage-
rites for/because today of-daughter your there-are.

EUC.   (*himself-with he-reflects*) O scheme audacious! Liar the-man
he-is: all [345] my gold to-find he-wants. Wait, cooks all.
Stand there.
(*Euclio his-house he-enters. At length from-the-house he-comes-
out and onto the-stage he-enters. A-pot in-his-hands he-carries*)

EUC.   (*himself-with he-reflects*) Now all the-treasure in this pot I-
carry. All [350] by-Hercules the-gold now me-with always
I-shall-carry. Go all inside. Cook, or depart from the-
house, rascals!
(*They-depart the-cooks. Euclio himself-with he-reflects*)
A-scheme bold it-is, when a-man poor with a-rich-man
business to-do/have he-wants. Megadorus gold my to-find
and [355] to-carry-off he-wants. He-sends therefore cooks
into my house. 'Cooks' I-say, but thieves they-are all!
Now what plan best it-is? Me unhappy!

Now learn the Learning Vocabulary at *GVE* p. 68.

EXERCISES FOR 1F

Page 69

Exercise

habere to have; *explicare* to explain; *celare* to hide; *inuenire* to find; *manere* to stay; **redire* to return; *ducere* to lead; *dicere* to say; *poscere* to demand; *stare* to stand; *rogare* to ask; *fugere* to escape; *amittere* to lose; **auferre* to take away; *facere* to make, do; **esse* to be.

Note: *indicates an irregular verb. If you have made any mistakes, check the **Conjugation** of the verb.

Pages 71–2

Exercises

1 *puer audax, puerum audacem, pueri audacis, puero audaci, puero audaci, pueri audaces, pueros audaces, puerorum audacium, pueris audacibus, pueris audacibus; omnis aqua, omnem aquam, omnis aquae, omni aquae, omni aquā, omnes aquae, omnes aquas, omnium aquarum, omnibus aquis, omnibus aquis; ingens periculum, ingens periculum, ingentis periculi, ingenti periculo, ingenti periculo, ingentia pericula, ingentia pericula, ingentium periculorum, ingentibus periculis, ingentibus periculis.*

*2	Noun	Case	Number	Gender	*omnis*	*ingens*	*audax*
	seruae	**gen.**	**s.**	**f.**	*omnis*	*ingentis*	*audacis*
		dat.	**s.**		*omni*	*ingenti*	*audaci*
		nom.	**pl.**		*omnes*	*ingentes*	*audaces*
	thesauri	**gen.**	**s.**	**m.**	*omnis*	*ingentis*	*audacis*
		nom.	**pl.**		*omnes*	*ingentes*	*audaces*
	oculos	**acc.**	**pl.**	**m.**	*omnīs (-es)*	*ingentīs (-es)*	*audacīs (-es)*
	dominus	**nom.**	**s.**	**m.**	*omnis*	*ingens*	*audax*
	nominibus	**dat.**	**pl.**	**n.**	*omnibus*	*ingentibus*	*audacibus*
		abl.	**pl.**		*omnibus*	*ingentibus*	*audacibus*

consilium	nom. acc.	s. s.	n.	omne omne	ingens ingens	audax audax
cenā	abl.	s.	f.	omni	ingenti	audaci
turbarum	gen.	pl.	f.	omnium	ingen-tium	auda-cium
ciui	dat.	s.	m.	omni	ingenti	audaci
pecunias	acc.	pl.	f.	omnīs (-es)	ingentīs (-es)	audacīs (-es)
puellā	abl.	s.	f.	omni	ingenti	audaci
periculo	dat. abl.	s. s.	n.	omni omni	ingenti ingenti	audaci audaci
ignis	nom. gen.	s. s.	m.	omnis omnis	ingens ingentis	audax audacis
animis	dat. abl.	pl. pl.	m.	omnibus omnibus	ingen-tibus ingen-tibus	audaci-bus audaci-bus

3   *ingentem* acc. sing. masc./fem.: *deum* acc. sing. masc.; *audax* nom. sing. masc./fem. *or* nom./acc. sing. neut.: *consilium* nom./acc. sing. neut., *homo* nom. sing. masc., *dominus* nom. sing. masc.; *omnium* gen. pl. masc./fem./neut.: *coquorum* gen. pl. masc.; *tristes* nom./acc. pl. masc./fem.: *animos* acc. pl. masc., *domini* nom. pl. masc., *filiae* nom. pl. fem., *aedīs* acc. pl. fem.; *facilia* nom./acc./pl. neut.: *scelera* nom./acc. pl. neut.; *difficili* dat./abl. sing. masc./fem./neut.: *coquo* dat./abl. sing. masc., *filia* abl. sing. fem., *exitio* dat./abl. sing. neut.

Page 73

Exercises

1(a)   Therefore the bold cook wishes to cook a huge dinner.
 (b)   Why do you want to know all the names of the cooks?
 (c)   However you have a bold plan in mind.
 (d)   When you want to come into the house, call us at once.
 (e)   Every poor man wants to do bold crimes.
 (f)   A huge crowd of bold men is approaching the house of Megadorus.

2(a) Many women neither sleep nor cook dinner.
  (b) He is taking the goods away.
  (c) You (pl.) want to know everything.
  (d) Handsome men love beautiful women.
  (e) Everyone wants to have money.
  (f) Many men flee, but many stand firm.
  (g) A rich man does not love a poor one.
  (h) All good men care for citizens.
  (i) Wicked men consider wicked deeds.
  (j) Money worries everybody.

3(a) Every age [of life] is both short and frail.
  (b) Old age is an incurable disease.
  (c) Anger is a short madness.
  (d) Man is an animal possessing reason.
  (e) The way to a happy life is easy.
  (f) It is difficult not to write satire.
  (g) It is difficult suddenly to lay aside a long-lasting love.
  (h) To change nature indeed is difficult.
  (i) Woman is a fickle and changeable thing.
  (j) An old man who is a soldier is a disgraceful thing; love in an old man is a disgraceful thing.

Page 74

Reading exercises

*****1**(a) The intellect (subj.) of man is forced (verb) to choose (infin.)
Perfection (obj.) of the life, or of the work.
  (b) To err (subj., infin.) is (verb) human, to forgive (subj., infin.) divine.
  (c) And that same prayer (subj.) does teach us (obj.) all to render (infin.)
The deeds (obj.) of mercy.
  (d) We'll (subj.) teach (verb) you (obj.) to drink (infin.) deep.
  (e) To make (subj., infin.) dictionaries (obj.) is (verb) dull work.
  (f) Love (subj.) looks (verb) not with the eyes but with the mind,
And therefore is (verb) wing'd Cupid (subj.) painted (verb) blind.
*****2**(a) *uult*: Where does the poor man want to have a huge dinner?
  (b) *uis*: Where do you wish to enter?
  (c) *uult*: Every poor man wishes to bear the worries of a rich man.
  (d) *uolumus*: We slaves wish to love beautiful girls and to carry off our master's gold.

(e) *uolunt*: All citizens want to bear an easy burden.

(f) *uultis*: You never wish to cook dinner at Euclio's house.

Pages 74–5

Reading exercise / Test exercise

Omitted.

**English–Latin

Latin–English omitted.

(a) *cenamne in aedibus Euclionis, uiri pauperis, coquere uultis?*

(b) *serui audaces fugere ex aedibus uolunt.*

(c) *quae femina seruum audacem inuenire non uult?*

(d) *domini ubi cenam magnam uolunt, coquum bonum rogant.*

(e) *femina pulchra turbam magnam fert.*

(f) *apud tamen diuitem cenae optimae sunt.*

DELICIAE LATINAE: 1F

Page 76

Word exercises

1. For meanings, consult an English dictionary: civilised > *ciuis*; nihilistic > *nihil*; cook > *coquus*; dormitory > *dormio*; fugitive > *fugio*; negotiate > *negotium*; initial > *ineo*; invention > *inuenio*; science > *scio*; emit > *mitto*.

2. facile; audacious; omnibus; arid; lapidary; tonsure.

Real Latin

Sayings of Cato

Sleep as much as is enough.

Avoid gambling.

Avoid prostitutes.

Vulgate

Blessed are the poor, for yours is the kingdom of God. (Luke 6.20)

Giovanni Cotta

I'm in love – a fact I admit – with my Lycoris,
As young men do love pretty girls;
My Lycoris loves me, as I think,
As good girls love young men.

Mottoes

Do right and fear nothing.
On the side of God and one's father.
Victory loves care, i.e. success depends on close attention to detail.

I G *(Text pp. 17–20)*

NOTES FOR I G

Page 17

358–9   *dic mihi* ... *mihi custos*: 'say *to me*', 'a guard *for me*'. You will have to work out whether 'to' or 'for' is the best answer for this new range of words.

Page 18

370–1   *quid mihi* ... *aufers*: *mihi* here means 'from me', as frequently in this passage with *aufero*, 'I take x *from* Y'.

373   *quid* ... *est*: 'what business is there to you with me?', i.e. 'what business *do you have* with me?' See **GVE 48** 2 p. 79 for clauses like 'there is to you' meaning 'you have'.

377   *redde* ... *mihi*: i.e. 'give [it] back to me'. Latin often omits such words (pronouns): supply them in English from the context, e.g. l. 379 *rogas?* 'are you asking *me*', l. 381 *da mihi* 'give *it* to me' and frequently from now on.

Page 19

410   *summā pulchritudine, nullā continentiā*: we would join these two with 'and' or 'but' in English. Cf. l. 425.

413   *de filiā: filiā* has a long -*ā* here, the marker of the ablative in
       first declension nouns. Cf. l. 425, and contrast the short -*a*
       of *culpa mea* (nominative) at l. 420.

418   *es*: not 'you are', but 'be!' (imperative). So also ll. 424, 427.
       For *bono animo* see *animo bono* in the vocabulary.

427   *mihi ignosce*: 'pardon me!' Some Latin verbs put the direct
       object in the dative, as here, not the accusative.

TRANSLATION OF 1G

EUCLIO
       Look! A-shrine I-see. Who god of-the-shrine he-is? Ah.
       Trust it-is. Say to-me, Trust, *you*? you-wish for-me a-
       guard good to-be? For now to-you I-bring [360] all gold
       my; the-pot of-gold full well guard, Trust! Stop thieves
       all. Now to-shrine your gold my I-entrust. Gold in shrine
       your placed it-is.
       (*Euclio into the-house he-returns. Onto the-stage he-enters Stro-
       bilus the-slave. All Euclio's words he-hears*)
STROBILUS
       [365] Gods immortal! What I-hear? What he-says the-
       man? What he-does? Gold? to-the-shrine he-entrusts?
       Gold? in the-shrine placed it-is? Why into the-shrine not
       I-enter and the-gold from-the-man unhappy I-take-away?
       (*Strobilus into the-shrine he-goes-in. Euclio however he-hears and
       from-the-house he-comes-out. Strobilus in the-shrine he-finds*)
EUC.   [370] Go outside, worm! Why into the-shrine secretly
       you-creep? What from-me from the-shrine you-carry-off,
       rascal? What you-do?
       (*Euclio at-once to-the-man blows he-gives*)
STR.   What to-you business me-with there-is? Why me you-
       flog?
EUC.   Most-floggable-one, still me you-ask, thief, triple-thief?
       What from-me from the-shrine [375] you-take-away?
STR.   Nothing from-you I-take-away.
EUC.   Come, give-back at-once to-me.

S T R. What you-want me to-you to-give-back?

E U C. You-ask?

S T R. [380] Nothing from-you I-take-away.

E U C. Come, give to-me.

S T R. Nothing I-have. What you-wish for-you?

E U C. Show to-me hand your.

S T R. To-you I show.

E U C. [385] Come, hand to-me show the-other.

S T R. There for-you.

E U C. I see. Come, the-third also show.

S T R. The-man mad he-is!

E U C. Say to-me, what from the-shrine you-take-away?

S T R. [390] The-gods me they-destroy! Nothing I-have, nothing from the-shrine I-take-away!

E U C. Come again to-me show your-hand right.

S T R. There.

E U C. Now left also show.

S T R. Look both I-hold-out.

E U C. [395] Give-back to-me what mine it-is.

S T R. Say to-me, what me you-wish to-you to-give-back?

E U C. Without-doubt you-have.

S T R. I-have *I*? What I-have?

E U C. Not to-you I-speak. Come, give-back to-me.

S T R. [400] Mad you-are!

E U C. I-am-lost! Nothing he-has the-man. Go-away at-once, rascal! Why not you-go-away?

S T R. I-go-away.

(*Euclio into the-shrine he-goes-in. The-gold he-finds, and from the-shrine he-carries. In another place secretly he-conceals*)

E U C. [405] I-am-done-for, I-am-lost! To-where I-run? To-where not I-run? (*To-the-audience*) Hold [= *tene-o tene-re* 'I hold', 'I take'], hold the-thief! But who the-thief he-is? What thief I-say? I-do-not-know, nothing I-see, blind I-go. Who pot my of-gold full he-takes-away from-me? (*To-the-audience*) Say to-me, audience, who the-pot he-has? You-do-not-know? O me unhappy!

[410] (*Onto the-stage there-enters Lyconides, a-young-man of/ with-great beauty, of/with-no restraint*)

LYCONIDES

What man before house our he-is-weeping? By-Pollux, Euclio it-is, Phaedra's father. Without-doubt *I* I-am-lost. For Euclio a-man of/with-great uprightness he-is; for-a-fact everything about his-daughter he-knows. What for-me better it-is to-do? Better it-is for-me to-depart or to-stay? By-Pollux, I-do-not-know.

EUC.　[415] Hey *you*, who you-are?

LYC.　*I* I-am unhappy.

EUC.　More-precisely *I* I-am.

LYC.　Be of/with-good spirit [cheerful].

EUC.　What to-me you-say? Why me of/with-good spirit to-be you-wish?

LYC.　[420] The-deed mine it-is, I-confess, and the-blame mine.

EUC.　What *I* from you I-hear?

LYC.　Nothing except true. The-deed mine it-is, the-blame mine.

EUC.　O rascal, why *you* you-touch what mine it-is?

LYC.　I-do-not-know. But of/with-spirit content be [= calm, collected]! Me pardon!

EUC.　[425] Shame on-you! A-young-man of/with-great boldness, of/with-no restraint you-are! Why *you* what mine it-is you-touch, shameless-one?

LYC.　Because-of wine and love. Of/with-spirit content be! Me pardon!

EUC.　Rascal, shameless-one! Too cheap wine and love it-is, if for-a-drunkard it-is-permitted whatever-he-likes to-do.

LYC.　[430] But *I* a-young-man of/with-great uprightness I-am, and to-have I-wish what yours it-is.

EUC.　What you-say to-me? Shameless-one, at-once to-me hand-back what mine it-is.

LYC.　But what you-wish me to-you to-hand-back?

EUC.　[435] That which from-me you-take-away.

LYC.　But what it-is? Nothing from-you I-take-away! Say to-me, what I-have which yours it-is?

EUC.　The-pot of-gold full I-say! Give-back to-me!

Now learn the Learning Vocabulary at G*VE* p. 78.

EXERCISES FOR 1 G

Pages 79–80

Exercises

1   *seni misero, senibus miseris; puellae audaci, puellis audacibus; puero in-genti, pueris ingentibus; oneri multo, oneribus multis; consilio audaci, consiliis audacibus.*

2   *animo, uirtuti, audaciae, diuitibus, oneri, filiis, aquae, domino, ignibus, dis, feminis, coronae, consilio.*

*3 *seruis ingentibus, mihi, seni misero, uxoribus malis, nobis, tibi.*

4(a) Then the Lar of the household gives Euclio a pot full of gold.

(b) The wretched old man however entrusts all the gold to the shrine.

(c) But the bold slave wants to take the gold away from the wretched old man.

(d) However, Euclio shouts in this way to the wicked slave: 'What business have you got in the shrine? What are you taking away from me?'

(e) Therefore the slave is afraid and doesn't take away the gold from Euclio.

(f) But Euclio takes away the pot from out of the shrine, because now he doesn't want to entrust the gold to the god.

Pages 80–1

Exercises

1   *sene misero, senibus miseris; puella audaci, puellis audacibus; puero in-genti, pueris ingentibus; onere multo, oneribus multis; consilio audaci, consiliis audacibus.*

2   *curā, animo, audaciis, homine, uxore, pecuniā, filiis, domino, ignibus, honoribus, femina, coronis, consilio, scelere.*

*3 *in fano, a feminā, ex aquis, in scelere, ex animo, in consiliis, ex ignibus.*

4(a) Euclio is a man of the highest self-control.

(b) Lyconides is a young man of the highest beauty, [but] of no self-control.

(c) Be of a calm frame of mind, my son.

(d) You are a slave-woman of the highest boldness [and] the highest beauty, [but] of no self-control.

(e)   I am in a cheerful frame of mind, because I have as my daughter a girl of the highest goodness.

5(a)   Fortune helps the brave.
(b)   No one is faithful in love.
(c)   All art is an imitation of nature.
(d)   Truth lies open for everyone.
(e)   Death is common to every age.
(f)   The gods care for great things, but do not bother with small ones.
(g)   The British have long hair, and have every part of their body shaved except their head and upper lip.

Pages 81–2

Reading exercises

*1(a)   The bold slave says many wicked things to the wretched old man.
(b)   Show me ointment [and] garlands and gold.
(c)   There is too much worry for my wife at home.
(d)   Why do you not give back my gold to me?
(e)   I promise my daughter to you because you are a good neighbour.
(f)   Beautiful wives always take away gold from rich men, because they want to give much money to the cooks.
(g)   I give you many slaves and much money.
(h)   I never entrust anything to a bold slave and a beautiful slave-woman.
(i)   I wish to promise my daughter to a rich man, because I have no dowry.
(j)   We have a garland at home, you [pl.] have ointment.

*2   (possible answers)
(a)   *dant*: All citizens give money to good men.
(b)   *das*: Why do you give me gold?
(c)   *est*: We are in a cheerful frame of mind.
(d)   *credit*: Euclio entrusts the gold to the shrine, not to the bold man.
(e)   *aufers*: Why do you take away all the garlands and all the ointment from us?
(f)   *est*: Bold girls and handsome young men have no self-control.
(g)   *celo*: I hide from the man my daughter's dowry.
(h)   *promittit*: Why does your father not promise you as a wife to me?
(i)   *est*: You villain, what business do you have in my house?
(j)   *dat*: Boldness gives courage to every good young man.

Pages 82–3

Reading exercise / Test exercise

Omitted.

**English–Latin

Latin–English omitted.

(a) *Phaedra puella summa pulchritudine est.*
(b) *aequo animo es et aurum seruo aufer.*
(c) *omnes senes ciuibus bonis aulas pecuniae plenas reddunt.*
(d) *uos autem quare coronam iuueni aufertis?*
(e) *quid uobis negoti est in fano Laris mei?*
(f) *est mihi filius optimus, iuuenis summis uirtutibus.*

DELICIAE LATINAE: 1 G

Page 83

Word-building

Exercise

e- + *uoco* I call out, summon; *circum-* + *duco* I lead round; *per-* + *facilis* very easy; *trans-* + *mitto* I send across; *re(d)-* + *eo* I return; *pro-* + *uideo* I see in advance; *e-* + *fero* I carry out; *prae-* + *facio* I make in charge (of); *a-* + *mitto* I send away (also 'I lose'); *re-* + *do* I give back; *sub-* + *duco* I take from under, withdraw, remove (sometimes implying 'by stealth'); *e-* + *duco* I lead out; *sub-* + *eo* I go under; *per-* + *multus* very many; *ante-* + *fero* I carry in front; *trans-* + *do* I give across, I hand over; *per-* + *facio* I do to the end, I complete; *circum-* + *do* I surround; *de-* + *duco* I lead down; *re-* + *fero* I bring back; *de-* + *uoco* I call away; *sub-* + *mitto* I let down; *per-* + *sto* I stand firmly.

Page 84

Exercise

1. listener; manager; harassing; invention; plan(ning); diction; trouble-maker; promise; misdeed; favour; dwelling.

2. *uexation-is, diction-is, habitation-is, inuention-is, auditor-is, turbator-is.*

Real Latin

Vulgate

Give us this day our daily bread and forgive us our trespasses. (Luke 11.3–4)

Mottoes

Not for ourselves, but for everyone.
Not for myself, but for God and the King.
Not for myself, but for my fatherland.
For God, King and Country.
For God, Fatherland and you.
Glory to God.

Section Two
Plautus' Bacchides

2 A *(Text pp. 26–31)*

The translation remains very literal, but reverts to regular English word-order. The subject-matter may encourage you to make a more colloquial translation for yourself.

In this Section, the future tense is introduced, 'I shall/will –', e.g. 1.14 *poteris* 'you will be able' (future), contrasted with *potes* 'you are able' (present). These new forms are all given individually in the vocabulary.

Page 27

10   *uolo ... fallere*: 'I want you to deceive the old man' or 'I want the old man to deceive you'? Obviously the first (from context), but double accusatives are common with infinitives and care needs to be taken.

11–12   *facile erit senem ... decipere*: 'it will be easy' expects 'to x' – solved only with *decipere* at the end of the sentence 'to deceive'. This in turn explains *senem* accusative 'to deceive the old man'.

14   *facile*: here an adverb, 'easily' (contrast *facile erit* l. 11 above). So also **Text** ll. 15, 21, 32 etc.

16   *decipere*: why infinitive? Solved by *difficile est* 'it is difficult to'.

18–19   *senem pecuniam*: two accusative nouns, solved by *habere nolo*

'I do not want x to have y', obviously 'the old man to have the money'. Compare *Text* l. 20, where *nos pecuniam* is solved by *habere mauis*. Note this very common pattern and be ready to hold double accusatives until they are solved.

20   *seni dare*: precede with 'and' or 'but' and supply 'it' ('the money') as the object of *dare*.

25   *multa mala*: neuter plural, 'many evil [things]'. See **GVE 14** Notes 7, p. 23. Cf. *Text* l. 33 *omnia* 'everything' (see **GVE 47** p. 72), l. 39 *uera* 'true things', 'the truth'.

Page 28

46   *quam*: here 'than'.

48   *nomen est mihi Chrysalo*: lit. 'the name is for me Chrysalus', i.e. 'my name is Chrysalus'. One might expect *Chrysalus*, but *Chrysalo* is attracted into the dative because *mihi* is dative.

Page 29

58–61   An extended image from laying siege to a city, in this case, the old man.

68   *stilum . . . linum*: the *tabellae* are wooden tablets with waxed inner surfaces, on which the message was scratched with the *stilus*. When the message had been written, the tablets were closed face to face and bound with *linum*. The knot of the *linum* was then sealed with wax (*cera*), and imprinted with the signet ring of the sender.

74   *tu alteram . . . alteram*: *alter* (here feminine, *altera*) means you are talking about one *or* the other of two people. So the first *altera* refers to one woman, the second to the other.

Page 30

82   *ita ut esse uolumus*: 'as we wish [it] to be'.

112–15 See these notes on *Text* l. 68 above.

Page 31

124   *meum*: supply *officium*.

TRANSLATION OF 2A

The play's characters [= The cast list]
Nicobulus, a rich old man, Mnesilochus' father, a man of the highest seriousness, [but] of no wisdom.
Mnesilochus, Nicobulus' son, lover of the one Bacchis [Bacchis 1].
Pistoclerus, Mnesilochus' friend, lover of the other Bacchis [Bacchis 2].
[5] Chrysalus, Nicobulus' slave, a man of the highest astuteness.
Cleomachus, a soldier, the other lover of Bacchis 1.

(*Enter Mnesilochus, Pistoclerus, [and] Chrysalus*)

MNESILOCHUS

> Listen to me, Chrysalus. For you are a slave of great astuteness and of much intelligence. I want you to manufacture a second way [to get] to my father. [10] I want you to trick the clever old man cleverly, and to take the gold away from the old man. Surely it will be easy to deceive the old man, a man of great stupidity [and] of no intelligence.

CHRYSALUS

> I can't.

MNE. You can't? Go on and you will easily be able [to].

CHR. [15] How, you criminal, will I easily be able [to]? Who is now able to manufacture a second way [to get to] the old man? It's difficult enough to deceive [him] once. But now our old man considers me untruthful, therefore I shall not be able to deceive the old man for a second time. But I prefer you to have the money; I don't want the old man to have the money.

MNE. [20] If you prefer *us* to have the money, [and] you don't want to give [it] to the old man, come, Chrysalus, do everything. Go on and you will easily be able [to].

CHR. But Mnesilochus, your father knows *everything*. What can I do? He considers me untruthful and will never believe me, even if I say to the man 'Don't believe me.'

PISTOCLERUS

> [25] And he's saying many bad things about you, Chrysalus.

CHR. What's your father saying about me?

MNE. He is speaking thus about you: 'If Chrysalus says to me
      "Look, I see the sun", then I refuse to believe Chrysalus.
      For it won't be the sun, but the moon. If Chrysalus says to
      me "It's day", I won't believe [him]. For it will be night,
      [30] not day.'

CHR. Your father is speaking thus? The gods are preserving me!
      Be of good heart. I'll easily deceive the man today, by
      Hercules! Listen. I have a bold plan. But first tell me –
      what do you prefer? For today I can do everything.

MNE. [35] We prefer today to have both the girls and the money.

CHR. So today you will have both the girls and a huge [sum of]
      money. For I shall give [it] to you. Today both the girls
      and the money will be yours.

MNE. You will give [them] to us? Will the girl be mine? I don't
      want you to make a joke. I prefer you to tell the truth.

CHR. [40] I am not making a joke, for today [your] father will
      give you a huge [sum of] money. Today, Mnesilochus,
      you'll have your girl, just as your heart hopes.

MNE. Will I have my girl? Do you promise?

CHR. Thus I promise. It will be an easy thing. For [your] father
      will give you everything.

PI.   [45] Then indeed, Chrysalus, we will give huge thanks to
      you. Now – what do you want us to do? For we prefer to
      help [rather] than do nothing.

CHR. I want you to do nothing except make love. But how
      much gold do you want to have for yourselves? Ask [and]
      I shall give it to you. For my name is Chrysalus [Goldie].
      But now how much gold will be enough for you, Mnesi-
      lochus? Tell me.

MNE. [50] I want you to give me two hundred coins for Bacchis.

CHR. I will give [them] to you.

MNE. But two hundred coins won't be enough for us, because
      after [our] victory we will have expenses. For after [our]
      victory, we will run up great expenses.

CHR. [55] First I'll take action about the two hundred coins,
      then about the expenses. Everything will be easy for me.

MNE. But what plan do you have? What will you do? Tell me. I
      want to hear.

CHR. You will hear. Concerning the two hundred coins, I shall first aim a catapult at our old man. If the catapult destroys [his] tower and ramparts, I shall at once invade [60] the ancient town through the gate. If I capture the town, you'll carry your gold away from the town in baskets. Then you'll be able to give [it] to [your girl], just as your heart hopes, Mnesilochus. The matter will be easy, the road smooth.

PI. Our heart [= hopes] is in your hands, Chrysalus.

CHR. [65] If you want to help, you'll go off inside, Pistoclerus, to Bacchis and you'll quickly bring in . . .

PI. What? Tell me and I'll do [it] at once. What shall I bring in?

CHR. You will bring in a stylus, wax, tablets [and] thread.

PI. I'll do [it] now.

[70] (*Pistoclerus exits from the stage* [*to go*] *to Bacchis*)

MNE. What will you do now? Tell me.

CHR. You have your Bacchis. Does Pistoclerus have a mistress?

MNE. Yes indeed: the other Bacchis [2].

CHR. [So] you [have] the one, [and] Pistoclerus has the other Bacchis? Where's [75] your dining couch?

MNE. What's the problem? Why do you want to know?

CHR. You don't know my plan, but it'll be huge.

MNE. Give me your hand and come with me to the doors.

CHR. Look, [here's] my hand. Lead on.

[80] (*Chrysalus gives Mnesilochus his hand and approaches the doors*)

MNE. Look inside.

CHR. Good. The place is very beautiful thus, [exactly] as we want [it] to be.

(*Re-enter Pistoclerus onto the stage*)

PI. As you command thus do I do.

CHR. [85] What do you have?

PI. I have everything. I'm bringing stylus, wax, tablets and thread.

CHR. Good. Now Mnesilochus, you'll take the stylus.

MNE. What next?

CHR. I'll speak, [and] you will write my words. For I prefer you to write, because [90] thus your father will recognise the letters [handwriting] when he reads [it]. Be of good spirit! Write!

MNE. What things shall I write?

CHR. I'll tell [you]. Write 'Mnesilochus greets [his] father. But now, father, I don't want Chrysalus to deceive you again. For ...'

PI. [95] Wait while he writes. You're speaking too quickly, Chrysalus.

CHR. The hands of lovers ought to be swift.

MNE. My hand is swift, Chrysalus.

PI. No, you will have a swift hand when you are holding the money in your hand.

MNE. Speak.

CHR. [100] 'For, my father, Chrysalus is devising tricks, because he wants to deceive you again. For he wants to take the gold from you and he's saying "Today, I'll take the gold away from the stupid old man."' Write [that] next to [it].

MNE. I will write [it] alongside. Speak now.

CHR. 'And he's saying "Today I'll give you the gold, Mnesi-lochus, [and] you'll [105] be able to give the gold to [your] mistresses." But, father, I bid you to beware.'
(Chrysalus is silent while Mnesilochus writes)

MNE. Speak now.

CHR. Write also ...
(Chrysalus says nothing but thinks to himself)

MNE. [110] Speak now, [and] I'll write [it].

CHR. 'But, father, I don't want you to beat Chrysalus. I prefer you to bind Chrysalus' hands, [and] keep Chrysalus at home.' You, give [me] the wax and thread. Come, tie [it] up, [and] seal [it] quickly.

MNE. I shall tie [it] up, [and] seal [it].
[115] *(Mnesilochus ties up and seals the tablets)*

MNE. I beg [you], why do you want me to send such a letter to [my] father? What plan do you have? What use will it be if my father is wary and binds you and keeps you at home?

CHR. Because I want the matter to be thus. Surely you are able to take care of yourself? I shall take care of [120] my job. Give [me] the tablets.

MNE. Take [them].

CHR. Pay attention, Mnesilochus, and you, Pistoclerus. I want
      you to lie down with your mistresses in the dining room
      now. Do not get up, until I give the signal. You take care
      of your job, [and] I shall take care [125] of mine.

MNE. O excellent general!

PI.   And bold slave!

CHR. Now you ought to be making love to your mistresses.

MNE. We're off!

      [130] (*Exeunt Mnesilochus and Pistoclerus to the dining room*)

Now learn the Learning Vocabulary at *GVE* p. 87.

EXERCISES FOR 2A

Page 89

Exercises

1   *celabunt*, they will hide, *celabit*, 1; *inueniet*, he will find, *inuenient*, 4;
     amittes, you (s.) will lose, *amittetis*, 3; *habebimus*, we shall have, *habebo*,
     2; *coquent*, they will cook, *coquet*, 3; *iubebit*, he will order, *iubebunt*, 2;
     uerberabis, you (s.) will beat, *uerberabitis*, 1; *credet*, he will believe,
     credent, 3; *capietis*, you (pl.) will capture, *capies*, 3/4; *scribam*, I shall
     write, *scribemus*, 3; *facient*, they will do, *faciet*, 3/4; *audietis*, you (pl.)
     will hear, *audies*, 4.

*2   *credunt, credent*, they will believe; *salutat, salutabit*, he will greet;
     scribit, scribet, he will write; *fers, feres*, you (s.) will bear; *estis, eritis*,
     you (pl.) will be; *it, ibit*, he will go; *rogo, rogabo*, I shall ask; *curant,
     curabunt*, they will take care of.

3   *do, dabit*, he will give, *dabunt*, they will give; *clamo, clamabit*, he will
     shout, *clamabunt*, they will shout; *maneo, manebit*, he will wait, *man-
     ebunt*, they will wait; *taceo, tacebit*, he will be silent, *tacebunt*, they will
     be silent; *duco, ducet*, he will lead, *ducent*, they will lead; *posco, poscet*,
     he will demand, *poscent*, they will demand; *dormio, dormiet*, he will
     sleep, *dormient*, they will sleep; *uincio, uinciet*, he will bind, *uincient*,
     they will bind; *capio, capiet*, he will capture, *capient*, they will cap-
     ture; *fugio, fugiet*, he will flee, *fugient*, they will flee; *sum, erit*, he will
     be, *erunt*, they will be; *redeo, redibit*, he will return, *redibunt*, they will
     return.

*4   You will hear *audies*; they will call *uocabunt*; I shall make *faciam*; we
will speak *dicemus*; you (pl.) will be silent *tacebitis*; he will lead *ducet*;
we will love *amabimus*.

5   *ducent* they will lead; *uerberabo* I shall beat; *duces* you (s.) will lead;
amabunt they will like; *fugiemus* we shall flee; *mittes* you (s.) will send;
decipies you (s.) will deceive.

All other verbs in this exercise are in the Present Tense.

If you have given the wrong answer in any of these exercises,
check that you have identified the **conjugation** of the verb cor-
rectly, or check whether the verb is **irregular**.

Page 90

Exercises

1   you (s.) wish *uis*; we prefer *malumus*; they refuse *nolunt*; he can *potest*;
we will prefer *malemus*; you (pl.) do not wish *non uultis*; you (s.) are
able *potes*; they will refuse *nolent*.

2   *est* he is, *erit* he will be; *possunt* they can, *poterunt* they will be able;
uoles you (s.) will wish, *uis* you wish; *malent* they will prefer, *malunt*
they prefer; *non uis* you (s.) do not wish, *noles* you (s.) will not wish;
erimus we shall be, *sumus* we are; *nolumus* we do not want, *nolemus* we
shall not want.

Page 93

Exercises

*1   beautiful hand *manus pulchra*; large hand *manus magna*; my hand
manus mea; swift hand *manus celeris*.

Note: *man-us, -us* (fourth declension) is a feminine noun.

Declension: *manus pulchra/celeris, manum pulchram/celerem, manus pulchrae/
celeris, manui pulchrae/celeri, manu pulchrā/celeri; manus pulchrae/celeres, manus
pulchras/celerīs, manuum pulchrarum/celerium, manibus pulchris/celeribus, manibus pulchris/celeribus.*

Note: *magn-a* and *me-a* decline as *pulcher*.

2   *uiā* ablative sing. (without macron = nominative); *amicae* dative sing.
or genitive sing. *or* nominative pl.; *nocte* ablative sing.; *manui* dative
sing.; *celeri* dative *or* ablative sing.; *officio facili* dative *or* ablative sing.;

scelere audaci ablative sing.; *soli* dative sing.; *nummis ducentis* dative *or* ablative pl.; *astutiae tuae* dative sing. *or* genitive sing. *or* nominative pl.; *sumptui magno* dative sing.

If you have made any mistakes, check the **declension** of the nouns and adjectives.

Page 94

Exercises

1(a) Today our old man will give you two hundred coins in the hand.
(b) What do you want me to do? For I prefer to help [rather] than to do nothing.
(c) If the old man considers [lit. will consider] me a liar, I shall want to play many tricks.
(d) I shall do my duty; I prefer you to do yours.
(e) If I can [lit. shall be able to] remove the gold [away] from the old man, you will be able to give two hundred coins to your friends.
(f) Give me your hand, I beg you; I shall give you mine.
(g) If you wish to trust a woman, you want to write in running water.
(h) If you can [lit. will be able to] get the gold away from the old man, Chrysalus, I shall consider you a slave of great astuteness.
(i) While the night is silent, thieves prefer to commit wicked crimes [rather] than sleep.
(j) Take the wax, tablets [and] pen away from me; today I do not wish to write.

2(a) Experience is the best teacher.
(b) But who will guard the guards themselves?
(c) The deeds of mortals never fool the gods.
(d) It is rage that helps lions, fear stags, vehemence the hawk and flight the dove.
(e) A great man can emerge from a hovel, a beautiful and mighty heart can emerge from an ugly and lowly little body.
(f) No man can be happy without virtue.
(g) Without control no house or state can survive.

Pages 95–6

Reading

*1 The infinitive phrase is marked in italic, the object in bold italic.

(a) ***Man good*** *than bad daughter my to-home to-lead* I-prefer.
(b) ***Slave*** *man to-be of-great boldness* I-do-not-wish.

(c)   **You** *your job,* **me** *to-do mine* master orders.

(d)   **Masters** *to-beat slaves bold* citizens prefer.

(e)   *Wives husbands to-love* I-order (see the next exercise).

*2

See ***1** above.

(a)   *uxores amare.*

(b)   *uiros amare.*

*3(a)   You me to believe *iubeo*: I order you to believe me.

(b)   The slave to the old man the way to find another *uolo*: I want the slave to find another way to the old man.

(c)   Coins two hundred to get than nothing to have *malo*: I prefer to get two hundred coins than to have nothing.

(d)   Girl-friend me to love my *iubes*: you order me to make love to my girl.

(e)   Stiluses and wax and tablets you to bring *iubet*: he orders you to bring stiluses, wax and tablets.

(f)   Men from the town to go out bold *iubemus*: we order the bold men to go out of the town.

(g)   Chrysalus again father to deceive my *uolumus*: we want Chrysalus to deceive my father again.

(h)   A slave perfume, garlands a slave-girl to bring to me *nolunt*: they do not want the slave to bring me perfume, nor the slave-girl [to bring me] garlands.

(i)   Gold to Lar my than to slave bold to entrust *mauultis*: you prefer to entrust your gold to my Lar [rather] than to the bold slave.

(j)   To/from friends to take away bold coins you two hundred *iubemus*: we order you to take two hundred coins away from your bold friends.

*4(a)   It.

(b)   Her.

(c)   Them.

(d)   It.

(e)   It.

Pages 96–7

Reading exercise / Test exercise

Omitted.

**English–Latin

Latin–English omitted.

(a) *Mnesilochus Chrysalum iterum senem miserum decipere uolet.*
(b) *audacis serui astutias quam mendacis amicae audaciam semper malet.*
(c) *Chrysalus, uir magna astutia, ducentos nummos senis facile auferre poterit.*
(d) *furis manus semper celeris est.*
(e) *senes iuuenibus pecuniam dabunt multam.*
(f) *erunt iuuenibus magni sumptus, quod amicas habent pulchras.*

DELICIAE LATINAE: 2A

Page 98

Word exercise

For meanings consult an English dictionary.

lunatic > *luna*;   style > *stilus*;   official > *officium*;   adjutant > *adiuuo*;
nocturnal > *nox*;   solar > *sol*;   manual > *manus*;   mendacious > *mendax*;
credible > *credo*;   scribble > *scribo*;   a   posse > *possum*   (infinitive   *posse*);
beneficial > *beneficium*; reiterate > *re- iterum*; sumptuary > *sumptus*.

Real Latin

Pages 99–100

Martial

I do not like you, Sabidius, and I cannot say why.
This is the only thing I can say, I don't like you. (1.32)

You mix me Veientian wine, when you drink Massic.
I prefer smelling the Massic, [rather] than drinking [sc. the Veientian]. (3.49)

Vulgate

You will not be able to see my face: for a man shall not see me and
live. (Exodus 33.20)
Thou shalt not kill ... thou shalt not commit theft ... thou shalt
not covet thy neighbour's house; nor shalt thou desire his wife, nor

his servant, nor his serving-girl, nor his ox, nor his ass. (Exodus
20.13)
And I say unto you ... 'Seek and ye shall find.' (Luke 11.9)

Mottoes

Virtue overcomes all.
Love conquers all.
Work conquers all.
Truth conquers all.
All things are good to the good.

2 B *(Text pp. 31–4)*

NOTES FOR 2B

In this Section, we concentrate on a new type of verb with new
endings, called 'deponent', e.g. **Text** l. 132 *persequor* 'I pursue', l.
135 *loquor* 'I speak', l. 136 *loqui* 'to speak', etc. These are all individually glossed in the Vocabulary.

Page 31

138–40 *erit ... dabo ... erit ... exibit...*: these are future tense in
Latin, but English translates them 'is', 'give', 'is' and 'he
comes out'. Watch out for other places where English
tenses do not correspond to the Latin.

139   *tam*: 'as' prepares the way for *quam*, 'as'; cf. *ut ... ita / ita ...
ut.*

Page 32

151   *loquere*: imperative, not infinitive (see Vocabulary).

166–7   Plautus' comedies are full of such lively images, cf. the
image of the siege at **Text** p. 29, l. 58ff.

180   *obsignatas*: add 'them', referring to *tabellas*.

Page 33

193   *quem di diligunt*: for the background to this famous sentiment, see **Text** p. 47.

195   *tanti*: 'worth as much' looks forward to *quanti* 'as'. Cf. note on **Text** l.139 above.

200   *plus auri*: 'more [of] gold', cf. *satis, nimis, quantum, quid* **GVE 31** p. 51; **GVE 40** p. 62.

201   *tum*: 'then' looks forward to *ubi* 'when' (not 'where').

203–4   *loquere . . . sequere*: imperatives, not infinitives.

TRANSLATION OF 2B

CHRYSALUS

You look after your job [and] I'll look after mine. (*Talks to himself*) It's a big, more precisely crazy, business I am pursuing. I have a bold and difficult enough task. Will I be able to complete today a thing so difficult? But I am a slave of great astuteness [and] of the highest intelligence, [**135**] Nicobulus is an old man of no wisdom. Why am I talking to myself like this? It's necessary to do the business and not talk [about it].

But now I want the old man to be angry. For I will not easily carry out my trick if the old man is calm when I give the letter into [his] hands. If he is angry, I will make him as roasted as a chick-pea. [**140**] I'll go up to the house. Then, when he comes out, I'll immediately give the tablets into the old man's [lit. to the old man] hands.

(*Nicobulus comes out of the house onto the stage and talks to himself*)

NICOBULUS

I'm angry because I cannot find Chrysalus. But if I catch the villain, I will beat [him].

CHR.   [**145**] (*He speaks to himself*) I'm safe, the old man's angry! Now I'm going up to the man.

NIC.   Who's speaking near by? It's Chrysalus, as I think.

CHR.   (*He speaks to himself*) I'll go up to [him].

(*Chrysalus goes up to the old man*)

NIC.   [**150**] Good slave, greetings. You are silent? Why? Do not keep silent, scoundrel [lit. source of crimes], but speak. For I know all your crimes from Mnesilochus.

CHR.   Is Mnesilochus accusing me? Am I bad [and] criminal? Just look at the fact[s]: I will keep quiet.

NIC.   What matter are you talking [about], you scoundrel? Are you threatening me? Don't [155] threaten *me*, Chrysalus, I'm warning you.

CHR.   I'm not threatening you, master. Soon you will know your son's character; thus I promise. Now take the tablets. For Mnesilochus orders me to bring the tablets and to give [them] into your hands. He wants you to read [them] and carry out all its words [instructions].

NIC.   [160] Give.

CHR.   Take. Recognise the seal.

NIC.   It is the seal of Mnesilochus. But where is my son?

CHR.   I don't know.

       (*Nicobulus reads the tablets. Meanwhile Chrysalus talks to himself*)
       [165] I forget everything. I remember nothing. I'm ignorant of everything. I know myself to be a slave. I do not know even that which I know. Hoorah! Now our thrush is going after the worm from the trap ...

NIC.   Don't go away, Chrysalus. Wait. Now I'm going into the house; soon I'll come out to you.
       [170] (*Exit Nicobulus from the stage into the house*)

CHR.   O stupid man! How you are trying to deceive me! But I shall say no word: the old man's coming out.
       (*Nicobulus advances from the house onto the stage. Slaves come out with Nicobulus*)

NIC.   Slaves, follow [me]. You, bind Chrysalus' hands at once.

CHR.   [175] What's happening? What's the matter? Don't bind my hands, master.

NIC.   Don't beg [me], villain. (*To the slave*) Thrust your fist [against him] if he says a word. (*To Chrysalus*) I have in my hand Mnesilochus' tablets. What do the tablets say? Do you know, or not?

CHR.   Why do you ask me? As you received the tablets from Mnesilochus, thus sealed [180] I bring them to you.

NIC.   Ha! You, scoundrel! Are you saying 'Today I'll take the gold from the stupid old man'?

CHR.   Am I speaking thus? I do not remember. I forget everything.

NIC. Don't lie. You remember everything well, [185] you forget no word.

CHR. What man thus announces my words?

NIC. No man, but the tablets of Mnesilochus announce the matter. The tablets order me to bind your hands.

CHR. Ah! Your son is making me a Bellerophon; for I [190] bring the tablets, and because of the tablets you'll bind me. O foolish [man], foolish [man], you are ignorant of everything. I order you to beware.

NIC. What are you saying? Why are you ordering me to beware? Reply to me!

CHR. (*He does not reply but mocks the old man*) [He] whom the gods *love* dies young. But no god loves Nicobulus; for he's [195] a very old old man; he's worth as much as a rotten mushroom.

NIC. Slaves, take Chrysalus off inside and bind [him] to a column vigorously. (*To Chrysalus*) You'll never take [my] gold from me.

CHR. But you will soon give [it].

NIC. I'll give [it]? I will never give [it], scoundrel.

CHR. [200] And you will order me to take away more gold. For your son is in great danger. You will wish to free Chrysalus then, when you know the matter. But I will never accept my freedom.

NIC. Speak up, scoundrel. What danger is my son in?

CHR. Follow me. You'll know soon, as I think.

NIC. [205] But to where do I follow you? Don't be silent, but go on.

CHR. I shall go on.
(*Nicobulus follows Chrysalus to the house*)
Look. Look into the house.
(*Nicobulus looks inside*)
[210] Do you see a party? Whom do you see on the one couch?

NIC. On the one couch I see Pistoclerus and Bacchis.

CHR. Pray tell [me], who are on the other couch?

NIC. Poor me! I'm lost!

Now learn the Learning Vocabulary at *GVE* pp. 101–2.

EXERCISES FOR 2B

Page 104

Exercises

Remember to check the **conjugation** of each verb.

1   *precatur* he prays, *precantur* they pray; *mentiris* you (s.) lie, *mentimini*
you (pl.) lie; *pollicemur* we promise, *polliceor* I promise; *sequuntur* they
follow, *sequitur* he follows; *minaris* you (s.) threaten, *minamini* you
(pl.) threaten; *loquimini* you (pl.) speak, *loqueris* you (s.) speak; *mentior* I lie, *mentimur* we lie; *opinare* you (s.) think / think! (imper.),
opinamini you (pl.) think / think! (imper.); *progredimini* you (pl.)
advance, *progrederis* you (s.) advance; *loqueris* you (s.) speak, *loquimini*
you (pl.) speak; *pollicere* you promise (s.) / promise! (imper.), *polli-
cemini* you (pl.) promise / promise! (imper.); *minamur* we threaten,
minor I threaten.

Note: -*re* endings may be indicative or imperative.

2   we threaten *minamur*; he promises *pollicetur*; they forget *obliuiscuntur*;
you (pl.) remember *recordamini*; you (s.) speak *loqueris*; I am following *sequor*; advance! (s.) *progredere!*; beg! (s.) *precare!*; talk! (pl.) *loquimini!*; promise! (s.) *pollicere!*

3   Infinitives: *amare* to love; *uocare* to call; *habere* to have; *loqui* to speak;
inuenire to find; *progredi* to advance; *mentiri* to lie; *opinari* to think;
ducere to lead; *inire* to go in; *iubere* to order.

Imperatives: *minare* threaten! (s.); *pollicere* promise! (s.); *sequere* follow! (s.); *audi* listen! (s.); *dormi* sleep! (s.); *precare* pray! (s.); *inueni* find!
(s.); *loquere* speak! (s.); *progredere* advance! (s.).

*4   *habeo* I have, *habere*, *habe!*; *curo* I care for, *curare*, *cura!*; *minor* I
threaten, *minari*, *minare!*; *loquor* I speak, *loqui*, *loquere!*; *audio* I hear,
audire, *audi!*; *duco* I lead, *ducere*, *duc!* (irregular); *mitto* I send, *mittere*,
mitte!; *precor* I pray, *precari*, *precare!*; *fugio* I flee, *fugere*, *fuge!*; *credo* I
trust, *credere*, *crede!*

Page 105

Exercise

noli + Infinitive: don't (s.) follow *noli sequi*; don't (pl.) threaten me *nolite
mihi minari*; don't (s.) be stupid (m.) *noli stultus esse*; don't (pl.) send the

letter *nolite litteras mittere*; don't (s.) hide the pot *noli aulam celare*; don't (pl.) lead the slaves *nolite seruos ducere*.

Exercise

*Declined in full: *omnis res, omnem rem, omnis rei, omni rei, omni re, omnes res, omnīs (-es) res, omnium rerum, omnibus rebus, omnibus rebus; pulcher dies, pulchrum diem, pulchri diei, pulchro diei, pulchro die, pulchri dies, pulchros dies, pulchrorum dierum, pulchris diebus, pulchris diebus; mea res, meam rem, meae rei, meae rei, mea re, meae res, meas res, mearum rerum, meis rebus, meis rebus; tristis dies, tristem diem, tristis diei, tristi diei, tristi die, tristes dies, tristīs (-es) dies, tristium dierum, tristibus diebus, tristibus diebus.*

Pages 106–7

Exercises

1(a) N: Don't threaten me, Chrysalus.
        C: But master, I'm telling you how it is. (Lit. = as the thing is.)
 (b) The bold slave has a head full of tricks.
 (c) The slaves soon leave the house and follow the old man.
 (d) But who is speaking? I think it's Chrysalus. (Lit. = as I think it's Chrysalus.)
 (e) Look inside, my master. What do you see in the house? It's a bad thing I think.
 (f) Chrysalus tells his master to take care and calls him ignorant of all things.
 (g) Find out everything. I prefer you to remember [rather] than forget.
 (h) As you promise, so I want it [the thing] to be.
 (i) What do you think? Look! The slave threatens me, next he lies, then he begs and beseeches me.
 (j) Advance, my Nicobulus, and threaten Chrysalus at once.

2(a) Love is (an) unsuspecting (thing). (OVID)
 (b) It is a great thing to be quiet. (MARTIAL)
 (c) There will be crimes as long as there are men. (TACITUS)
 (d) Human affairs are frail and perishable. (CICERO)
 (e) It is sweet and honourable to die for one's country. (HORACE)
 (f) It is Roman to do and suffer brave deeds. (LIVY)

Reading (markers underlined)

(a) <u>Then</u> you will find out everything, my master, <u>if</u> you want to know, <u>when</u> you see your son in the house of the Bacchides.

(NB all the tenses in the Latin in this sentence are **future**, but need not be translated as such.)

(b) <u>As</u> you say the thing to me, <u>so</u> I think, <u>because</u> I trust you.

(c) Our old man is worth <u>as much</u> <u>as</u> a stinking mushroom, <u>as</u> Chrysalus thinks, <u>because</u> he is a slave of the utmost boldness.

(d) <u>Because</u> I want you to know everything, I will order you to look inside the house, <u>where</u>, <u>if</u> you have eyes, you will soon see your son with his girl friend.

(e) But <u>if</u> I can (shall be able to) give the old man the letter <u>at the time</u> <u>when</u> I want to, he will be <u>as</u> roasted <u>as</u> a roasted chick pea, <u>as</u> I think.

Page 108

Reading exercise / Test exercise

Omitted.

**English–Latin*

Latin–English omitted.

(a) *noli seni misero* [dative] *minari, serue.*

(b) *ubi rem recordamini, pericula recordamini* [or *in animo habete*]; *animus numquam mentitur.*

NB *recordor* = recall *and* remember.

(c) *serui autem, omnium rerum nescii, periculi* [genitive] *obliuiscuntur.*

(d) *puellae omnes ex aedibus egrediuntur.*

(e) *nos non mentimur, sed ita tibi* [or *uobis*] *loquimur ut res est.*

(f) *sequere me in aedis, mi fili, et deos precare.*

DELICIAE LATINAE: 2B

Page 109

Word exercise

Use an English dictionary to check meanings.

perfect > *perficio*; capital > *caput*; verb > *uerbum*; irate > *iratus*; maximise > *maximus*; legible > *lego*; advent > *aduentus* ('arrival'); opinion > *opinor*; loquacious > *loquor*; progressive > *progredior*; stultify > *stultus*; oblivious > *obliuiscor*; record > *recordor*; literate > *litterae*.

Everyday Latin

A *non sequitur* 'does not follow'.

Real Latin

Martial

Since you do not publish your poems, you criticise mine, Laelius.
Either stop criticising mine, or publish your own.

Page 110

Sayings of Cato

Walk with the good.
Guard your possessions.
Read books.
Do not poke fun at a man in distress.

Vulgate

'Go in to Pharaoh and say to him: "This is what the Lord God of the Hebrews says: Let my people go".' (Exodus 9.1)
'Suffer the little children to come unto me and forbid them not; for of such is the kingdom of God.' (Luke 18.16)

Mottoes

Don't annoy a lion.
Don't lie.
Don't touch me.
While I grow, I hope.
While I breathe, I hope.
While I am on guard, I care.
While I live, I hope.
Until crucifixion.
Do and hope.

2 C *(Text pp. 34–7)*

NOTES FOR 2C

Page 34

214   *ille homo . . . illum*: *ill-* means 'that' (adjective, going with a noun) or 'he, she, it' (pronoun, on its own), with the suggestion of 'the person *over there*'. So here, *ille homo* means 'that man', *illum* means 'him'. It is very important that you get used to this distinction. To help you on your way, we list the usages up to *Text* l. 224: 215 *ille* 'he', pronoun; 216 *illa mulier* 'that woman', adjective; 217 *illa* 'she', pronoun; 218 *illae mulieres* 'those women', adjective; 220 *illa mulier* 'that woman', adjective; 221 *illa* 'she', pronoun; 223 *illa* 'she', pronoun; 224 *illa* 'she', pronoun.

Page 35

231   *hic*: 'this' (adjective). Like *ille*, *hic* is used as an adjective 'this' or a pronoun 'he, she, it' (with the suggestion of 'the person *here*'). Consider *Text* l. 247 *hos seruos* 'these slaves' (adjective) as in 251; 268 *hic* 'he, the person here'; 274 *hunc* 'him'; *huic* 'to him here'.

234–5   *exheredem uitae*: another lively and amusingly paradoxical image from will-making.

237   *uir*: 'husband'.

257   *paciscere*: imperative, like *Text* l. 268 *sequere*, l. 277 *loquere*. Distinguish carefully between these *-ere* imperative forms in deponent verbs, and *-ere* infinitives in 3 and 3/4 conjugation active verbs, like *opprimere* (*Text* l. 258). The deponent has its infinitive form in *-i*, e.g. *Text* l. 256 *pacisci*, l. 263 *polliceri*.

Page 36

282–4   Observe that the Roman pantheon contains well-known anthropomorphic deities like Jove, Juno, etc. who are identified with Greek gods, but also abstractions like *Spes*,

Ops and *Virtus* (often moral) and specifically Roman gods like Summanus.

Page 37

291   *crucem*: a reference to crucifixion, a standard mode of capital punishment for slaves.

TRANSLATION OF 2C

CHRYSALUS
    Who is that man? Do you recognise him?

NICOBULUS
    [215] I recognise [him]: it's Mnesilochus.

CHR.   Tell me, does that woman seem to you beautiful?

NIC.   She seems fairly beautiful to me.

CHR.   Oooh! How beautiful are both women. How sweet the one, how charming the other.

NIC.   [220] Tell me, I pray, who is that woman?

CHR.   What do you think? Does she seem to be a prostitute or not?

NIC.   She is obviously a prostitute, as I think.

CHR.   You are wrong. She is not a prostitute.

NIC.   What is she, I pray?

CHR.   [225] You'll know soon ...
    (*Cleomachus, a soldier and lover of the one Bacchis* [1], *enters. He does not see Chrysalus and Nicobulus. He is angry and talks to himself*)

CLEOMACHUS
    Is Mnesilochus, Nicobulus' son, trying to detain my woman by force?

NIC.   [230] (*he hears Cleomachus' words*) Who's that?

CHR.   (*he speaks to himself*) The gods are preserving me! This soldier is coming right on time for me!

CLE.   (*he speaks to himself*) That Mnesilochus thinks me not a soldier but a woman. Surely I can defend my woman? I will quickly make him lifeless, if I meet [him], and disinherited [235] from life.

NIC.   Chrysalus, who *is* that? Why is he threatening my son?

CHR.   He's that woman's man.

NIC.   What? [Her] man?

CHR.   [Her] man, I say.

NIC.   [240] Is she married [to him], I pray?

CHR.   You'll soon know.

NIC.   I'm done for, poor me!

CHR.   What now? Does Chrysalus seem to you a criminal? Am I bad? Come now, bind me, [and] listen to your son. [245] Now you know his character clearly.

NIC.   What shall I do now?

CHR.   Tell these slaves to release me quickly. For if you do not release me, he will openly catch the man soon.

CLE.   (*he speaks to himself*) How I wish to catch him with her openly! [250] Then I will kill them both.

CHR.   Do you hear his words? Why do you not order these slaves to release me?

NIC.   (*to the slaves*) Release this man. I'm done for, poor me! How I am afraid!
(*The slaves release Chrysalus' hands*)

CLE.   [255] (*he speaks to himself*) Then that woman will not be able to mock me.

CHR.   (*to Nicobulus*) You will be able to make a bargain with him, if you give him money ...

NIC.   I beg, make a bargain with him, in whatever way you want. Just be careful. For I do not want the soldier to catch them openly and kill them.

CHR.   I'll go up to him and act assiduously.
[260] (*He goes up to the soldier; Nicobulus cannot hear their conversation*)
Hey you, why are you shouting?

CLE.   Where's your master?

CHR.   Nowhere. I don't know. You want me to promise you two hunded coins now? I'll promise these coins, if you keep quiet.

CLE.   [265] I prefer nothing to those two hundred coins.

CHR.   Therefore I shall promise the coins if you keep quiet and do what I order.

CLE.   As you think, thus I shall do.

CHR.   This is Mnesilochus' father. Follow [me], [and] he will promise [them] to you. You ask for that gold.
       [270] (*Chrysalus leads the soldier to Nicobulus*)

NIC.   What's happening?

CHR.   This soldier will accept two hundred gold coins.

NIC.   You are saving me. How soon shall I say 'I shall give [them]'?

CHR.   (*to the soldier*) You ask this man, (*to Nicobulus*) you promise the coins to this man.

NIC.   [275] I promise. Ask.

CLE.   Will you give [me] two hundred gold Philip coins?

CHR.   Say 'I will give [them].' Reply.

NIC.   I will give [them].

CHR.   (*becomes angry and addresses the soldier*) What now, vile man? What do you want? [280] Do you suspect Mnesilochus to be with that woman?

CLE.   Yes, indeed, she is too.

CHR.   By Jove, Juno, Ceres, Minerva, Latona, Hope, Ops, Virtue, Venus, Castor, Pollux, Mars, Mercury, Hercules, Summanus, Sun, Saturn and [285] all the gods, I swear: he is neither sleeping with her nor walking nor kissing [her].

NIC.   How my slave does swear! The perjuries of this slave are preserving me.

CLE.   So where's Mnesilochus now?

CHR.   The man is absent; but she is visiting the temple of Minerva. Go, see.

CLE.   [290] So I'm going off to the forum.

CHR.   Or to a bad end, by Hercules.

Now learn the Learning Vocabulary at *GVE* p. 113.

EXERCISES FOR 2C

Pages 115–16

Exercises

*1   *hic seruus, hunc seruum, huius serui, huic seruo, hoc seruo, hi serui, hos seruos, horum seruorum, his seruis, his seruis; ille miles, illum militem, illius* *militis, illi militi, illo milite, illi milites, illos milites, illorum militum, illis militibus, illis militibus; haec serua, hanc seruam, huius seruae, huic seruae, hac serua, hae seruae, has seruas, harum seruarum, his seruis, his seruis; illud periculum, illud periculum, illius periculi, illi periculo, illo periculo, illa pericula, illa pericula, illorum periculorum, illis periculis, illis periculis; hoc uerbum, hoc uerbum, huius uerbi, huic uerbo, hoc uerbo, haec uerba, haec uerba, horum uerborum, his uerbis, his uerbis; illa mulier, illam mulierem, illius mulieris, illi mulieri, illa muliere, illae mulieres, illas mulieres, illarum mulierum, illis mulieribus, illis mulieribus.*

2 genitive; ablative; nominative; dative; nominative *or* accusative; dative *or* ablative; (optional); nominative; ablative; nominative *or* accusative; accusative; dative *or* ablative; dative; (optional).

3 *hunc militem; illi seni; huius puellae; illa consilia; haec pericula; illius feminae.*

4 *hi thesauri* nom. pl.; *illius thesauri* gen. sing.; *illas sorores* acc. pl.; *hae sorores* nom. pl.; *illa res* nom. sing.; *has res* acc. pl.; *illae res* nom. pl.; *huius manus* gen. sing.; *illae manus* nom. pl.; *hae manus* nom. pl.; *illas mulieres* acc. pl.; *hae mulieres* nom. pl.; *illi puero* dat. sing.; *hoc puero* abl. sing.; *illae feminae* nom. pl.; *huic feminae* dat. sing.; *illius feminae* gen. sing.; *hic dies* nom. sing.; *illos dies* acc. sing.; *hi dies* nom. pl.

5 *huius amici*, this friend's, *huius lunae*, this moon's, gen. sing. masc./ fem./neut.; *illum puerum*, that boy, *illum fratrem*, that brother, acc. sing. masc.; *illā uxore*, [by] that wife, *illā manu*, by that hand, abl. sing. fem.; *hoc officium*, this duty, *hoc nomen*, this name, *hoc aurum*, this gold, nom./acc. sing. neut.; *haec corona*, this crown, *haec manus*, this hand, *haec res*, this thing, nom. sing. fem.; *haec opera*, these works, *haec negotia*, these businesses nom./acc. pl. neut.; *illos ciuīs*, those citizens, *illos deos*, those gods, acc. pl. masc.

Optional revision

Omitted.

Pages 116–18

Exercises

1 with these women, on that head, to this thing, through that crowd, with this prostitute, from that danger.

*2 *in hanc scaenam, cum illa muliere, per haec incendia, cum illis fratribus, in hoc oculo, in illud oppidum, per haec pericula.*

3(a)   If that soldier catches Mnesilochus with Bacchis, he will kill them.
 (b)   This Bacchis seems to be the girl friend of Mnesilochus, that one of Pistoclerus.
 (c)   That young man loves this woman, and this one loves that one.
 (d)   Nicobulus hears the words of that soldier, then he clearly gets to know the character of his son.
 (e)   All prostitutes seem evil to this slave and excellent to those young men.
 (f)   That slave tries to deceive this old man.

4(a)   The one salvation for the conquered is to hope for no salvation.
 (b)   We cannot change the past.
 (c)   We always strive towards the forbidden and yearn for what has been denied.
 (d)   Once spoken the word flies beyond recall.

*Reading

(a)   That soldier (subject) this woman (object) to/for this young man (dative) to believe (NB takes dative)
ille miles hanc mulierem huic iuueni credere <u>uult</u>.
That soldier wants this woman to believe this young man.

(b)   that ... slave (object) of this old man
illum huius senis seruum <u>uideo</u>.
I see that slave of this old man.

(c)   this gold (object) to/for that soldier this slave (subject)
hoc aurum illi militi hic seruus <u>dat</u>.
This slave gives this gold to that soldier.

(d)   with this woman that young man (object) this soldier (subject) soon
cum hac muliere illum iuuenem hic miles mox <u>uidebit</u>.
This soldier will soon see that young man with this woman.

(e)   to this ... woman he (subject) all these coins (object) to give
huic ille feminae hos nummos omnis dare <u>mauult</u>.
He prefers to give all these coins to this woman.

Reading exercise / Test exercise

Omitted, apart from choice of word: *uidet, est, illa, meretricis, uirum, ualde, uxorem, exsoluere, milite, multos, audire, decipere, ille, de Mnesilocho.*

**English–Latin

1(a) *illius filiam hic amat.*
 (b) *pater huius iuuenis diues esse uidetur.*
 (c) *illas meretrices arbitror.*
 (d) *hoc bonis ciuibus magnum officium est.*
 (e) *ille miles hanc mulierem defendere uult.*
 (f) *mores harum malos arbitror.*

2   CHR.   *quis est hic homo?*
    NIC.   *est filius meus Mnesilochus.*
    CHR.   *bella cum muliere esse uidetur. quid opinaris?*
    NIC.   *bella est, sed quis est? dic mihi, precor.*
    CHR.   *illumne uides?*
    NIC.   *militemne illum dicis?*
    CHR.   *ita.*
    NIC.   *age nunc.*
    CHR.   *ita faciam. huius mulieris uir est.*
    NIC.   *quid dicis? sed haec mulier plane meretrix est.*
    CHR.   *hocne arbitraris? scies mox omnia.*
    NIC.   *quid? nuptane est illa? perii. me miserum! scelestum iuuenem!*

DELICIAE LATINAE: 2C

Page 118

Word exercise

Use an English dictionary to check the meanings.

military > *miles*; le, la, il, la > *ille, illa*; conative > *conor*; arbitrate > *arbitror*; meretricious > *meretrix*; morals > *mores*.

Real Latin

Martial

My Rome praises, loves and sings my books of poems.
    Every pocket has one [sc. in it] and every hand too.
But look! One fellow blushes, goes pale, looks bewildered, yawns, hates.
    This is what I want: now my poems please me. (6.60)

Mottoes

This emblem is not a burden, but an honour.
This [is] the task.
This [is] the task of virtue.

2 D *(Text pp. 37–41)*

NOTES FOR 2D

In this Section we concentrate on introducing a new tense, 'I -ed',
'I have -ed', the so-called perfect, e.g. **Text** l. 292 *fecerunt* 'they
perpetrated', l. 293 *aedificauerunt* 'they built', l. 295 *ceperunt* 'they
captured', etc.

Page 37

292   Note the long, boastful comparison between Chrysalus'
        activities and the Trojan War, cf. **Text** p. 29, ll. 57ff.

Page 38

305   *huic stulto seni*: dative 'to the disadvantage of this old man',
        in English 'this old man's'.

306   *Ilio*: for the dative case, see on **Text** p. 28, l. 48.

312   *ubi miles fugit*: Latin 'when the soldier fled', but English
        prefers 'when the soldier *had* fled'.

Page 39

328   *tacitus*: adjective 'silent', describing the subject 'he'. Lit. 'he
        silent heard/wrote'. English prefers the adverb, 'silently', or
        'in silence'.

336   *ades*: 'be present', imperative of *adsum*. So also in **Text** l.
        340.

Page 40

346   *nihil*: looks forward to *consili* 'no [lit. nothing of] plan'.

349   *illius*: direct object of *misereor*, one of a few verbs that put

their direct object in the genitive. Cf. **Text** p. 19, l. 427 for verbs taking the dative.

350   *tuus*: i.e. 'your son'.

359   *facis*: here 'you are acting', cf. **Text** l. 365.

TRANSLATION OF 2D

CHRYSALUS

The sons of Atreus, as the story is, did a very great deed. For the gods built the town [of] Troy (the King of Troy was Priam), but the sons of Atreus captured [it] with weapons, horses, an army, [**295**] excellent soldiers [and] in the tenth year. But this was a deed of no value. For I will take my master by storm in one hour, without an army [and] without soldiers! O Troy, O fatherland, O Pergamum, O old man Priam, you are done for: for you unhappily [and] badly have lost two hundred gold coins, and soon will lose another two hundred. For I have brought these sealed tablets. More precisely, they are not tablets, but a Wooden Horse. As the Greeks [**300**] at that time sent a Wooden Horse against Troy, so I at this time will send these tablets against the old man. And, as there were armed soldiers in the Wooden Horse, so there are letters in these tablets. Thus have I conducted the matter well. And this horse will make an attack not on a stronghold [citadel] but upon [**305**] a strongbox [money-chest] and will destroy this stupid old man's gold. So I shall make the name of the old man Ilium; I'm Agamemnon and Ulysses, son of Laertes, and I'm now besieging Ilium. As I've heard, Ulysses was a man of the highest boldness, great astuteness [and] the highest intellect. I am both bold and astute. For the slaves of Nicobulus found me but [**310**] I deceived the old man and thus saved myself at that time. Not long afterwards, I fought with the soldier Cleomachus and routed the man. When the soldier fled, I fought with the old man. Him I easily conquered and immediately captured the spoils. For

Nicobulus has promised two hundred coins and soon will give [them] to the soldier. Now I want to capture [315] a second two hundred coins. For as the expenses were great, when the sons of Atreus captured Ilium, so our expenses will be great! For when soldiers capture a city, they ought to celebrate a triumph.

(*Nicobulus comes out of the house*)

But I see Priam before the gate. I shall go up to him.

NICOBULUS
[320] Who is it?

CHR. O Nicobulus!

NIC. What's happening? Did you perform that deed?

CHR. You ask? I have performed [it]. Come here.

NIC. I'm coming. What did you say to Mnesilochus? What did he do?

CHR. [325] I am an excellent orator. I reduced the man to tears; so violently did I curse and reprimand him.

NIC. What did he say?

CHR. He made no reply [word]; in silence [silent] he heard my words; in silence he wrote these tablets and gave them to me sealed. He ordered me [330] to give [them] to you. But I am afraid. For I suspect these tablets to be like the others. Examine the seal. Is it his?

NIC. I recognise [it]. It is his. I want to read these through.
(*Nicobulus undoes the tablets*)

CHR. (*aside*) Hoorah! Now Ilium's destruction is at hand. The Wooden Horse is worrying the old man! [335]

NIC. Chrysalus, come here.

CHR. Why do you want me to be at your side?

NIC. I want you to hear these words.

CHR. I don't want to know.

NIC. [340] Nevertheless be at hand.

CHR. Why?

NIC. Silence! I order you to be at hand.

CHR. I will be at hand.
(*Nicobulus undoes the tablets and reads them through*)
[*English passage*]

N I C.   [**345**] What do you think now, Chrysalus?

C H R.   At this time I shall give you no advice. For I do not wish to act according to my own opinion. But, as I think, you ought to give the gold ... but I neither order nor forbid nor recommend [this].

N I C.   I feel sorry for him.

C H R.   [**350**] He's yours. It's not surprising.

N I C.   What shall I do? I'll bring out the two lots of two hundred coins. Wait here. I'll soon come from the house to you, Chrysalus.

(Nicobulus enters the house from the stage)

C H R.   The destruction of Troy is happening! The Greeks are destroying Troy! Look, the old man [**355**] is bringing out the booty. I shall now keep quiet.

N I C.   Take this gold, Chrysalus. Go, [and] bring [it] to [my] son. I however shall go to the forum and give the coins to the soldier.

C H R.   For my part, I shall not accept those coins. I don't want you to give [them] to me.

N I C.   Indeed take [them]. You are acting annoyingly.

C H R.   [**360**] I won't take [them].

N I C.   But I beg [you].

C H R.   I refuse.

N I C.   Why?

C H R.   I don't want you to give me the gold.

N I C.   [**365**] Oh, you are acting annoyingly.

C H R.   Give [them to me], if it is necessary.

N I C.   Take care of this. I'll soon return here.

(Exit Nicobulus)

C H R.   Yippee! I have seen to this! For you at this time are a most wretched old man. [**370**] How well I have con- ducted the matter! I have saved myself and captured the city. But I am a slave of great astuteness and highest intel- lect. Now I shall return to the house and bring this booty to Mnesilochus.

Now learn the Learning Vocabulary at *GVE* pp. 121–2.

EXERCISES FOR 2D

Page 126

Exercises

1 All these verbs follow the patterns set out on **GVE** p. 122.

clamo, clamaui, clamauisti etc.; *uideo, uidi, uidisti* etc.; *uinco, uici, uicisti* etc.; *uincio, uinxi, uinxisti* etc.; *abeo, abiui* (or *abii*), *abiuisti* (or *abiisti*) etc.; *sum, fui, fuisti* etc.; *do, dedi, dedisti* etc.; *capio, cepi, cepisti* etc.; *fero, tuli, tulisti* etc.; *facio, feci, fecisti* etc.

If you made a mistake in forming these perfects, check the perfect **stems** on **GVE** pp. 123–6.

2 *deleuisti* you (s.) destroyed, *deleuistis*; *gesserunt* they did, acted, *gessit*; *uicit* he conquered, *uicerunt*; *adfuistis* you (pl.) were present, *adfuisti*; *solui* I released, *soluimus*; *pugnauimus* we fought, *pugnaui*; *abiistis* you (pl.) went away, *abiisti*.

3 *do*, you (s.) gave; *credo*, he believed; *adfero*, they brought; *sum*, he was; *debeo*, you (pl.) owed; *maneo*, I remained; *opprimo*, we surprised; *scribo*, they wrote; *adiuuo*, you (pl.) helped; *tango*, he touched; *amitto*, you (s.) lost; *dico*, we said; *exeo*, he went out.

*4 *dedi, pugnauimus, deleuisti, amauit, adfuerunt, uicistis, exii, necauerunt, respondit, gessisti, perfecimus, tulistis.*

5

Pres.	*dormit*	*dormiunt*
Fut.	*dormiet*	*dormient*
Perf.	*dormiuit*	*dormiuerunt*

Pres.	*est*	*sunt*
Fut.	*erit*	*erunt*
Perf.	*fuit*	*fuerunt*

Pres.	*pugnat*	*pugnant*
Fut.	*pugnabit*	*pugnabunt*
Perf.	*pugnauit*	*pugnauerunt*

Pres.	*aufert*	*auferunt*
Fut.	*auferet*	*auferent*
Perf.	*abstulit*	*abstulerunt*

Pres.	*delet*	*delent*
Fut.	*delebit*	*delebunt*
Perf.	*deleuit*	*deleuerunt*

Pres.	*redit*	*redeunt*
Fut.	*redibit*	*redibunt*
Perf.	*rediit*	*redierunt*

Pres.	*gerit*	*gerunt*
Fut.	*geret*	*gerent*
Perf.	*gessit*	*gesserunt*

Pres.	*decipit*	*decipiunt*
Fut.	*decipiet*	*decipient*
Perf.	*decepit*	*deceperunt*

*6   *stabit* future; *dederunt* they gave; *credet* future; *aderis* future; *uicisti* you conquered; *pugnabunt* future; *soluunt* present; *delent* present; *gerent* future; *mansi* I remained; *inuenistis* you found; *perficies* future; *diligis* present; *habes* present; *monuistis* you warned.

Page 127

Exercise

1(a)   Mnesilochus silently listened to the words of Chrysalus.
 (b)   I fought with a soldier, now I shall fight with an old man, now however I am silent.
 (c)   A long time afterwards the Greeks captured the city of Troy.
 (d)   At this time of night everyone ought to be asleep.
 (e)   Silently thieves enter the house secretly by night.
 (f)   As the Greeks sent the horse against Troy at that time, so today Chrysalus will send writing tablets against his master.

2(a)   The defender of a fault says to me, 'We also did this as young men.'
 (b)   Tell me, what have I done, except that I have not loved wisely?
 (c)   We were Trojans: Troy was [Troy has existed, is a 'has been'].
 (d)   You have played enough, eaten and drunk enough; it is time for you to leave.
 (e)   Nature has given us the seeds of knowledge; it has not given knowledge.

Pages 127–9

*Reading exercise

A very bold man (a), at that time (c), on this night (c), about your danger (b), in the silent night (c), by sad old men (b), a very astute slave (a), with me (b), in many hours (c), a long time afterwards (c), a very beautiful woman (a), out of the forum (b), at that time of night (c), with my wife (b), in ten years (c).

Reading exercise / Test exercise

Omitted.

**English–Latin

1(a)   *iuuenis in aedibus stetit tacitus.*
 (b)   *senexne aurum militi dedit?*
 (c)   *equos contra urbem Troiam miserunt.*

(d)   *hac nocte meum dominum uici et multam praedam cepi.*
(e)   *hoc anni tempore omnes domi manere debent.*
(f)   *milites signum uiderunt et mox contra urbem progredientur[†].*

† For this future tense, see **GVE 68**, p. 135.

2   NIC.   *quid facere debeo, Chrysale? dic mihi.*
      CHR.   *dicere nolo.*
      NIC.   *dic, quaeso. quid faciam? nam rem bene gerere uolo.*
      CHR.   *rem bene geres, ut ego opinor, si aurum filio tuo dabis. sed ego*
             non iubeo.
      NIC.   *pecuniam ei dabo. mane hic! mox huc reueniam. (Nicobulus in*
             aedis intrat).
      CHR.   *adest exitium senis [or seni]! ut eum decepi! nunc Mnesilochus*
             amicae satis pecuniae dare poterit.

DELICIAE LATINAE: 2D

Real Latin

Page 129

Vulgate

In the beginning God created heaven and earth. (Gen. 1.1)
Therefore the Lord God formed man from the mud of the earth
and breathed into his face the breath of life. (Gen. 2.7)
But on the seventh day is the sabbath of your God; thou shalt not
perform any task during it, thou and thy son and thy daughter, thy
servant and thy maidservant, [nor] thine ox .... for in six days the
Lord made the heaven and the earth and the sea. (Exodus 20.10–
11)

Mottoes

Nothing without God.
Nothing without labour.
Nothing without a reason.
Not without God.
Not without reason.
Not without effort.
Not without justice.
Not without danger.

Page 130

Exercise

1. *iuuenis* young man, *iuuentus* youth; *scio* I know, *scientia* knowledge; *timeo* I fear, *timor* fear; *uir* man, *uirtus* manliness, courage; *pulcher* beautiful, *pulchritudo* beauty; *pauper* poor, *paupertas* poverty; *prae-* before *dico* I say, *praedictio* prediction; *facilis* easy, *facilitas* ease; *prae-* at the head of, *praetor* praetor (a magistrate); *male-* badly, *facio* I do, *malefactor* evildoer; *clamo* I shout, *clamor* shout(ing); *ciuis* citizen; *ciuitas* citizenship; state; constitution.

2. *uirtutis; pulchritudinis; paupertatis; facilitatis; timoris; praetoris.*

3. *Scipio; Cicero; legio; longitudo; uictor; cupiditas; eruptio; iuuentus; libertas; explorator.*

4. Scipio; Cicero; legion; length; victor; lust; eruption; youth; liberty; spy.

Page 131

Exercise

familia household, + *-ris* = *familiaris*, to do with the household; *facio* I do, + *-ilis* = *facilis*, do-able, thus easy; *audio* I hear, + *ibilis* = *audibilis*, audible; *in-* not + *credo* I believe, + *-ibilis* = *incredibilis*, incredible; *fero* I bear, + *-ilis* = *fertilis*, fertile; *scaena* stage, + *-icus* = *scaenicus*, pertaining to the stage; *fur* thief, + *-iuus* = *furtiuus*, pertaining to thieves; *senex* old man, + *-ilis* = *senilis*, pertaining to old men; *honor* honour, + *-bilis* = *honorabilis*, honourable; *ignis* fire, + *eus* = *igneus*, made of fire, fiery; *oculus* eye, + *-eus* = *oculeus*, full of eyes; *aqua* water, + *-arius* = *aquarius*, pertaining to water; *pecunia* money, + *-osus* = *pecuniosus*, full of money; *uir* man, + *-ilis* = *uirilis*, pertaining to men; *uxor* wife, + *-ius* = *uxorius*, pertaining to wives; *domus* house, + *-icus* = *domesticus*, pertaining to the house; *nomen* name, + *iuus* = *nominatiuus*, pertaining to naming; *do* I give, + *-alis* = *dotalis*, pertaining to a dowry; *animus* mind, spirit, + *-osus* = *animosus*, full of spirit; *ciuis* citizen, + *-ilis* = *ciuilis*, pertaining to citizens; *iuuenis* young man, + *-ilis* = *iuuenilis*, pertaining to young men.

Word exercise

praeda booty (*ae* becomes *e* in English); *annus* year; *per-* through, *annus* year; *annus* year, *uers-* turn; *mille* 1,000, *annus* year; *tempus* (stem *tempor-*)

time; *urbs* city; *tacitus* quiet; *pugna* battle; *deleo* I destroy; *debeo* (stem *debit-*) I owe; *soluo* I release; *ante-* before, *camera* room.

2 E *(Text pp. 41–6)*

NOTES FOR 2E

Here we concentrate on the future of deponent verbs, e.g. **Text** l. 391 *adgrediar et alloquar* 'I shall advance and address'.

Page 42

379   A comic list of amusing insults, underlined by alliteration (repetition of sounds, especially at the beginning of a word).

Page 43

418   Plautus starts here a comic image – the old men are like sheep, who have strayed from their flock (**Text** l. 420), been sheared (l. 426), lost their lambs (l. 439), etc.

Page 44

438   *malum . . . nobis minamini*: 'you threaten evil to/on us'.

467   *fieri*: 'to become', infinitive of *fio* (see **Learning Vocabulary** 2D).

Page 45

478   *ei mihi*: 'Alas for me!'

Page 46

490   *satis, satis . . . est*: 'That's quite enough of your . . .'

TRANSLATION OF 2E

(*Enter onto the stage Philoxenus, Pistoclerus' father, and talks to himself*)

PHILOXENUS
How my son's life worries me! I have been a young man and at that [375] time I did all those things, but in moder-

ation. I wanted him to behave himself as he wanted, but I
didn't want him to play about too much.
(*Enter Nicobulus onto the stage. He doesn't spot Philoxenus, but
talks to himself*)

NICOBULUS

[Of all those] who were and will be stupid, senseless, silly,
mushrooms, dull, blockheads, [**380**] blabberers, I alone
beat all of them because of my stupidity. I am lost! I am
dead! For Chrysalus today has torn me to pieces [and] has
despoiled poor me. The soldier Cleomachus told me
everything. That 'woman' of Cleomachus is a prostitute:
the soldier doesn't have a wife. I, the most stupid of all
men, have promised coins for a prostitute to that [**385**]
soldier. But I am especially angry because Chrysalus, a
slave of the highest wickedness, has deceived me.

PHI.   (*he has heard the voice of Nicobulus*) Who's talking?
(*He spots Nicobulus*)
But whom do I see? This indeed is Mnesilochus' father.

NIC.   [**390**] (*he spots Philoxenus*) Hoorah, for I see Philoxenus,
an ally of my trouble. I shall approach him and talk to
him.
(*Nicobulus approaches Philoxenus*)
Greetings, Philoxenus.

PHI.   And to you. Where are you coming from?

NIC.   [**395**] From where an unhappy, down-on-his-luck man
[comes].

PHI.   By Pollux, that's where I am.

NIC.   Therefore we have a similar fortune.

PHI.   It is so. But you, say what is worrying you.

NIC.   Chrysalus, an excellent fellow, has ruined my son, your
son, [**400**] me and all my property. For both Mnesilochus
and Pistoclerus have mistresses.

PHI.   How do you know?

NIC.   I have seen them.

PHI.   I'm done for.

NIC.   [**405**] Why are we delaying? Why do we not call our sons
out? Shall we try to call them out?

PHI.   I'm not bothered.

NIC.   We'll try. Come with me. Will you follow me to the house of the Bacchises?

PHI.   I'll follow you. Off you go.

NIC.   [410] We'll both advance and try to save our sons at the same time.
       (*They both advance on the Bacchises' house*)
       Hey, Bacchis, open the doors, unless you prefer us to break the doors down.

BACCHIS (1)
       (*she speaks inside*) Who's shouting? Who's saying my name and [415] knocking at the house?
       (*Enter the Bacchises from the house*)

NIC.   Me and him.

B. I   What's the problem? Who has brought these sheep here?

NIC.   Those very wicked women are calling us sheep!

SISTER (2)
       [420] Their shepherd's asleep; they are going far from their flock, bleating.

B. I   But by Pollux, they're in a good condition; neither of them seems to be dirty.

S. 2   They both seem to be shorn.

PHI.   Those prostitutes seem to be mocking us. Shall we put up with this?

NIC.   [425] I won't put up with this.

B. I   In my view the shepherd has shorn them twice this year. What do you think?

S. 2   By Pollux, certainly someone has shorn this sheep twice today.

B. I   Shall we try to bring them inside?

S. 2   [430] But they're not worth a thing: for they have neither milk nor wool. Shall we go back inside, sister?

B. I   Yes. I will follow you.
       (*The Bacchises return to the house*)

NIC.   Wait. These sheep want you.

B. I   [435] This is a miracle – their voice is human. These sheep are calling us.

NIC.   These sheep will give you a great load of trouble [big, bad thing].

s. 2   But why are you threatening us with trouble?

PHI.   Because you've got our lambs shut in.

NIC.   [440] If you don't bring them out to us, we will be rams and charge into you.

B. I   Sister, will you speak in private with me?

s. 2   I will [speak]. What is it?

B. I   I want you to come over here.

s. 2   [445] I shall come. Speak.
        (*The sister goes up to Bacchis: they converse in secret*)

NIC.   Where are they going off to?

B. I   (*she points at Philoxenus*) I am giving that old man to you. I want you to calm him pleasantly. I'll go up to this angry man. Thus, we'll try [450] to drive them both inside here.

s. 2   I shall see to my duty charmingly, though it's nasty to embrace death.

B. I   Do as I told you.

s. 2   Be quiet; you do your [duty] [and] I'll try to do mine.

NIC.   [455] What are they secretly deliberating in counsel?

PHI.   What do you say, man?

NIC.   What do you want of me?

PHI.   I'm of no value.

NIC.   Why are you worthless? Tell me.

PHI.   [460] Do you see this woman (*he indicates the sister*)?

NIC.   I see [her].

PHI.   The woman's not bad.

NIC.   She by Pollux [is] bad, and you [are] of no value.

PHI.   Why [say] much? I'm in love.

NIC.   [465] You're in love?

PHI.   Yes indeed.

NIC.   You rotten man – you dare to become a lover as an old man?

PHI.   I do dare. What is it?

NIC.   Because it's a disgrace.

PHI.   [470] Why [say] much? I'm not going to rebuke my son and you ought not to rebuke yours. If they're in love, they're acting wisely.
        (*The Bacchises return to the old men*)

B. I   Will you follow this way, sister?

s. 2   I will follow.

NIC.   [475] What now? Will you actually give us back [our] sons? If you don't give them back, I'll give you great trouble.

B. I   I will put up with [that]. For I will not feel pain if *you* beat me.

NIC.   How persuasive she is. Alas for me, I'm afraid.

s. 2   This one's more calm.

B. I   [480] Come with me this way and rebuke your son there, if you want.

NIC.   Will you get away from me, villain?

PHI.   (*speaks to sister*) I beg you, take me inside.

s. 2   What a charmer you are!

PHI.   You do know my conditions?

s. 2   [485] You want to be with me.

PHI.   That's what I want!

NIC.   O most wicked man!

PHI.   Yes, I am.

B. I   Come inside with me this way. There you'll have food, wine, perfumes . . .

NIC.   [490] That's enough already of your party. My son and Chrysalus have taken away from me four hundred Philipcoins. I can't forget.

B. I   Well, what if I return half your gold – will you come in with me?

PHI.   He will do it; he'll forget everything.

NIC.   [495] Not at all. I refuse. I prefer to take revenge on those two [i.e. his son and Chrysalus].

PHI.   (*he gets angry*) You too, worthless man? You are worth as much as a rotten mushroom! Bacchis will give you half the gold. Take it.

B. I   If you take it, by Pollux I'll lie down with you, I'll love you, I'll embrace you.

NIC.   [500] I'm done for. I'm saying no with difficulty.

B. I   Do yourself a favour while you are alive. Life, by Pollux, isn't long. And if you lose this chance today, it won't ever happen afterwards in death.

NIC.   What do I do?

PHI. [505] What ought you to do? You're actually asking?

NIC. I want to, and I'm afraid.

B. I What are you afraid of?

NIC. Surely my son and slave will want to laugh at me?

B. I I won't let them.

NIC. [510] Because of you, I am becoming wicked. Take me in.

B. I The day is passing, go inside and lie down. Your sons are waiting for you inside.

S. 2 It's evening. Will you follow us?

NIC. We'll follow, like slaves.

Now learn the Learning Vocabulary at *GVE* p. 134.

EXERCISES FOR 2E

Pages 135–6

Exercises

1 *opinabor, opinaberis* etc. and *conspicabor, conspicaberis* etc. – as for *minabor GVE* pp. 134–5; *uidebor, uideberis* etc. – as for *pollicebor GVE* pp. 134–5; *irascar, irasceris* etc. *obliuiscar, obliuisceris* etc. – as for *loquar GVE* pp. 134–5; *mentiar, mentieris* etc. – as on *GVE* p. 135; *egrediar, egredieris* etc. and *patiar, patieris* etc. – as for *progrediar* on *GVE* p. 135.

2 I shall think *opinabimur*; you will lie *mentiemini*; he/she will pray *precabuntur*; you will seem *uideberis*; you will speak *loquemini*; we shall promise *pollicebor*.

*3 *precaberis*; *minabitur*; *uidebuntur*; *loquemini*; *progrediar*; *opinabimur*; *conabuntur*; *sequetur*.

*4 *minabitur* he/she will threaten; *precabuntur* they will pray; *opinabor* I shall think; *uidebimini* you will seem; *conspicabitur* he/she will catch sight of; *sequetur* he/she will follow; *loquentur* they will speak.

5 *arbitraris* you think; *conatur* he/she tries; *patiuntur* they suffer; *loquimini* you speak; *sequimur* we follow; *adgrederis* you go up to; *moror* I delay; *opinamur* we think; *progredimini* you advance; *uidetur* he/she seems; *mentior* I am lying.

6 *dedit* he gave, perfect; *conaberis* you will try, future; *mentitur* he lies, present; *uidebitur* he will seem, future; *fecerunt* they made, perfect; *amant* they like, present; *delent* they destroy, present; *dicent* they will

say, future; *loqueris* you (s.) will speak, future; *tulisti* you (s.) have carried, perfect.

Pages 136–7

Exercises

1(a) Nicobulus called his son a worthless young man.
 (b) Philoxenus, however, considered mistresses nothing but good.
 (c) Nicobulus is threatening Bacchis with death if she will not release his son.
 (d) Because he is in love, Philoxenus seems to Nicobulus to be as valuable as a rotten mushroom.
 (e) Bacchis! I order you to embrace that old man. I shall embrace this one.
 (f) Sister! I shall deal with the old man just as you ordered, although it seems a great evil to me to embrace death.
 (g) In my opinion, both old men will soon advance to the doors.
 (h) It is just as I said. The old men are advancing to the doors.

2(a) The humble have a hard time when the powerful disagree. (PHAEDRUS)
 (b) Divine nature gave the fields, human skill built the cities. (VARRO)
 (c) [For] I remember, I remember and I shall never forget that night. (CICERO)
 (d) Here, where Rome, the capital of the world, now is, was a tree, grass, a few cattle and the odd cottage. (OVID)
 (e) Religion produced wicked and impious deeds. (LUCRETIUS)
 (f) Nobody was an utter scoundrel suddenly. (JUVENAL)

Page 137

Optional supplementary revision sentences

Omitted.

Pages 137–9

Reading and Reading exercise / Test exercise

Omitted, apart from answers to 1.

1(a) + *quod amator ...*
 (b) + *nisi bonum.*

(c) + *quam uitam.*
(d) + *nisi nobis ...*
(e) + *quamquam Mnesilochum ...*
(f) + *dum uiuis.*
(g) + *ubi ad fores ...*

**English–Latin

1(a) *nisi pecuniam (meam) mihi reddes, te necabo.*
(b) *nihil nisi seruus mendax me sollicitat.*
(c) *ille senex tanti est quanti seruus scelestus.*
(d) *filium meum, si ad me adgredi audebit, amplexabor/complectar.*
(e) *illo tempore nullam uocem nisi tuam audire poteram.*
(f) *quamquam uita bonum est, mors ad ianuas et diuitum et pauperum adibit.*

2   NIC.   *Philoxene, homo nihili es. quamquam senex es, amator tamen fieri audes.*

         PHI.   *noli me castigare, Nicobule. et si uis filium castigare, intra. si intrabis, mulieres te curabunt.*

         BAC. 1   *ducentos nummos reddam, senex, si intrabis, et te amplexabor.*

         NIC.   *perii. difficile est, quod scelestos castigare uolo. intrabo tamen, quamquam me scelestum habebo.*

         SOR. 2   *bene. bene tibi facis, ut debes, dum uiuis. in morte nulla te amplexabitur amica.*

DELICIAE LATINAE: 2E

Page 139

Word exercise

uita life; *malum* evil; *uox* voice, *fero* I carry; *ambi-* both, *dexter* right (hand); *castigo* I punish; *sollicitus* worried; *patior* I endure; *mors* death; *accipio* I receive.

Consult an English dictionary for meanings.

Page 140

Exercise

Consult an English dictionary for meanings.

Adjectives: *lego* I read + *-ibilis*; *sub-* beneath + *mergo* (stem *mers-*) I sink + *-ibilis*; *in-* not + *audio* I hear + *-ibilis*; *in-* not + *re-* back + *uoco* I call + *-abilis*; *miles* soldier + *-arius*; *capio* (stem *capt-*) I take + *-iuus*; *laudo* I praise + *-abilis*; *urbs* city + *-anus*; *scaena* stage + *-icus*; *nuptiae* marriage + *-alis*; *in-* not + *pecunia* money + *-osus*; *filius* son + *-alis*; *uideo* (stem *uis-*) I see + *-ibilis*.

Nouns: *frater* brother + *-itas*; *soror* sister + *-itas*; *sub-* beneath + *mitto* (stem *miss-*) I send + *-io*; *nomino* (stem *nominat-*) I name + *-io*; *audio* (stem *audit-*) I hear + *-io*; *uicinus* neighbouring + *-itas*; *admoneo* (stem *admonit-*) + *-io*; *sto* (stem *stat-*) I stand + *-io*; *uideo* (stem *uis-*) I see + *-ibilitas*; *uideo* (stem *uis-*) I see + *-io*; *mitto* (stem *miss-*) + *-io*; *longus* + *-itudo*; *insto* I urge + *-antia*; *adrogo* I claim + *-antia*; *re-* back, again + *plico* (stem *plicat-*) I fold + *-io*; *fugio* (stem *fugit-*) I flee + *iuus*.

Real Latin

Martial

You are the only one who has farms, Candidus, and the only one [who has] cash,

The only one who has gold coins, and the only one [with] expensive agate jars,

You're the only one who has Massic wines and the only one [who has] Caecuban wine of Opimius' vintage.

And you're the only one who has a heart, and the only one [who has] wit.

You're the only one who has everything – don't think I want to deny it!

But the wife you have, Candidus, [you share] with everyone [lit. with the people]. (3.26)

Page 141

Vulgate

Six days shalt thou work, and thou shalt perform all thy tasks ... thou shalt not commit adultery ... thou shalt not speak false witness against thy neighbour. (Exodus 20.9ff.)

Mottoes

For God and fatherland/freedom/the church.
For God, for the King, for the fatherland, for the Law.
For faith and fatherland.

For fatherland and freedom/king/religion/virtue.
To live and die for one's country.
For king and people.
For King, Law and the people.
For sport and prey.

Section Three
Plautus' Amphitruo

3 A *(Text pp. 48–50)*

NOTES

The translation remains close to the Latin but becomes moderately colloquial here and there.

In this Section we concentrate on *is, ea, id,* 'that', pl. 'those', and 'he, she, it', which functions as an adjective and pronoun, like *ille* and *hic*. Thus **Text** l. 8 *eae* 'that'; l. 10 *eius* 'of him, his'; l. 11 *is* 'that'; and so on. All are in the vocabulary.

We also introduce comparative and superlative adjectives – 'longer', 'long-est' in English, most commonly *-ior, -issimus* in Latin (e.g. **Text** l. 19 *longissima* 'very long', 'longest', l. 25 *audacior* 'bolder', 'more bold').

Page 49

9   *Amphitruonis*: 'of Ampitruo', i.e. 'belonging to Amphitruo'. *uiri* and *ducis* (genitive) both refer to him.

13   *omnes*: does not necessarily mean 'they all': wait for the verb *nouistis*.

14   *Amphitruonis*: genitive, after *similem*, 'resembling Amphitruo'. *similis* also takes the dative (l. 17, *Amphitruoni*).

18   *omnium*: 'of all [nights]'.

25   *quam*: you have learned *quam* as meaning 'how!' With

comparatives, it means 'than' – here 'braver *than* I'. Slaves
in Plautus are typically boastful.

Page 50

31   The night turns out to be long because Jupiter has ex-
        tended it in order to spend as much time in bed with
        Alcumena as possible. Sosia amusingly develops the idea of
        night and the sun being drunk.

44   *hominem stultissimum*: accusative, used to express an
        exclamation.

TRANSLATION OF 3A

Cast list
Amphitruo, general of Thebes' legions, husband of Alcumena; a
man of the highest courage.
Alcumena, wife of Amphitruo; a most loyal woman.
Sosia, Amphitruo's slave; wholly deficient in intelligence.
[5] Jupiter, king of the gods; Alcumena's lover.
Mercury, messenger of the gods; a highly intelligent god, the spit-
ting image of Sosia.

MERCURY
        My name is Mercury; I'm a god – highly intelligent, and
        full of tricks. This city is Thebes. That house belongs to
        Amphitruo, a man of the highest courage and bravery,
        general of [10] Thebes' legions. His wife is Alcumena, a
        deeply loyal and chaste woman. That Amphitruo has gone
        off with his army and is at this moment in time waging war
        against the Teleboae; and that Alcumena is pregnant by
        him. But my father, king of the gods – you all know him:
        he's free and easy in these matters – has turned himself into
        Amphitruo's look-alike [15] and has secretly made love to
        Alcumena. So she's now pregnant from two sources – a
        human, and highest Jove. My father, looking like Amphi-
        truo, tonight is tucked up inside with her, and for that
        reason this is an extended night. This night, in fact, is the

longest of them all. I, Mercury, messenger of the gods, have assumed the likeness [20] of Amphitruo's slave, Sosia. So now I look like Sosia. Today however Amphitruo and his slave will return home from the army. Look! That slave's now coming. He'll try to get into that house, but I'll keep him away from it [that house].

(*Enter Sosia, Amphitruo's slave*)

SOSIA

[25] What man is bolder, what man more undaunted, what man braver than I?

MER. (*to himself*) Who is stupider?

SOS. The fact is, to be precise, I am the boldest of all men, the most undaunted, the bravest.

MER. The most stupid.

SOS. [30] I am the boldest because I've been walking all alone all through this extremely long night. {For} what night is longer than this? What blacker than this? By Pollux, Nocturnus is rather drunk and sound asleep – that's my belief. The Great Bear isn't moving in the sky, the moon isn't changing, and Orion, the evening star and [35] Pleiades aren't setting either. That's the way all those constellations are standing stock-still and day is never breaking. I'll never see a longer night – nor a blacker.

MER. Carry on, Night, as you are now doing. You'll never give better service to a better master!

SOS. [40] All the same, I have seen one night longer than this. {For} there was this one occasion when my master flogged me and I was hung up there all night. That night was longer than this! But now it's my belief the sun's nodded off, well and truly drunk.

MER. What a fantastically stupid fellow! I will never see a fellow more stupid [45] than him.

SOS. Now I shall enter my master's house. I shall obey Amphitruo's order and announce his victory to Alcumena. You see, we defeated the enemy, we stormed their town, took loads of booty. Now, I'll briefly think about my speech – [50] how shall I announce the triumph to Alcumena?

What shall I say to her? (*He thinks briefly*) This is what I'll tell her!

Now learn the Learning Vocabulary at GVE p. 143.

EXERCISES FOR 3A

Pages 144–5

Exercises

*1   s.: *id bellum, id bellum, eius belli, ei bello, eo bello,* pl.: *ea bella, ea bella, eorum bellorum, eis bellis, eis bellis;* s.: *ea urbs, eam urbem, eius urbis, ei urbi, eā urbe* pl.: *eae urbes, eas urbes, earum urbium, eis urbibus, eis urbibus;* s.: *is dux, eum ducem, eius ducis, ei duci, eo duce,* pl.: *ei duces, eos duces, eorum ducum, eis ducibus, eis ducibus.*

Note: *bellum* is 2nd declension neuter; *urbs* is 3rd declension feminine; *dux* is 3rd declension masculine.

*2   gen. sing., nom. pl., dat. sing., dat./abl. pl., acc. sing., gen. pl., nom./acc. pl., nom. sing., acc. sing., acc. pl.

3   (*per*) *eos dies; eam uictoriam; eius belli; eis regibus; eos duces; id imperium; ei amicae; ei mores; eius; eis; eius; ei; ei; ea nocte.*

4   *uiri, patres* (nom. pl.), *feminae, exercitui, puero* (dat. sing.). *ei* is nom. pl. masc. *or* dat. sing. masc./fem./neut.; *amicae, res* (nom. pl.). *eae* is nom. pl. fem.; *imperia, capita* (nom./acc. pl.), *astutia, uirtus, urbs, manus* (nom. sing.). *ea* is nom./acc. neut. pl. or nom. fem. sing; *operis, pueri, rei, exercitūs* (gen. sing.). *eius* is gen. sing. masc./fem./neut.; *signis, meretricibus, uiris, moribus. eis* is dat./abl. pl.

5   in that town; because of that courage; at their house; at that time; along/through that road; with her; on that night; into that city; for those hours; towards those soldiers; through that night; for many days; in that year; that time.

6   *cum eis feminis; eā horā; apud eum; in eam scaenam; in eis urbibus; ob ea pericula; eis noctibus; propter id bellum; per eas horas.*

7(a)   hae: These women are beautiful.
 (b)   *illos:* Do you see those soldiers?
 (c)   *eius:* It's enough of that war.

(d)   *illius*: That man's head is huge.
(e)   *earum*: A crowd of those women is coming in.

Page 147

Exercise

diem longiorem, longissimum; nocte longiore, longissimā; milites celeriores, cele-rrimi (-os); oculo celeriore, celerrimo; aedes ingentiores, ingentissimae (-as); fami-liam ingentiorem, ingentissimam; manus pulchriores, pulcherrimae (-as); mulierum pulchriorum, pulcherrimarum; consilia stultiora, stultissima; homini stultiori, stul-tissimo; operum stultiorum, stultissimorum.

Pages 148–9

Exercises

1   *liber* free, *liberior* freer, *liberrimus* freest, most free, very free etc.; *fortis* brave, *fortior* braver, *fortissimus* bravest etc.; *bonus* good, *melior* better, *optimus* best; *niger* black, *nigrior* blacker, *nigerrimus* blackest; *similis* like, *similior* more like, *simillimus* most like; *magnus* big, *maior* bigger, *maximus* biggest; *celer* quick, *celerior* quicker, *celerrimus* quickest; *paruus* small, *minor* smaller, *minimus* smallest; *scelestus* wicked, *scelestior* more wicked, *scelestissimus* most wicked; *stultus* stupid, *stultior* more stupid, *stultissimus* most stupid; *malus* bad, *peior* worse, *pessimus* worst; *tristis* sad, *tristior* sadder, *tristissimus* saddest; *facilis* easy, *facilior* easier, *facillimus* easiest; *multus* much, *plus* more, *plurimus* most; *ingens* huge, *ingentior* huger, *ingentissimus* hugest.

2(a)   [Throughout] that night the king of gods and men stayed with that woman in the house.
(b)   Her husband, Amphitruo, left home with a very strong army.
(c)   She thinks Jupiter [is] Amphitruo because he made himself like Amphitruo.
(d)   That god is loving her throughout the whole night because he has never seen a more beautiful woman than her.
(e)   He made that night longer because of Alcumena.
(f)   Or rather, he made that night the longest of all nights.
(g)   Mercury, his son, is a god of the highest cunning. In fact he is more cunning than all the gods and men.
(h)   He made himself very like the slave Sosia.

(i)   Amphitruo will return home this night because he has been suc-
      cessful in war and has carried off a very great victory.
(j)   I have never seen a more stupid slave than Sosia, [or] a more
      wicked god than Mercury on the stage.

3(a) Later thoughts, so they say, are accustomed to be wiser. (CICERO)
 (b) Golden reins / a golden bridle don't/doesn't make a horse better.
      (SENECA)
 (c) I see better things and I approve of them, [but] I pursue worse
      things. (OVID)
 (d) No slavery is more degrading than [a] voluntary [one]. (SENECA)
 (e) Love reason: love of this will arm you against the most difficult
      situations/things. (SENECA)

Pages 149–50

*Reading

(a)   *quam hanc*: I have never seen a longer night than this.
(b)   *quam ille*: This slave is bolder than that one.
(c)   *quam huic*: I shall give that old man more gold than this one.
(d)   *quam illo*: Night is blacker at this time than at that.
(e)   *quam hic*: That man is more courageous than this one.
(f)   *quam mendacem*: I prefer a very foolish slave to a deceitful one.
(g)   *quam hoc*: I shall never be able to bear greater danger than this.
(h)   *quam illi*: There were never braver soldiers than those.
(i)   *quam eum*: Have you ever seen a man more like a god than him?
(j)   *quam eas*: Shall I ever spot more beautiful women than those?

Pages 150–1

Reading exercise / Test exercise

Omitted.

**English–Latin

1(a) *haec uictoria maior erat quam illa.*
 (b) *illis annis, multi milites fortissimi, propter imperium regis stultioris,*
      bellum longissimum gerebant.
 (c) *nihil melius est quam officium ciuium optimorum.*
 (d) *sapientia deorum maior est quam hominum.*
 (e) *frater meus similior est patri/patris quam mihi/mei.*
 (f) *nihil peius est quam hoc malum.*

2 SOS.   *quis est melior quam ego?*

MERC.   *quis putidior?*

SOS.   *immo uero, ego optimus sum omnium seruorum, omnium hominum fortissimus.*

MERC.   *et stultissimus stultorum.*

SOS.   *audacior sum quia, hac nocte longissima, per has uias solus ambulo neque certe nigriorem nec longiorem quam hanc umquam uidi. cur luna non se mutat neque haec signa occidunt? numquamne dies apparebit?*

MERC.   *te, nox, ut nunc pergis, pergere uolo. numquam enim officium maius patri meo quam hoc facies.*

DELICIAE LATINAE: 3A

Page 151

Word exercise

uictoria; bellum; imperium; rex; urbs; longus; summus; liber; meditor; fortis.

3 B *(Text pp. 50–2)*

NOTES

You have already met the perfect tense ('I -ed', 'I have -ed') of active verbs (Section 2D). Here we introduce the perfect tense of deponent verbs. This tense has the same meaning, but a different formation, involving parts of *sum*, e.g. **Text** l. 53 *adgressi sunt* 'they attacked', l. 60 *adlocutus est* 'he addressed', etc.

Remove *sum*, however, and you are left with the so-called perfect participle, 'having -ed', e.g. **Text** l. 53 *adgressi* 'having attacked', etc. These too we examine.

Notice that participles can build up quite complex clauses around themselves, as if they were main verbs. One can say 'They fiercely attacked the troops of the enemy with spears'; but one can also say 'Having fiercely attacked the troops of the enemy with spears, they [did something else].'

Page 50

53   *adgressi sunt . . . adgressi*: 'they attacked . . . having attacked'. Watch out for this common pattern – 'X -ed. Having -ed,

x then . . .' This device rehearses the new perfect forms and the new perfect participle together.

54 *hanc praedam adepti*: 'having gained this booty'. A perfect participle can control an object – here *hanc praedam* 'this booty'.

60–1 *si uos . . . adepti . . . uultis*: 'if you, having gained xyz, [you] wish to . . .' – a long 'if' clause. Hold on!

Page 51

68–9 *uos . . . egressi . . . deducite*: Latin commonly says '[You] having done x, do y!' English more commonly says '[You] do x and y' – here, '[You] get out . . . and lead off . . .' Hint: turn Latin perfect participles into main verbs in English. Latin 'X, having done A and having done B, did C' becomes English 'X did A and did B and did C'. Try this with **Text** ll. 70–2.

70 *multa . . . minati*: 'having threatened many things *to/against* our army'.

77 *uicti*: here as subject of the sentence, 'the [ones] having-been-conquered', 'the vanquished'.

78 To hand over 'altars' and 'hearths' was to hand over the care of gods and homes to the victors. The victors would use them now.

79 Note asyndeton (no 'and') in this sentence. Sosia is whipping up the excitement.

81–2 *se tulit*: 'he bore himself', i.e. charged. *se* can mean 'himself' and 'themselves' – hence **Text** l. 82 'the troops *se tulerunt*' 'bore themselves'.

84 *hoc*: neuter object, 'this thing', 'this'.

Page 52

89 *adeptus*: singular, because it refers to Amphitruo.

91 *nos*: object of *precati*.

92 *diuina humanaque*: i.e. the altars and hearths.

94 *meae*: agrees with *dominae*; *haec* is neuter plural object, 'these things'.

94–6 Note the string of nominative participles referring to 'I' (Sosia, the speaker) – *ingressus, locutus, exsecutus.*

TRANSLATION OF 3B

SOSIA

'We were at peace and leisure. The Teleboae, fantastically fierce men, attacked us. Attacking with such speed and such ferocity, they seized massive booty. Having seized this, they returned home. [55] Our citizens wanted revenge on them, since the Teleboae had broken the law [lit. were unjust] and our reason for war was most just. So our soldiers, bravest of men, advanced in ships to that land. Having reached there, they quickly disembarked. After disembarking, they at once pitched camp. Amphitruo addressed the enemy through ambassadors, [60] as follows: "O Teleboae, if you, who seized so much booty in Argive territory, want to return it all to us, Amphitruo will withdraw his army home, without war; he will leave your territory and leave you in [lit. give you] peace and quiet. If you refuse and do not return everything to us, he will attack your city and destroy it." Thus [65] spoke Amphitruo's ambassadors. But the Teleboae replied as follows: "Thebans, you can depart at once. Our soldiers are men of the highest ferocity, the greatest courage. We shall wage war, if we must, and we can well look after ourselves and ours. So you, leaving our territory, take off your army."

[70] 'So the Teleboae, with that fierce reply [lit. having spoken fiercely] and with many threats [lit. having threatened many things] against our army, ordered Amphitruo to withdraw his army from their territory at once. Amphitruo therefore wanted revenge on the enemy and at once led all the army out of camp. The Teleboae led their legions out from the town. We drew up our legions; the enemy [75] drew up theirs. Then the generals came out into the middle and conversed apart from the mass of other ranks. After a brief conversation [lit. having conversed], they agreed: "After the battle, the defeated party will hand over their

city, altars, hearths and themselves to the victors." These were the terms of battle. On both sides trumpets sounded, the earth thundered, the cry went up to the heavens. [80] Amphitruo prayed to Jupiter and encouraged the army. With these prayers and encouragement [lit. having prayed to Jupiter and having encouraged the army], he launched himself bravely into battle. The troops on both sides did likewise [lit. launched themselves into battle].

'At last, as we wished, we got the upper hand [lit. our hand overcame them], but the enemy did not flee. Amphitruo, seeing this, ordered the cavalry to launch themselves [85] boldly into battle. So they did [lit. they launched themselves into battle], and boldly trampled down the enemy troops. Then the enemy took to flight. We fought till evening. Finally night came and broke off the battle. So at that time we bravely conquered our enemy. Having gained this [so] magnificent victory, [90] Amphitruo next day received the enemy embassy into the camp. The embassy, after setting out gloomily from the city and praying earnestly to us, handed over themselves, their city, their children and all things sacred and secular into Amphitruo's jurisdiction.'

This is what I'll tell my mistress. Now I'll go into the house [lit. having gone into the house] and [95] carry out that instruction of Amphitruo. When I've told Alcumena everything and followed my orders, I'll return with all speed to Amphitruo.

Now learn the Learning Vocabulary at *GVE* p. 154.

EXERCISES FOR 3B

Pages 157–8

Exercises

*1   *meditat-us/a/um sum, es, est; meditat-i/ae/a sumus, estis, sunt.*

And so on with: *conatus, uisus, oblitus, profectus, mentitus, progressus, passus* (as on *GVE* pp. 154–5).

2   *locutus sum* I spoke, *locuti sumus* we spoke; *uisum est it* seemed, *uisa sunt* they (neut.) seemed; *recordata est she* remembered, *recordatae sunt* they (fem.) remembered; *mentiti sumus* we (masc.) lied, *mentitus sum* I (masc.) lied; *ingressae sunt* they (fem.) entered, *ingressa est* she entered; *pollicita es* you (fem.) promised, *pollicitae estis* you (fem.) promised; *secuta sunt* they (neut.) followed, *secutum est* it followed; *adeptus est* he got/obtained, *adepti sunt* they (masc.) got.

3   *uideor:* he seemed; *adipiscor:* she got; *obliuiscor:* I forgot; *ingredior:* we (fem.) entered; *loquor:* you (pl.) spoke; *proficiscor:* they set out; *fio* [**GVE** p. 157]: it became/happened.

4   *minata est; profecti sunt; hortatus sum; uisa es; oblitae sumus; pollicitus est* [*promisit* exists too]; *factum est; mentiti estis.*

5   *irascitur* he/she is angry, *irascuntur* they are angry, *irascetur* he/she will be angry, *irascentur* they will be angry, *iratus/a est* he/she was angry, *irati/ae sunt* they were angry; *minatur* he/she threatens, *minantur* they threaten, *minabitur* he/she will threaten, *minabuntur* they will threaten, *minatus/a est* he/she threatened, *minati/ae sunt* they threatened; *pollicetur* he/she promises, *pollicentur* they promise, *pollicebitur* he/she will promise, *pollicebuntur* they will promise, *pollicitus/a est* he/she promised, *polliciti/ae sunt* they promised; *mentitur* he/she lies, *mentiuntur* they lie, *mentietur* he will lie, *mentientur* they will lie, *mentitus/a est* he/she lied, *mentiti/ae sunt* they lied; *patitur* he/she suffers, *patiuntur* they suffer, *patietur* he/she will suffer, *patientur* they will suffer, *passus/a est* he/she suffered, *passi/ae sunt* they suffered.

Page 158

Exercises

1   *locutus* having spoken, *loquor; profectus* having set out, *proficiscor; adeptus* having gained, *adipiscor; iratus* having become angry, *irascor; conatus* having tried, *conor; precatus* having prayed, *precor; suspicatus* having suspected, *suspicor; pollicitus* having promised, *polliceor; hortatus* having encouraged, *hortor; uisus* having seemed, *uideor; egressus* having gone out, *egredior; factus* having become, *fio.*

2(a)   He caught the soldier after he [the soldier] entered.
 (b)   The men thought a little, then came [after thinking a little the men came].
 (c)   He told a lot of lies, then went [he left after telling a heap of lies].
 (d)   Having advanced quickly from the city, the army soon pitched camp.

(e)   Having said these [things]/This [woman], having spoken, [she]
       went out.

Page 159

*Exercise

(a)   She (subject) writhed (verb) about, convulsed (participle) with
       scarlet (adjective) pain.
(b)   Naked (adjective) she (subject) lay (verb), clasped (participle) in my
       longing (adjective) arms.
(c)   I (subject) saw (verb) three (adjective) ships go sailing (participle) by
       on Christmas day (construe with both).
(d)   Know (verb) you (subject) not / Being (participle) mechanical (ad-
       jective) you (subject) ought (verb) not walk / Upon a labouring
       (adjective) day?
(e)   See (verb)! from the Brake the whirring (adjective) Pheasant (sub-
       ject) springs (verb),
       And mounts (verb) exulting (participle) on triumphant (adjective)
       Wings:
       Short (adjective) is (verb) his (adjective) Joy (subject); he (subject)
       feels (verb) the fiery (adjective) Wound,
       Flutters (verb) in Blood, and panting (participle) beats (verb) the
       Ground.

Page 160

Exercise

1   *audacter* boldly; *male* wickedly; *bene* well; *libere* freely; *magnopere*
    greatly; *multum* much; *celeriter* fast; *pulchre* beautifully; *paulum* slightly.

2   *stulte* stupidly; *bene* well; *fortiter* bravely; *longe* far; *similiter* in the same
    way; *saeue* wildly; *tacite* silently; *magnopere* greatly; *celeriter* fast/swiftly;
    multum much; *misere* unhappily.

3   [The successful orator] will speak ... seriously, sternly, fiercely,
    powerfully, passionately, plentifully, bitterly, affably, gently, pre-
    cisely, flatteringly, kindly, sweetly, briefly and wittily.

Pages 162–4

Exercises

1(a)   The bold soldier wildly attacked the enemy – even though the
        latter was angry and had made lots of threats [the enemy was

angry and made many threats, but the bold soldier attacked him wildly].

(b) The cavalry, after leaving their camp, quickly advanced to the city [leaving their camp, the cavalry quickly advanced to the city; the cavalry left their camp and quickly advanced to the city].

(c) The king got hold of a fast ship and fled far from his land.

(d) To his wife who had spoken much, her husband replied fiercely.

(e) When the ambassadors had spoken to the enemy, having returned to the camp, they reported their words to our leader.

(f) After encouraging his soldiers, the commander took himself boldly off to the battle.

(g) After suffering the ferocity of our cavalry, the enemy fled into their town and hid themselves away there.

2(a) It's not living that's good, but living well. (SENECA)

(b) No-one puts on a toga unless he's dead. (JUVENAL)

(c) The wealth of many exceptionally powerful people rules out loyal friendships: for not only is Fortune herself blind, she also generally renders blind those she has embraced. (CICERO)

Reading

*1(a) So Amphitruo, having encouraged the soldiers at that time, took himself off to the battle.

(b) The commander spoke to the soldiers and, having promised [them] the plunder after the victory, gave the sign.

(c) The wife of Amphitruo, when she saw her husband in the street, left her house.

(d) To his wife, when she made many prayers and recalled the faithfulness of her husband, Amphitruo nevertheless made no reply.

(e) But the slave, having told many lies, easily deceived his master.

*2(a) to citizens who have gained leisure and peace.

(b) the ambassadors after they had spoken these words.

(c) a band of slaves who had set out for the camp of the enemy.

(d) to that woman who had secretly followed her husband into the war.

(e) the commander, who had advanced to the enemy army.

(d) The soldiers spoke foul words

(b) The commander of the enemy upbraided

(a) War seems to be the greatest evil

(e)   The legions followed
(c)   The masters killed

Reading exercise / Test exercise

Omitted.

**English—Latin

1(a)   *dux noster, exercitum hortatus, signum dedit.*
 (b)   *Amphitruo per legatos hostes allocutus est.*
 (c)   *omnes sapientiam adepti pacem et otium quam bellum malunt.*
 (d)   *ea hora hostes a castris profecti sunt.*
 (e)   *mihi plane eis loqui conato hostes ferociter sunt minati.*
 (f)   *hominem sic locutum necauerunt.*

2   *Teleboae, Amphitruoni per legatos allocuto* [or *ubi Amphitruo eos per
       legatos allocutus est*], *sic* [or *haec*] *responderunt: 'terram nostram adgressi
       estis. statim abite. nisi abibitis, pugnabimus.' Ita* [or *haec*] *dixerunt.
       Amphitruo autem, uir maxima uirtute, cum exercitu e castris progressus,
       suos hortatus est. deinde eos in proelium duxit. ingens erat proelium. dux
       autem noster, uictoriam adeptus illustrem, iam domum regressus est.*

DELICIAE LATINAE: 3B

Page 165

Word exercise

For meanings, consult an English dictionary.

copia plenitude + *-osus*; firm earth; *legatus; ager; otium; hostis; nauis; pax;
ferox; in-* not + *uinco* I defeat + *-ibilis; ex-* + *hortor; illustris; sui* himself +
caedo I kill.

Real Latin

Martial

Difficult [and] easy, sweet [and] bitter are you – the same person.
I cannot live with you, nor without you. (12.46)

Motto

A lamb in peacetime, [but] a lion in war.

3 C *(Text pp. 52–5)*

NOTES

Here we concentrate on future participles, 'on the point of -ing', 'about to –'. These are formed by taking the last principal part of a verb and adding *-ur-us -a -um* (cf. fut*ur*e), e.g. **Text** l. 97 *facturus* 'about to do', *ingressurus* 'about to enter', etc. You have already met this principal part of deponent verbs; now you meet the 4th p.p. of active verbs.

Page 52

101   *sui similior*: 'more like himself'.

103   Mercury will play a slave at a typical (comic) slave's game. Check the meaning of this string of ablatives *malitiā . . . ui*.

113   *si quis*: 'if anyone'. *quis* means 'anyone' in a *si* clause.

Page 53

125   *cuius*: 'whose', genitive of *quis* 'who?'

Page 54

140   *filium*: describes *Sosiam*.

142–4   A series of puns dependent on the possible range of meanings of *consutus* 'stitched' and Latin's use of the ablative (see **GVE 84** p. 172).

147   *cui*: 'to/for whom?' (dative) – virtually the same as 'whose?' at **Text** l. 125.

161   *nonne*: this useful little word asks a question in such a way as to suggest that 'yes' is the answer. Translate 'surely', or construct a question with some form of 'aren't I / isn't he?' (etc.), e.g. 'I am Sosia, aren't I?' or 'Aren't I Sosia?'

173   *eun-dem*: is *ea id + dem* means 'the same'. Check running vocabulary.

175   *totus*: 'whole' i.e. all over, in every respect.

176   *cicatrosum*: from the floggings disobedient slaves could receive, cf. **Text** p. 50, l. 41.

TRANSLATION OF 3C

MERCURIUS

What's that slave about to do? Is he going to enter this house? Is he going to tell all about Amphitruo's victory? I shall go up to him and drive him very quickly away from this house. Never [100] will I allow this fellow today to reach the house. Since my shape is similar to his – to be precise, he is no more like himself than I am – I shall adopt an absolutely identical character. So I shall be wicked, cunning, sharp, and drive him at full speed away from this house with evil, tricks, cleverness, deceptions, [and] force.

[105] (*Sosia, about to enter the house, sees Mercury*)

SOSIA

Now I am about to enter the house and recount my master's achievements . . . but who is this fellow? Whom do I see before my master's house? I beseech you, by Hercules, how powerful he is! Never seen anyone more powerful. I don't like this much – I can see [lit. for sure] my reception is going to be a fisty one. [110] I'm most unhappy!

MER. I've got some weight in this fist, but even more in that one . . .

SOS. Help! He's weighing his fists! He wants to give me a fisty welcome [lit. welcome me with his fists].

MER. If anyone comes here, he'll eat a knuckle sandwich [lit. fists].

SOS. No, thank you. I've just had dinner.

MER. [115] One touch with this fist [lit. if this fist touches his face] and it'll be fillet of face [lit. it will be boned].

SOS. He wants to fillet me with his fists? Misery me! I'll be worth about as much as an eel.

MER. Someone's talking round here.

SOS. Saved! He hasn't seen me! You see, my name's not Someone. [120] It's Sosia.

(*Mercury sees Sosia*)

MER. And where are you off to, you most miserable wretch? Tell me, who are you? {Are you} slave or free? Speak up, scum [lit. worst]!

SOS. I'm a slave, about to enter my master's house.

MER. [**125**] Whose slave {are you}? Why are you chattering silently to yourself on the point of entry into this house? What are you about to report? Tell me, scum of the world [lit. worst of all].

SOS. I'm about to go into that house. {For} my master told me to [lit. ordered this]. I'm his slave, you see.

MER. Get lost, fount of iniquity! You're worth nothing! If you don't buzz off quickly, it'll [**130**] be all the more quickly I fillet you with these fists, scoundrel! You'll be worth about as much as an eel!

SOS. If you intend to exercise your fists on me, why not limber them up on the wall first?

MER. If you don't buzz off at once...

SOS. [**135**] But I live here and I'm this household's slave.

MER. Who's your master?

SOS. Amphitruo, best of men, and his wife Alcumena, loveliest of women.

MER. And what's your name, scum?

SOS. [**140**] The Thebans call me Sosia, son of Davus.

MER. What are you saying? You're an outrageous liar [lit. you are lying, most outrageous man]. *You*'re Sosia? *I*'m Sosia. Don't come here with your second-hand tricks.

SOS. Actually it's the tunic I've come with that's second-hand, not my tricks.

MER. {But} you're lying! You've come with your feet, not your tunic.

[**145**] (*Mercury beats up Sosia violently with his fists*)

SOS. I'm done for!

MER. You actually shouting, worthless fellow? Whose slave are you now?

SOS. I'm Amphitruo's Sosia.

MER. *I*'m Sosia, not you.

[**150**] (*Mercury beats him up more violently with his fists*)

SOS. I'm done for! I'm dead!

MER. You shouting, worthless fellow? Shut up.
SOS. I will.
MER. Who's your master? Whose slave are you now?
SOS. [155] I don't know. Whom would you like most of all?
MER. That's better [lit. you're speaking better things]. OK then [lit. what therefore?]. What's your name now?
SOS. I don't know. Got a choice [lit. what do you want?]?
MER. Very good [lit. you speak very good things]! Are you Amphitruo's Sosia?
SOS. Definitely not.
MER. [160] Excellent reply. No-one is Amphitruo's slave but I.
SOS. (*to himself*) No-one's worse than this worst [of all]. Aren't I Amphitruo's slave Sosia? Aren't I now standing in front of our house? Aren't I speaking? Don't I live here? Isn't this fellow thrashing me with his fists? Aren't I about to go into our house?
       [165] (*Mercury stops Sosia as he prepares to enter the house*)
MER. What are you saying? You call the house yours? But this house is mine, not yours, worthless fellow. Don't lie.
       (*Mercury thrashes Sosia extremely severely with his fists*)
SOS. I'm dead! Who am I, if not Sosia? I'm asking you.
MER. [170] When *I* do not wish to be Sosia, *you* will be. Now, when *I* am Sosia, get lost, scum.
SOS. (*to himself, after thinking a great deal*) There's no doubt his looks are very much like mine – {for he has the} same hat, same clothes, same height, same feet, same chin, same cheeks, [175] same lips, beard, nose, neck. He's like me in every respect. He's more like me than I am. If his back's covered in scars [lit. if he has a scarred back], no one could be more similar to me. But for my part, as a matter of fact, I'm the very same Sosia, best slave of the best master. {For} there's no slave better than I, no master better than Amphitruo.
       [180] (*On that note* [lit. *having spoken thus*], *exit Sosia*)

Now learn the Learning Vocabulary at *GVE* p. 167.

EXERCISES FOR 3C

Page 172

Exercises

1 about to enter, *intro*; about to shout, *clamo*; about to do, *facio*; about to have, *habeo*; about to advise, *moneo*; about to remain, *maneo*; about to hear, *audio*; about to lie, *mentior*; about to go out, *egredior*; about to lead, *duco*; about to capture, *capio.*

2 future (*scribo*), past (*loquor*), future (*ago*), future (*inuenio*), past (*sequor*), future (*egredior*), future (*accipio*), future (*sum*), past (*moror*), future (*gero*), future (*nuntio*), past (*suspicor*), future (*uinco*), past (*hortor*).

3 *iturus, facturus, defensurus, redditurus, risurus, positurus, uisurus, iussurus, decepturus.*

Pages 172–3

Exercises

*1(a) But the very bad man [= utter scoundrel] deceived me with tricks throughout all of my most wretched life.
 (b) Why therefore did he beat her fiercely with his fists?
 (c) This year I finished this house with my [own] hands.
 (d) Neither by cunning nor with tricks will you ever deceive the citizens.
 (e) The utter scoundrel conducted the business very well for himself, with enormous misdeeds and very great crimes.
 (f) Alcumena outdid all wives in goodness and restraint.

2(a) That slave is about to go into the house, isn't he?
 (b) I am going to beat him with my fists at the same time.
 (c) That man Sosia is about to act most foolishly, isn't he, if he wishes to enter this house?
 (d) I very much want to deceive that slave for this night with my appearance.
 (e) Sosia will never conquer me with his courage.
 (f) What does he think [is] about to happen? For at this hour I am about to take [his] name away from him by my trickery.

Pages 174–5

Exercises

1   *stultius stultissime; melius optime; putidius putidissime; miserius miserrime; pulchrius pulcherrime; celerius celerrime; audacius audacissime; peius pessime.*

2   *facillime* most/very easily; *astutius* more cunningly; *optime* very well, best; *fortius* more bravely; *magis* more; *minime* least / very little; *pulcherrime* most beautifully.

*3   a man of the highest courage; with the highest courage; a slave of the highest cunning; with the highest cunning; with hands and feet; this year; with the same appearance; with my fists; at the same time.

*4   *eodem die; uxor summā uirtute; summā uirtute; pugno meo; eodem anno; eisdem manibus; seruus summā audaciā; dolo.*

5(a)   All the future is uncertain. (SENECA)
 (b)   We live among things destined to die. (SENECA)
 (c)   It is always difficult to talk about future events. (CICERO)
 (d)   The same goodness is in man and god. (CICERO)
 (e)   A way is made by violence. (VIRGIL)

Pages 175–6

Reading exercise / Test exercise

Omitted.

**English–Latin

1(a)   *quid ille seruus acturus est?*
 (b)   *nonne proelium Alcumenae narraturus est?*
 (c)   *eodem tempore dolis et pugnis eum decepturus sum.*
 (d)   *huc enim ueni mortem ei minaturus.*
 (e)   *hoc dolo nomen ei auferre mihi placuit.*
 (f)   *ego nihil facilius, nihil melius, nihil celerius feci.*

2   MER.   *quis loquitur? eum, si inueniam, pugnis meis aggressurus sum.*
        SOS.   *mihi melius est tacere. si me illis pugnis tanget, certe tanti ero quanti murena.*
        MER.   *quo iturus es, sceleste? quis es tu? ciuisne es?*
        SOS.   *seruus sum.*

MER.   *plura quam haec mihi dicere te uolo. quid est nomen tibi?*
SOS.   *nomen mihi est Sosia* [or *Sosiae*].
MER.   *tu mentiris. mene dolis tuis decepturus es? nisi celeriter abibis, ego his pugnis te necabo.*

DELICIAE LATINAE: 3C

Page 177

Word exercise

For meanings, consult an English dictionary.

forma beauty; *pes* (*ped-*) foot; *melior* better; *peior* worse; *interrogo* I ask; *sto* I stand; *maneo* I remain (stem *mans-*); *uideo* I see (stem *uis-*); *re-* back + *teneo* (stem *tent-*) I hold; *possideo* (stem *possess-*) I possess; *pono* (stem *posit-*) I place; *uerus* true; *gero* (stem *gest-*) I carry; *soluo* (stem *solut-*) I release; *con-* + *coquo* (stem *coct-*) I cook; *e-* + *fero* (stem *lat-*) I carry; *futurus* about to be; *sto* (stem *stat-*) I stand; *amo* (stem *amat-*) I love.

Page 178

Real Latin

The Vulgate

From Sion there shall come forth a law, and the word of God from Jerusalem, and he shall judge between many peoples, and he shall control mighty nations afar off; and they shall beat their swords into ploughshares and their spears into pruning-hooks; nation shall not raise sword against nation; and they shall not learn to fight any more ... because all peoples, each and every one, shall walk in the name of their God; and we shall walk in the name of the Lord our God for ever and beyond. (Micah 4.2.5)

Mottoes

Not by force, but by intellect.
Not by force, but by virtue.
Not by force, but by free will.
Not by the sword, but through grace.
Not by songs, but by action.
Through talent and work.

Through talent and strength.
By fire and sword.
By industry and work.

Page 179

By industry and hope.
By industry and virtue.
By counsel and virtue.
By counsel and spirit.
By counsel and arms.
By faith and love.
By faith and mercy.
By faith and arms.
By faith and constancy.
By faith and diligence.
By faith and trust.
By faith and work.
By faith and hope.

3 D *(Text pp. 55–7)*

NOTES

New uses of the dative case dominate this Section, especially verbs which put their direct objects in the dative (e.g. **Text** l. 181 *nihil ei obstat* 'nothing obstructs *him*' (dat.)).

Note verbs which have only a third person singular form ('impersonal verbs'), e.g. *licet* 'it is permitted', *placet* 'it is pleasing', which also take the dative e.g. **Text** l. 181 *licet patri meo* 'it is permitted *to my father*', ll. 184–5 *Sosiae non placuit* 'it was not pleasing *to Sosia*', etc.

Page 55

182   *licuit*: note that this is followed by a dative and infinitive ('it was permitted *to* x [dat.] *to do* [infinitive] Y'). All such impersonal verbs in this Section follow this pattern.

187   *seruo suo*: dative after *iratus*, 'angry *at his slave*', cf. **Text** l. 190.

189 *tibi*: dative after *credo*, 'I believe you'.

Page 56

195 *mihi imperat*: *impero* takes the dative, 'orders me', as does *pareo* (*imperio*, 'obey the command').

199 *si cui*: 'if at/with anyone' (dative after *iratus*); so *si quibus* (plural), after *fauet*. Note the way *si quis* sets up expectations here, often solved by *is* or *ille*: 'if *anyone* does x, *that person* [*ille/is*] is . . .'

200 *curae est*: 'is *for* a concern [dative] to' in Latin, 'is a concern to' in English. We offer alternative literal translations of this idiom down to *Text* l. 205.

224 *est mihi*: a common dative construction, 'there is to me x', 'x is to me', i.e. 'I have x'.

TRANSLATION OF 3D

MERCURIUS

Now my father can [lit. it is permitted for my father] get on with making love to Alcumena. Nothing stands in his way. But what will that Sosia say to Amphitruo? 'I wasn't allowed to go into the house. A slave barred my way.' Then Amphitruo will say 'What do you mean? Why weren't you allowed [in]?' That Sosia will say 'Because Sosia didn't [**185**] agree.' Then Amphitruo [will say] 'What are you saying, worst of slaves?' And Sosia [will repeat] 'Sosia didn't agree. Sosia got in the way.' Then Amphitruo, very enraged with his slave, [will say] 'What are you telling me, scum? Sosia didn't agree? But *you*'re Sosia! You're lying, worthless wretch: I don't believe you.' [And] Sosia: 'Believe me, master. I'm not [**190**] lying, but telling you the truth.' So Amphitruo will get angrier with the slave and the slave with Amphitruo; Amphitruo won't believe that slave, nor vice versa [lit. not the slave Amphitruo]. All the time, my father will be allowed free access to [lit. to make love to] Alcumena. Aren't I a wicked, cunning, smart slave? {Aren't I} the best slave to the best

father? The fact is, if my father [195] gives me orders, I
follow him and obey his command. {So} I am to Jove as a
good son is to his father. If anything tickles my father, it
tickles me more. If anything does not tickle my father, it
tickles me less. If Jupiter gives me any orders, I obey him
at once. If he threatens me at all, I'm terrified. If he's angry
with someone, I'm angry with him too. If he favours any
people, those [200] men I favour as well. If Jupiter is worried about anyone, so am I [lit. he is a concern to me]. If
he hates anyone, so do I too [lit. he is an object of hatred
to me]. If something gives Jupiter pleasure, it gives me
pleasure [lit. it is a source of pleasure]. If Jupiter helps
anyone, I help him [lit. I am a help to that man]. If he
stymies anyone, I stymie them as well [lit. I am a hindrance
to them]. So I am an example to all sons, as my father [205]
is an example to all fathers!

But now this slave has very definitely decided to shut
up. {For} the door-hinges are creaking a bit and my father
is about to make his exit from the house.

(*Enter Jupiter and Alcumena. Jupiter, embracing her briefly,
addresses her*)

JUPITER [210]

Farewell, Alcumena, and look after yourself, I beg you,
since you will soon give birth. I must return to the army.

ALCUMENA

What's the matter with you, my husband? Why is it necessary for you to leave home so suddenly?

JUP.   Not because I am tired of you [lit. you are a source of
boredom to me], dearest wife, but when a general [215] is
not in charge of his army, a lot of problems can occur.
Cheer up!

ALC.   You arrived in the middle of the night, now you leave
early in the morning. Does this appeal to you? Why don't
you stay with me a little [longer] this time?

JUP.   My wife, leaving does not appeal to me in the slightest.
But I have to be in charge of my troops and give my
careful attention to everything. Believe me. [220] {For}
who wants to leave his wife?

ALC. I don't want you to go, my husband. I shall love you all the more if you don't.

JUP. Why are you holding me? Don't obstruct me. I must return at high speed to my troops.

Look: I have a golden dish. This dish belonged to the king of the Teleboae. [**225**] But I killed him in battle with my own hand. So now I have his dish – and this dish I shall give to you. You will have the king's dish. Which husbands do not like to give something to their wives? Take it ...

ALC. I do, and a million thanks, my husband.

JUP. Lead the way, Sosia. I'll follow in a minute. Is there anything you want, my wife?

ALC. [**230**] I want you to come back quickly! Give me a hug!

JUP. I shall – there [lit. just as you wish]. Cheer up! I shall be back very soon.

(*Jupiter embraces Alcumena and is about to leave. Alcumena goes into the house*)

JUP. Now, night, I dismiss you. The day will be shorter by the amount the night was longer. This is what lovers like most of all. Now I shall go and [**235**] follow Mercury.

(*Following Mercury, Jupiter departs*)

Now learn the Learning Vocabulary at G*VE* pp. 180–1.

EXERCISES FOR 3D

Pages 183–4

Revision exercises

1   1st and 2nd declensions: household *famili-ae*, *-is*; eye *ocul-o*, *-is*; plan/ advice/judgement *consili-o*, *-is*; mind/spirit/heart *anim-o*, *-is*; dinner *cen-ae*, *-is*; war *bell-o*, *-is*; god *de-o*, *-is*; crowd/mob *turb-ae*, *-is*; victory *uictori-ae*, *-is*; town *oppid-o*, *-is*; booty *praed-ae*, *-is*.

Note: All 1st and 2nd declension dative plurals end in *-is* (except *deabus*, *filiabus*); but **all** 3rd, 4th and 5th declension dative plurals end in *-bus*.

3rd, 4th and 5th declensions: father *patr-i, -ibus*; respect *honor-i, -ibus*; temple *aed-i*; *but* house/mansion *aed-ibus*; brother *fratr-i, -ibus*; sister *soror-i, -ibus*; wife *uxor-i, -ibus*; load/burden *oner-i, -ibus*; man *homin-i, -ibus*; citizen *ciu-i, -ibus*; hand/band *man-ui, -ibus*; day *di-ei, -ebus*; night *noct-i, -ibus*; work *oper-i, -ibus*; head/source/fount *capit-i, -ibus*.

*2   1st and 2nd declensions: much *mult-o, -ae, -o; -is*; unhappy/wretched *miser-o, -ae, -o; -is*; bad/evil *mal-o, -ae, -o; -is*; my *me-o, -ae, -o; -is*; your (s.) *tu-o, -ae, -o; -is*; our *nostr-o, -ae, -o; -is*; your (pl.) *uestr-o, -ae, -o; -is*.

3rd declension: every/all *omn-i, -ibus*; sad/gloomy *trist-i, -ibus*; huge *ingent-i, -ibus*; short/brief *breu-i, -ibus*; bold/brave *audac-i, -ibus*; this *huic, his*.

3   Four principal parts: *do dare dedi datus*, give; *sto stare steti statum*, stand; *iubeo iubere iussi iussus*, order; *possideo possidere possedi possessus*, possess/hold; *sum esse fui* (no supine, only a future participle: *futurus*), be *eo ire ii itum*, go/come; *fero ferre tuli latus*, bear/carry; *uolo uelle uolui* –, wish; *dico dicere dixi dictus*, say/speak; *duco ducere duxi ductus*, lead/ consider; *capio capere cepi captus*, take/capture; *gero gerere gessi gestus*, conduct; *uenio uenire ueni uentum*, come; *uinco uincere uici uictus*, defeat/conquer.

Three principal parts: *adipiscor adipisci adeptus*, get/gain/acquire; *adgredior adgredi adgressus*, go up to/attack; *loquor loqui locutus*, speak; *sequor sequi secutus*, follow; *proficiscor proficisci profectus*, set out; *hortor hortari hortatus*, encourage; *polliceor polliceri pollicitus*, promise; *mentior mentiri mentitus*, lie; *conspicor conspicari conspicatus*, catch sight of; *arbitror arbitrari arbitratus*, think/judge; *conor conari conatus*, try.

Pages 184–5

Exercises

1(a)   *mihi*: I am allowed to leave the house
 (b)   *seruum*: Mercury [has] attacked the slave with his fists.
 (c)   *huic*: The slave obstructed this man [*or* got in his way].
 (d)   *tibi*: I don't believe you.
 (e)   *illam*: The man [*or* her husband] loves her enormously.
 (f)   *uobis*: That slave is threatening you.
      (You threaten someone in the dative: **GVE** p. 183.)
 (g)   *patri*: A good son always obeys his father [**GVE** p. 182].
 (h)   *cenam*: The cook is at present preparing dinner.

(i)   *exercitui*: My master is in charge of the army.
(j)   *te*: I instruct you to enter the house.
(k)   *ei*: The commander gave him this order ['ordered this to him'].

For the following exercise look at **GVE** p. 183 ('predicative dative').

2(a)   The cavalry are a hindrance to the legion.
 (b)   Alcumena is a major concern of Jupiter's ['Alcumena is a great care to Jupiter'].
 (c)   This bad citizen is loathed by all decent people ['. . . is a loathing to all good men'].
 (d)   Amphitruo was the salvation of his citizens.
 (e)   I will be a help to this city [*or* I will go to the assistance of this city].
 (f)   This duty is a pleasure to me.
 (g)   This is your duty.
 (h)   Alas for me! I will be the destruction of all my [family].
 (i)   This will be a bad thing for you.
 (j)   The victory of Amphitruo is a benefit to all citizens.

*3(a) I had a good son.
 (b)   My wife has a very large dowry.
 (c)   Our citizens had no help.
 (d)   No-one has a good mistress.
 (e)   They have a son and a daughter.

4(a)   For a learned and educated man, living is thinking. (CICERO)
 (b)   No road is impassable to Virtue. (OVID)
 (c)   Injustice cannot befall [be done to] the wise man. (SENECA)
 (d)   Men believe their eyes more than their ears. (SENECA)
 (e)   [The man] Who mixes [Latin says 'mixed'] useful with pleasant, wins ['won'] every vote. (HORACE)

Pages 185–7

Reading exercise / Test exercise

Omitted, but we identify key dative constructions:

domino Amphitruoni . . . dicet; uxori . . . nuntiare; mihi . . . minatus est; mihi . . . obstitit; mihi . . . non licuit; tuo seruo maximo fuit impedimento; necesse . . . mihi; imperiis . . . parere; mihi . . . placet; mihi . . . fuit . . . uoluptati . . . oneri; seruo . . . respondebit; illi seruo ingenti . . . est; ei . . . est; mihi . . . abstulit; mihi . . . est.

**English–Latin

1(a) *ingentissimus mihi seruus obstitit.*
 (b) *pulchra seni est filia / seni pulchra est filia / habet filiam pulchram senex / senex pulchram habet filiam. . .*
 (c) *militibus meis licet mihi imperare / militibus meis mihi imperare licet.*
 (d) *Euclioni pecunia magnae uoluptati est / Euclioni pecunia ualde placet.*
 (e) *malus ciuis omnibus odio est.*
 (f) *omnes uolo imperiis meis parere / omnes imperiis meis parere mihi placet.*
 (g) *hoc officium uxori oneri erit.*
 (h) *dux, non milites, exercitui praeest.*
 (i) *celerrime tibi in patriam regredi necesse est / necesse est tibi celerrime in patriam regredi.*
 (j) *amatoribus ita placet.*

2   J U P.   *uale, uxor. necesse enim est mihi ad copias regredi.*
     A L C.   *quid tibi negoti est? sumne tibi iam taedio?*
     J U P.   *immo, magnae mihi es uoluptati. sed ubi dux exercitui non praeest, milites officiis operam non dant.*
     A L C.   *noli abire, mi uir. plus te amare potero, si mihi parebis.*
     J U P.   *noli mihi obstare. mox regrediar ita ut uis. nunc tamen mihi abire placet. uale.*

DELICIAE LATINAE: 3D

Page 187

Word exercise

Consult an English dictionary for meanings.

gratitude > *gratia* thanks; auxiliary > *auxilium* help; voluptuary > *uoluptas* pleasure; brevity > *breuis* short; minus > *minus* less; favour > *faueo* I support; licence > *licet* it is allowed; obstinate > *obsto* I stand in the way of; tenacious > *teneo* I hold; emperor > *imperator* general; impede > *impedimentum* hindrance; necessary > *necesse* necessary.

Everyday Latin

non nobis . . . 'Not unto us, Lord, not unto us, but to Thy name give the glory.'
te Deum . . . 'We praise Thee [as] God.'

Page 188

Real Latin

Martial

A boy like the Trojan slave [i.e. Ganymede], Faustinus,
One-eyed Lycoris loves. How well the one-eyed [woman] sees!
(3.39)

Vulgate

Glory to God in the highest, and on earth peace to men of good
will. (Luke 2.14)

Section Four
Provincial corruption:
the Verres scandal 73–71

4A (i)–(iv) *(Text pp. 69–72)*

NOTES TO 4A

Testing shows that the change in register from colloquial Latin in dialogue form to a continuous prose narrative causes problems. We therefore revert to a literal translation in Latin word-order throughout Section 4.

In these four passages, we introduce one new tense 'I was -ing' (the imperfect of active and deponent verbs). You will also meet two new infinitive forms: (1) 'to have -ed' (perfect active and deponent); (2) 'to be going to ...' (future infinitive active and deponent). The central feature of the texts, though, is the introduction of the Latin for 'that' clauses after verbs like 'I say', 'I deny' etc. (indirect statement), which Latin does with accusative and infinitive. Two little words (*iste* 'that of yours', or 'the defendant', *quidam* 'a') complete the package. From now on, all references are to **Text** unless otherwise indicated. **NB** these notes are no longer separated by page-number.

4A(i)

4   *seruos quosdam*: 'some slaves'. Latin does not have a word for 'a'. But *quidam* (like *qui* **GVE 29**) does duty for it when indefiniteness is emphasised. Other examples are in ll. 10 and 11.

5   *expugnabant*: '[they] began to storm'. This is the first example of the new tense, the imperfect, which is introduced

in this section. Note the marker, after the stem, *-eba-* or *-aba-*, to which the personal endings are added. The continuousness of the action is here contrasted with the 'finished' action *concurrerunt* ('they charged and began storming'). Other imperfects in this section are: *conabantur* (l. 7); *commouebant* (l. 8); *percrebrescebat* (l. 9); *fiebat* (l. 15).

6   *clamauere*: remember that this is an alternative 3 pl. perfect active form, for *clamauerunt*. You will find several more examples in 4A(ii).

9   *erat*: 'was'. This is the first example of the imperfect tense of *sum*, which is *irregular*. See **GVE 89 Notes 4** for the full forms.

      seruos ... expugnare: '[The rumour was] that slaves were storming the temple.' This is the first example of the use of an infinitive phrase which reports a statement. Note that the subject of the 'that' clause in English is expressed in the accusative case in Latin (*seruos*). See **GVE 98** for a full explanation. In 4A(i) other examples are: *seruos ... commouere* (ll. 10–11); *seruos ... conari* (ll. 13–14).

10–11 *seruos ... commouere*: the object of *commouere* is *simulacrum Herculis*. *quosdam* agrees with *seruos*.

13–14 *seruos ... conari*: *conari*, as usual, governs another infinitive (*commouere*) and *simulacrum* is the object of *commouere*.

15   *impetum*: take with *fecerunt* to complete the idiom *impetum facio* = 'I make an attack'.

17   *num*: 'Surely not ...?' See **GVE 93** and contrast *nonne* 'Surely ...?'

4A(ii)

21   *qui*: 'which', describing the river (*fluuius*) and subject of the verb *fluit*.

25–6 *uenere ... effregere ... intrauere*: alternative 3 pl. perfect active forms (see 4A(i) l. 6 note).

26–7   *homines . . . intrare*: see 4A(i) l. 9 note. Here *aedem* is the object of *intrare*.

31   *discam*: '. . . am I to say?' Not a *future* ('shall I say').

4A(iii)

40   *iste*: 'he'. Literally 'that [man] of yours'. Forms of *iste* are like those of *ille* (*GVE* 64). This pronoun/adjective is often used in court-speeches to refer disparagingly to the defendant.

43   *cuiusdam*: genitive of *quidam* ('a') referring to *serui* ('of a[n unnamed] slave').

46   *seruos . . . intrauisse*: 'that the slaves had entered'. Note that *intrauisse* (lit: 'to have entered') is the first example of the perfect infinitive active. For forms, see *GVE* 95. Further examples are *sustulisse* (ll. 47 and 49), *audiuisse* (l. 50).

46–7   *et signum loco sustulisse*: *seruos* is still the subject of this phrase. *signum* is the object of *sustulisse*.

47   *se . . . conspicatas esse*: 'that they all . . .' I.e. the same people as are the subject of *affirmarunt* (note that this is an alternative form of *affirmauerunt*). Note that *conspicatas esse* is the first example of the perfect infinitive deponent. The participle agrees in gender, number and case with *se*. As you can see, it is feminine (because the *sacerdotes* are in this instance priestesses). *omnia* is the object of *conspicatas esse*. For perfect infinitive deponent forms see *GVE* 96. A further example is *ingressum esse*, l. 48.

48   *negauit*: '[the senate] said [that the slave had] not [entered]'. In English the force of *negauit* might be got by using 'denied that . . .' Note that *illum seruum* is subject both of *ingressum esse* (*ingressum* agrees with it in gender, number and case: cf. *se . . . conspicatas esse* at l. 47 above) and of *sustulisse*.

49–50   *scelera peiora*: this is the object of the infinitive *audiuisse*.

51   *uos . . . audituros esse*: 'that you will soon hear . . .' *peiora* is the object of the infinitive *audituros esse*. This is the first instance of the future infinitive active (for forms, see *GVE*

97). *audituros* agrees in gender, number and case with *uos* (cf. *se ... conspicatas esse* l. 47, and *seruum ... ingressum esse* at l. 48). For further examples, see 4A(iv) ll. 58–9.

4A(iv)

53 *iubet*: sc. 'the people of Syracuse [to] ...'

56 *istius*: 'of the defendant / that man of yours [i.e. Verres]'. Genitive of *iste*, dependent on *imperio et auctoritate* ('by the power and authority of ...').

57–8 *Verrem ... ausurum esse*: 'that Verres would not dare ...' Another future infinitive. *ausurum* agrees with *Verrem*. Another example occurs below in l. 59 (*Verrem ... perfecturum esse*).

63–4 *quot ... tot*: lit. 'how many ... so many'. But in English these so-called 'correlatives' are better translated by 'as many ... as', with 'as many' translating *tot*, and 'as' *quot*.

64 *cuius*: 'whose', describing *is* 'he' and qualifying *nomen* (subject of *exit*).

66 *Syracusani*: understand 'replied'. The suppression of the verb is common in passages like this, where several spoken exchanges are reported.

69 *negauere fas esse*: 'they said that it wasn't right'. For *nego* see 4A(iii) l. 48 note. Note that *negauere* is an alternative form of *negauerunt* (3 pl. perfect active).

70 *dicam*: '... am I to say'. See note on 4A(ii) l. 31.

TRANSLATION OF 4A

4A(i)

Hercules' temple among the men of Agrigentum is not far from the forum. There there is a statue of Hercules himself a very beautiful [statue]. Although very many statues I have seen, judges, a more beautiful statue than that never I have caught sight of. To this temple Verres by night slaves certain [ones] [5] armed suddenly sent. These charged and were storming the temple, but the guards of the temple shouted and the slaves to resist and the temple to defend tried. But the slaves of Verres them with clubs and fists drove back and when the folding-doors of the temple they broke open, the statue they began to shift. Meanwhile rumour through the whole city began to spread; the rumour was the slaves the temple to be storming [= that slaves were storming]. [10] Suddenly a messenger a certain [one], into the forum very quickly entering, announced the slaves certain [ones] the statue of Hercules to be shifting [= that certain slaves were moving]. All the Agrigentines, when they arose and the weapons seized, in a short time to the temple from the whole city ran up. When to the temple they reached, they saw the slaves the statue with maximum force to shift to be trying [= that the slaves were trying to shift]. Then the Agrigentines, very greatly [15] angry, a charge suddenly they made; there occurred great stoning; the slaves of Verres fled.

Surely not crimes greater ever you have heard, judges? Surely not deeds more wicked ever you have learned of? Listen, judges, and your attention more carefully pay: soon both worse and more wicked [things] you will hear.

Now learn the Learning Vocabulary at GVE p. 190.
4A(ii)

[20] The Assorines later, men of highest bravery, this courage of the Agrigentines they copied. Chrysas a river is which through the territory of the Assorines flows. The Assorines this river [as] a god they consider and worship, and many respects to it they give. In its temple a statue of Chrysas is of marble made. But Verres, because of the unique of that temple sanctity, that to demand did not [25] dare. To Tlepolemus he gave and to Hiero the business. Those men by night came, the folding-doors of the temple they broke open and they entered. But the guards in time realised the men certain [ones] the temple to be entering [= that certain men were entering] (to the neighbours the signal on the horn they gave), and the Assorines from their fields began to rush. There fled Tlepolemus and Hiero.

Of the Mother Great a shrine among the men of Engyum there is. In this shrine there were breastplates and [30] helmets of bronze and jars huge. Those in that shrine Scipio placed, and name his inscribed. What more should I say? All those [things], judges, Verres removed; nothing in that most sacred shrine he left. You apparently alone, Verres, these monuments understand and evaluate, Scipio, a man of the highest learning and culture, these did not understand!

Now learn the Learning Vocabulary at *GVE* p. 191.

4A(iii)

[35] There is among the men of Catina a shrine to Ceres. But not it is permitted for men into shrine that to enter. Women and virgins the rites to carry out are accustomed. In that shrine a statue of Ceres there was very old. This statue slaves of Verres from that most sacred and ancient place by night removed. Next day priests of Ceres the matter to magistrates their reported; to all the matter [40] most shocking seemed. Then that man, because suspicion from himself to remove he wanted, a friend a certain [one] [of] his he ordered someone [else] to find and accuse. He did not wish for/ because Verres on a charge to be. The friend therefore that [one] the name of a slave a certain [one] reported; then this slave he accused, and witnesses false against him gave. The senate of the Catinensians the matter by laws their to judge decided and [45] the priests it summoned. When the senate about all matters asked, the priests replied the slaves of Verres into the temple by night to have entered and the statue from the place to have removed [= that the slaves entered ... and removed]; they asserted themselves all everything to have seen [= that they had all seen]. The senate therefore denied that slave into the temple by night to have entered and the statue to have removed [= that that slave entered ... and removed], and confirmed him innocent to be [= that he was]. I think judges you [50] crimes worse never to have heard [= that you have never heard]. But attention to me pay; for even worse I think you soon about to hear to be [= that you are about to / will hear].

Now learn the Learning Vocabulary at *GVE* p. 192.

4A(iv)

At Syracuse a law there is concerning the priesthood of Jupiter (for that priesthood the Syracusans consider most prestigious to be).

This law the Syracusans it orders three men from three tribes through votes to choose. Then [for] those three necessary it is to draw lots. [55] Thus one from the three the priest of Jupiter becomes. Theomnastus a certain, a friend of Verres, by that man's order and influence among three those was selected. Necessary therefore it was [for] those three to draw lots. The Syracusans, thinking Verres the lot to interfere with never about to dare to be [= that Verres would never dare] the result happily they awaited; they were hoping for/because Verres his ends not about to achieve to be [= that Verres would not achieve]. What did Verres? First that man forbade [60] to draw lots, and ordered the Syracusans outside the lot Theomnastus to select. The Syracusans denied that to happen to be possible [= that it was possible for that to happen]; furthermore, right they denied it to be [= that it was right]. There ordered therefore that man the Syracusans to him the law about the priesthood to read out. The law thus they read out 'As many men as through votes we have selected, so many lots into the jar we throw. That man priest becomes, whose name from the jar comes out.' Then Verres [65] 'How many men have you selected?' The Syracusans replied 'Three.' Verres 'It is necessary therefore three lots to throw in, one to draw out?' Syracusans 'Thus it is necessary.' Verres therefore the Syracusans he ordered three lots, all with the name of Theomnastus inscribed, into the jar to throw. There arose an outcry very great; the Syracusans denied [it] right to be. To all that thing most wicked appeared. What [70] more should I say? In that way Verres most important that of Jupiter priesthood to Theomnastus he gave.

Now learn the Learning Vocabulary at *GVE* p. 193.

EXERCISES FOR 4A

Pages 196–7

Exercises

Morphology

Note ***GVE*** page references throughout.

1 *uideor, uidebar* I was seeming (like *pollicebar* – p. 195; *expugno, ex-pugnabam* I was storming (like *amabam* – p. 194); *fio, fiebam* I was being made (like *capiebam* – p. 194); *peruenio, perueniebam* I was reaching (like *audiebam* – p. 194); *sum, eram* I was; *conor, conabar* I was trying (like *minabar* – p. 195); *iubeo, iubebam* I was ordering (like *habebam* – p. 194); *reduco, reducebam* I was leading back (like *dicebam* – p. 194); *irascor, irascebar* I was getting angry (like *loquebar* – p. 195); *facio, faciebam* I was making (like *capiebam* – p. 194).

2* *tenebas* you (s.) were holding, *tenebatis*; *loquebantur* they were speaking, *loquebatur*; *praeerat* he was in charge, *praeerant*; *minabamini* you (pl.) were threatening, *minabaris*; *imperabam* I was ordering, *imperabamus*; *ueniebatis* you (pl.) were coming, *ueniebas*; *audebant* they were daring, *audebat*; *obliuiscebaris* you (s.) were forgetting, *obliuisce-bamini*; *audiebat* he was listening, *audiebant*; *patiebamur* we were suffering, *patiebar*; *auferebamus* we were taking away, *auferebam*; *sequebar* I was following, *sequebamur*.

3 I used to think *arbitrabar*; he was abandoning *relinquebat*; they were throwing *coniciebant*; we used to follow *sequebamur*; you (s.) were reporting *deferebas/nuntiabas*; she was going out *exibat*; they were accustomed *solebant*; you (pl.) were *eratis*; we were stating strongly *affirmabamus*.

4*

	Present	Future	Imperfect	Perfect
sentio	*sentit*	*sentiet*	*sentiebat*	*sensit*
	sentiunt	*sentient*	*sentiebant*	*senserunt*
minor	*minatur*	*minabitur*	*minabatur*	*minatus est*
	minantur	*minabuntur*	*minabantur*	*minati sunt*
ueto	*uetat*	*uetabit*	*uetabat*	*uetuit*
	uetant	*uetabunt*	*uetabant*	*uetuerunt*
tollo	*tollit*	*tollet*	*tollebat*	*sustulit*
	tollunt	*tollent*	*tollebant*	*sustulerunt*
eo	*it*	*ibit*	*ibat*	*iuit*
	eunt	*ibunt*	*ibant*	*iuerunt*
sum	*est*	*erit*	*erat*	*fuit*
	sunt	*erunt*	*erant*	*fuerunt*

audeo	audet	audebit	audebat	ausus est
	audent	audebunt	audebant	ausi sunt
adipiscor	adipiscitur	adipiscetur	adipiscebatur	adeptus est
	adipiscuntur	adipiscentur	adipiscebantur	adepti sunt
uideor	uidetur	uidebitur	uidebatur	uisus est
	uidentur	uidebuntur	uidebantur	uisi sunt
teneo	tenet	tenebit	tenebat	tenuit
	tenent	tenebunt	tenebant	tenuerunt
adgredior	adgreditur	adgredietur	adgrediebatur	adgressus est
	adgrediuntur	adgredientur	adgrediebantur	adgressi sunt
mentior	mentitur	mentietur	mentiebatur	mentitus est
	mentiuntur	mentientur	mentiebantur	mentiti sunt
accuso	accusat	accusabit	accusabat	accusauit
	accusant	accusabunt	accusabant	accusauerunt
colo	colit	colet	colebat	coluit
	colunt	colent	colebant	coluerunt

Note: In the following answer imperfects are underlined.

5 *loquar* future; *sentiebat* he was feeling; *amabit* future; *negabat* he was denying; *solebunt* future; *audebant* they were daring; *ponam* future; *tollebatis* you (pl.) were removing; *reliquit* perfect; *habebit* future; *tacebant* they were silent; *opinaberis* future; *arbitrabaris* you (s.) were thinking; *expugnant* present; *repellebas* you (s.) were driving back; *iudicabatis* you were judging; *coniecistis* perfect.

If you got any of these wrong, check which **conjugation** the verb belongs to.

Page 197

Exercises

Note: The underlined forms are the ones that agree.

1 *istius*: *serui*, *feminae*, *templi*, *manūs*, *rei*, *custodis*, *impetūs* – gen. sing. masc./fem./neut.;
istā: *lege*, *uirginem*, *serui*, *sacerdote* (can be fem.), *negotio* – abl. sing. fem.;

isti: <u>serui</u>, <u>uirtuti</u>, <u>manui</u>, <u>negotio</u>, <u>milites</u> – dat. sing. masc./fem./neut. *or* nom. pl. masc.;
ista: <u>femina</u>, clamor, <u>res</u>, <u>simulacra</u>, puellā – nom. sing. fem. *or* nom./acc. pl. neut.

2   *serui istius* (gen. sing.); *isti* (nom. pl.); *negotio isti* (dat. sing.); *isto* (abl. sing.); *uirtuti isti* (dat. sing.); *custodibus istis* (dat./abl. pl.); *manus istius* (gen. sing.); *istae* (nom. pl.); *istas* (acc. pl.).

Page 198

Exercises

1   *seruorum quorundam* gen. pl., of certain slaves; *custodi cuidam* dat. sing., to a certain guard; *signa quaedam* nom./acc. pl. (neut.), certain statues; *clamores quosdam* acc. pl., certain shouts; *dolo quodam* abl. sing., by a certain trick; *iudicibus quibusdam* dat./abl. pl., for/by certain judges.

Note: In the following answer the underlined forms are the ones that agree.

2   *cuiusdam*: <u>serua</u>, <u>templi</u>, <u>sacerdotis</u>, custodum, <u>manūs</u>, impetu – gen. sing. masc./fem./neut.;
quaedam: <u>femina</u>, <u>res</u>, negotia, milites, <u>leges</u>, <u>loca</u> – nom. sing./pl. fem. *or* nom./acc. pl. neut.;
quidam: <u>custos</u>, <u>nuntius</u>, <u>pueri</u>, <u>milites</u>, <u>magistratus</u>, <u>iudices</u> – nom. sing./pl. masc.

Page 201

Exercises

1

	Present	Perfect	Future
sum	*esse*	*fuisse*	*futurus esse*
accuso	*accusare*	*accusauisse*	*accusaturus esse*
expugno	*expugnare*	*expugnauisse*	*expugnaturus esse*
confirmo	*confirmare*	*confirmauisse*	*confirmaturus esse*
iubeo	*iubere*	*iussisse*	*iussurus esse*
reduco	*reducere*	*reduxisse*	*reducturus esse*
tollo	*tollere*	*sustulisse*	*sublaturus esse*

conicio	conicere	coniecisse	coniecturus esse
egredior	egredi	egressus esse	egressurus esse
mentior	mentiri	mentitus esse	mentiturus esse
uenio	uenire	uenisse	uenturus esse
eo	ire	iuisse (iisse)	iturus esse

2* *passurus esse* future, *patior; loqui* present, *loquor; amauisse* perfect, *amo; sentire* present, *sentio; habiturus esse* future, *habeo; sustulisse* perfect, *tollo; minatus esse* perfect, *minor; uelle* present, *uolo; iturus esse* future, *eo; expugnare* present, *expugno; secutus esse* perfect, *sequor; poscere* present, *posco; posuisse* perfect, *pono; adeptus esse* perfect, *adipiscor; iudicasse* perfect, *iudico; reperturus esse* future, *reperio; deferre* present, *defero*.

3* to seem *uideri;* to have forbidden *uetuisse;* to be about to think *arbitraturus esse;* to report *deferre;* to have found *inuenisse;* to be about to remove *ablaturus esse;* to follow *sequi;* to have remembered *recordatus esse;* to be about to lie *mentiturus esse;* to promise *promittere;* to have spoken *locutus esse;* to be about to forget *obliturus esse*.

In the following answer infinitives are underlined, and we give the present infinitive of verbs that are not already in an infinitive form and the present indicative of those that are.

4 *solitus es* 2nd sing. perf., *solere; detulistis* 2nd pl. perf., *deferre;* confirmauere (= *confirmauerunt*) 3rd pl. perf., *confirmare;* affirmare present, *affirmo; sequere* imperative, *sequi;* coluisse perfect, *colo; puta* imperative, *putare;* hortatus esse perfect, *hortor;* reperire present, *reperio; mentire* imperative, *mentiri;* accusaturus esse future, *accuso; ausus est* 3rd pl. perf., *audere;* repellere present, *repello; loquere* imperative, *loqui;* expugnauisse perfect, *expugno;* auditurus esse future, *audio; deferebat* 3rd sing. imperfect, *deferre;* iudicaturus esse future, *iudico*.

Pages 203–4

Exercises

1*(a) Cicero states strongly that the people of Agrigentum have a statue of Hercules.

  (b) The people of Agrigentum were saying that Verres had not been a good praetor.

(c)   The story was that the man's slaves had entered the temple and had removed the statue.

(d)   Cicero said that a certain messenger had announced all these things to the people of Agrigentum.

(e)   I think that that man will always lie to you.

(f)   Cicero was of the opinion that no one would ever commit worse crimes than that man (the defendant).

(g)   Verres used to send his slaves to the temples, take gold from citizens, show favour to his friends, even against the law, [and] embrace all crimes.

(h)   I hear that Verres will report the name of a certain slave.

(i)   Verres, because he did not want to be incriminated, ordered a certain friend to lie.

(j)   I know that Verres was accustomed to accusing innocent men.

(k)   Surely you have never heard more wicked crimes, gentlemen of the jury?

(l)   Verres is a most wicked man, is he not?

(m)   I heard that the people of Agrigentum made an attack on Verres' slaves.

2(a)   Reason tells us that the gods exist. (CICERO)

(b)   The outcome taught [us] that fortune favours the brave. (LIVY)

(c)   I am a man: I think there is nothing that does not concern me. (TERENCE)

(d)   They say that Democritus was never in public without a smile. (SENECA)

(e)   A young man hopes that he will live for a long time. (CICERO)

(f)   Renown is a fickle and unstable thing. (SENECA)

(g)   Recently the illness of a certain friend reminded me that we are at our best when we are ill. For what sick man does avarice or lust ever worry? (PLINY)

(h)   Here, where Rome is now, an uncut wood used to grow green; such a great undertaking was pasture for a few oxen. (OVID)

Pages 204–6

Reading exercises

The following answer gives translations only. Where there is ambiguity, the more likely translation is given first.

1(a)   ... that the slaves will storm the temple.

(b)   ... that Verres has sent the slaves to the temple.
        (*or* ... that the slaves have sent Verres to the temple.)

(c)   ... that the people of Assorus worship Chrysas (the river-god).
       (or ... that Chrysas worships the people of Assorus.)
(d)   ... that Verres will accuse me.
       (or ... that I will accuse Verres.)
(e)   ... that they [he, she, or it] love the statues.
       (or ... that the statues love themselves.)
(f)   ... that Scipio was a man of the highest kindness.
(g)   ... that the women have spotted everything.
(h)   ... that that man will leave the city by night.
(i)   ... that a great uproar had taken place.
(j)   ... that he is going home.

In the next answer the introductory verb is in **bold**; the accusative
and infinitive is <u>underlined</u>.

2*   *Cicero <u>templum esse</u> apud Agrigentinos* **dixit**. *<u>id</u> **affirmauit** non longe a
       foro <u>esse</u>. in hoc templum <u>intrauisse</u> **dixit** Verris <u>seruos</u>. eos <u>Verrem misisse</u>
       Cicero **opinatus est**. Verres autem <u>se</u> hoc <u>fecisse</u> **negabat**. fama percre-
       brescebat Verris <u>seruos</u> in templum <u>ingressos esse</u> et <u>custodes</u> templum
       defendere <u>conatos esse</u>. magnum clamorem <u>custodes fecisse</u> **putauit** Cicero;
       Agrigentinos igitur ex urbe <u>progressos esse</u> et ad templum <u>uenisse</u>. <u>fugisse</u>
       tum <u>seruos</u> Verris **affirmauit**. Cicero **negabat** umquam <u>se</u> scelera peiora
       <u>auditurum esse</u>.*

       Translation:

       Cicero said that there was a temple belonging to [amongst] the
       people of Agrigentum. He declared that it was not far from the
       forum. He said that it was this temple that Verres' slaves had en-
       tered. Cicero was of the opinion that Verres had sent them. Verres
       however denied that he had done so. The story spread abroad that
       Verres' slaves had gone into the temple and that the guards had
       tried to defend the temple. Cicero thought that the guards had
       caused a great commotion; [and] that the people of Agrigentum
       had therefore come forth from the city and had come to the
       temple. He declared that, at that point, the slaves of Verres had
       fled. Cicero said that he would never hear worse crimes.

3(a)   acc. + infin.: They said that this could not happen.
 (b)   prolative infin.: He did not want you to do this.
 (c)   prolative infin.: I order you to remove the statue of Chrysas.
 (d)   acc. + infin.: He was declaring that the slaves had tried to kill him.
 (e)   acc. + infin.: The story was that Verres had removed the statue.

(f) prolative infin.: Gentlemen of the jury, all the people of Agrigentum were wanting me to prosecute Verres.

4 *Cicero dicit templum apud Agrigentinos esse non longe a foro. affirmat ibi esse simulacrum Herculis pulcherrimum. negat se pulchrius simulacrum quam illud umquam conspicatum esse. fama est ad hoc templum Verrem repente nocte seruos quosdam armatos misisse. dicit hos concurrisse et templum expugnauisse. affirmat custodes templi clamauisse et seruis obsistere templumque defendere conatos esse. dicit eos mox et peiora et scelestiora audituros esse.*

Pages 206–7

Reading exercise / Test exercise

Omitted.

**English–Latin

1(a) *arbitror Verrem hoc fecisse.*
(b) *Cicero dixit seruos in templum intrauisse.*
(c) *multi ciues ad urbem ueniebant, negotium faciebant, deinde domum regrediebantur.*
(d) *amicus Verris nomen cuiusdam serui detulit.*
(e) *nos omnes scimus istum scelestum esse.*
(f) *num arbitraris seruos simulacrum sustulisse?*
(g) *Cicero uir optimus erat, amicos libenter defendebat, numquam scelerum hostium nostrorum obliuiscebatur.*
(h) *Cicero arbitratur iudices numquam scelus peius audituros esse.*

2 *Syracusanis lex est de sacerdotio Iouis. Cicero dicit hanc legem Syracusanos iubere tres uiros creare; Syracusanis sortiri necesse esse; unum ex tribus sacerdotem fieri. affirmat Verrem amico cuidam, Theomnasto nomine, sacerdotium dare uoluisse; Syracusanos negauisse, Verrem dolo rem perfecisse.*

DELICIAE LATINAE: 4A

Page 208

Word exercises

For meanings, consult an English dictionary.

clamour > *clamor* shout; custodial > *custos* guard; temple > *templum* temple; repulsion > *repello* (stem *repuls-*) I drive back; renunciation > *renuntio*

I select, return; total > *totus* whole; pugnacious > *pugno* I fight (cf. *ex-pugno* I storm); convention > *con-* together + *uenio* (*uent-*) I come; sign > *signum* sign, statue; cult > *colo* (stem *cult-*) I worship; relic > *relinquo* (stem *relict-*) I leave; sensibility > *sentio* (stem *sens-*) I feel; sacerdotal > *sacerdos* (stem *sacerdot-*) priest; conjecture > *conicio* (stem *coniect-*) I throw; putati-ve > *puto* (stem *putat-*) I think; veto > *ueto* I forbid; legal > *lex* (stem *leg-*) law; amicable > *amicus* friend; defamation > *de-* down + *fama* reputation; impetuous > *impetus* attack; judicial > *iudico* I judge; triumvirate > *tres* three + *uir* man.

Page 208

Real Latin

Catullus

My woman says she prefers to marry no one
   Rather than me, not even if Jupiter himself were to ask her.
[That's what] she says: but what a woman says to a passionate lover
   One should write in the wind and fast-flowing water. (Poem 70)

Martial

You promise everything, when you have been drinking all night long.
   In the morning, you give [me] nothing. Pollio, drink in the morning! (12.12)

Page 209

Philo swears he has never dined at home. And this is [the case].
   He does not dine, whenever no one has invited him [to dine out]. (5.47)

Aulus Gellius

When I tell a lie and say that I am lying, am I lying, or telling the truth?

An epitaph

I am what you will be, [and] I was what you are.

4 B (i)–(iv) *(Text pp. 73–5)*

NOTES TO 4B

In these four passages, we concentrate upon some new uses of the ablative case. A summary of the forms and uses will be found in **GVE 100A**. The individual references to earlier discussion are: **GVE 10, 23, 49, 67, 84**. There is also a new and uncomplicated use of the genitive ('a man of great wisdom'). Three new pronouns/ adjectives complete the haul of new grammar (*alius* 'other', *aliquis*/ *aliqui* 'someone/some', *ipse* 'actual, self'). You will need to be sure of the accusative and infinitive construction for reported statement ('x said that …') before you continue.

4B(i)

73   *ipsi*: 'themselves' nom. pl. m. It agrees with *Lampsaceni*. See **GVE 103** for forms.

74   *quietiores … hominibus*: 'more peaceful than …' The comparative adjective is here followed by plain ablative (of comparison: see **GVE 100B 1**). See also ll. 79, 80 and 84 below. Compare the construction you already know, with *quam* 'than', as in ll. 72–3 and *(malunt)* in ll. 74–5 below.

         ut Graeci: 'as Greeks'.

74–5   *otio uti et pace frui*: note that the verbs *utor* 'I use' and *fruor* 'I enjoy' take ablative objects. See **GVE 100B 4**.

75   *Lampsacum*: 'at/to Lampsacum'. Names of towns behave like *domus* (**GVE 30**) in not taking a preposition after verbs of motion (see further **GVE 110**).

79   *uiros peiores … turpioresque*: 'men worse and more revolting than …' Comparative adjectives followed by ablative (of comparison). See note on l. 74 above and **GVE 100B 1**.

80–1   *scitis Verrem … cupiuisse*: 'you know that Verres desired …' If you had trouble with this accusative and infinitive construction, return to **GVE 98–9** and do or repeat some of the exercises which follow the grammar.

81   *feminas ... pulchriores*: 'women more beautiful than ...' Comparative adjectives followed by ablative (of comparison). See *GVE* 100B 1.

4B(ii)

83   *miro artificio*: 'by ...' Ablative of means. See *GVE* 84.

86   *meliorem Lampsacenis*: 'better than ...' Comparative adjective followed by ablative (of comparison).

84–5   *esse hominem*: 'that he was a man ...', continues the reported statement after *detulit*. The same verb is also understood before *eum ... habere* (ll. 85–6) and *illam ... esse* (l. 86).

85   *hominem ... multi honoris, magnae existimationis*: 'a man of' (as in English). See *GVE* 101.

85–6   *filiam ... eximiae pulchritudinis*: 'a daughter of ...' (as in English). See *GVE* 101. Compare *uirginem ... summā ... modestiā* (ll. 86–7), where the ablative of description is used (see *GVE* 49).

87   *ut ... audiuit*: 'when ...' (*ut* can also mean 'as').

87–8   *summā cupiditate*: 'with ...' (ablative of accompanying circumstances). See *GVE* 100B 2.

90   *altero consilio*: object (ablative) of *usus*. See *GVE* 100B 4.

92   *summā celeritate*: 'with ...' Ablative of manner. See *GVE* 100B 3.

93   *se ... solere*: understand 'he said ...' as introductory verb, even though the previous verb was *negauit* ('he denied').

94   *dicam*: '... am I to say' (not 'shall I say').

4B(iii)

97–8   *uir aliis prouincialibus ... hospitalior*: 'a man more hospitable and friendlier than ...' Comparative adjectives followed by ablative (of comparison).

97   *multo*: 'much' (qualifying *hospitalior* and *amicior*). See **GVE 100B 5**.

108   *alius ex alia parte*: lit. 'another person from another part'. Translate as in the vocabulary and see **GVE 102 Note 1**.

115   *eodem animo*: translate 'of . . .' (ablative of attendant circumstances). See **GVE 100B 2**.

4B(iv)

122   *omnibus aliis . . . turpiorem*: 'more disgraceful than . . .' Comparative adjective followed by ablative (of comparison).

       multo: 'much' (qualifying *hospitalior* and *amicior*). See **GVE 100B**.

125   *his uerbis*: ablative object of *usi* (nom. m. pl. participle of *utor*). See **GVE 100B 4**.

NB *aliquis* 'someone' is not used in the text of 4B. However, you have already met an example in 4A(iii), l. 41: *amicum . . . iussit aliquem reperire* 'he told his friend to find someone'.

TRANSLATION OF 4B

4B(i)

A town there is in the Hellespont Lampsacum, judges. This town more famous and more renowned is than any other of Asia town, and themselves / the very men of Lampsacum more law-abiding than all other men. They prefer for/because like Greeks leisure to use and peace [**75**] to enjoy than riot to raise. Verres once arrived at Lampsacum with great disaster and almost destruction of the state. The men of Lampsacum the defendant / that man they led to Janitor a certain host, and retinue his all [of it] among other hosts they lodged. As the habit was of him, at once he ordered retinue his, men worse than all others and more disgusting, to find a [**80**] woman than the others more beautiful. You all know, judges, Verres women than others more beautiful always to have desired.

Now learn the Learning Vocabulary at GVE p. 210.

4B(ii)

There was a friend of the defendant / that man Rubrius a certain, a
fellow made for his [Verres'] lusts. That fellow, who with skill
amazing these things all to look into was accustomed, to him reported a man there to be Philodamus better than all other men of
Lampsacum; to be [85] a man among them of much respect, of
great reputation; him a daughter to have of outstanding beauty;
but that [girl] a virgin to be of the highest integrity, chastity and
discretion. Verres, as these things he heard, with the greatest desire
burned. At once he said himself to Philodamus about to move to
be. His host Ianitor, nothing suspecting, but thinking himself
Verres to have offended, [90] the fellow with all force to hold
back began. Verres therefore, another scheme using, Rubrius to
Philodamus to move ordered. Philodamus, when these things he
heard, with all speed to the defendant / that man came. He denied
this duty his to be, he denied himself him about to welcome to be;
himself praetors and consuls to welcome to be accustomed, not
their friends. What more should I say? That man the whole of
him the request [95] ignored and slaves his to take Rubrius to
Philodamus ordered, although that man Rubrius to receive not
had duty.

Now learn the Learning Vocabulary at *GVE* p. 211.

4B(iii)

Philodamus, a man than other provincials always much more wel-
coming and friendly, himself that Rubrius to home his welcomed;
and because he did not want unwilling to seem, a great party he
prepared. Not only [100] Rubrius retinue all to invite did he order,
but even son his out to a neighbour certain he sent for dinner. But
Verres Rubrius the daughter of Philodamus to carry off ordered.
Rubrius therefore with retinue his with all speed to the party
came; they lay down; there arose discussion among them; in Greek
fashion they drank; and at this time with conversation and pleasure
the party [105] they filled. After the thing enough to grow warm
seemed, Rubrius 'Please', he said, 'Philodamus, why to us daughter
your not you call?' Philodamus, a man of the highest seriousness,
very greatly angry became; strongly he denied women to be owing

[ought] in a party with men to lie down. Then different [ones] from different sides 'Call the woman' said; and at the same time slaves his Rubrius ordered the door [110] to shut. This when Philodamus understood, slaves his to himself he summoned and ordered them himself himself to ignore, his daughter with all force to defend, the matter to his son with all speed to announce. Uproar meanwhile arose through the whole house. Rubrius himself Philodamus with water boiling soaked. These things when the slaves of Philodamus to his son announced, at once home he hurried. All [115] the men of Lampsacum, as soon as these things they heard, with the same mind were and at the house of Philodamus by night gathered. That man, when he saw himself by his desire and lust such riots to have incited, to escape wanted.

Now learn the Learning Vocabulary at *GVE* p. 212.

4B(iv)

These things when all the men of Lampsacum with the same sentiment and anguish discussed, with sword and stones the door to cut down began, and at that time with fire to surround. [120] Citizen Romans certain, who at Lampsacum were doing business, with all speed ran together. They begged and beseeched the men of Lampsacum; they agreed Verres to be the worst and than all others much more disgusting; but they said the men of Lampsacum the fellow criminal to spare to be owing [ought], rather than a praetor Roman to kill; [in] this for/because way the crime of them less [125] to be about to be. These words using, at last the men of Lampsacum from violence they restrained.

Now learn the Learning Vocabulary at *GVE* p. 213.

EXERCISES FOR 4B

Page 216

Exercises

1*(a)   *comite claro, comitibus claris; calamitate magnā, calamitatibus magnis; conuiuio Graeco, conuiuiis Graecis; amico nobili, amicis nobilibus;*

magistratu innocenti, magistratibus innocentibus; formā turpi, formis turpibus; re Romanā, rebus Romanis.

(b) The ablatives are: *comitibus, Asiā, conuiuiis, sermone, ui, amico, diebus, homine turpi, uiro nobili, manu celeri.*

(c) *ingenti*: dat./abl. sing. – *templo, uirgine, curā; audacibus*: dat./abl. pl. – *feminis, sacerdotibus; solā*: abl. sing. fem. – *uirtute; magnis*: dat./abl. pl. – *pueris, manibus; tanto*: dat./abl. sing. masc./neut. – *proelio, praetore; longiore*: abl. sing. – *periculo, uiā.*

NB: most third declension nouns have ablative singular ending in *-e.*

If you have made any mistakes, check carefully the **declension** of the nouns and adjectives.

2(a) The man was much better than all the others.
 (b) He said that he had not killed [lit. He denied himself to have killed] the man with the utmost force.
 (c) That man / the defendant beat the door with rocks.
 (d) Cicero asserted that the Agrigentini were very brave men [lit. men of great courage].
 (e) Praetors, very serious men [lit. men of the highest seriousness] do not enjoy parties.
 (f) The Lampsaceni used to conduct their business in the Greek manner.
 (g) Greeks prefer to pass their life in leisure and peace [rather] than in war and disasters.
 (h) Cicero thought that Verres was [lit. thought Verres to be] worse than the other praetors.
 (i) The story was that Verres' slaves had used the utmost violence [*utor* takes the ablative].
 (j) At that time Ianitor came to Verres with the utmost speed and tried to detain him with many words.

Pages 217–18

Exercises

1 *alius*: nom. sing. masc. – *comes; alii*: dat. sing. m. f. n. *or* nom. pl. masc. – *Lampsaceno, sermones, ianuae; alia*: nom. sing. fem. *or* nom./acc. pl. neut. – *conuiuia, uirgo; aliā*: abl. sing. fem. – *calam-*

itate; *aliqua*: nom. sing. fem. *or* nom./acc. pl. neut. – *mulier, uerba*; *aliquā*: abl. sing. fem. – *re, seruā*.

2*(a) Different people say different things (**GVE 102 Note 1** p. 217).
 (b) Some were Lampsaceni, the others were Agrigentini.
 (c) Different people are making an attack on the town in different places.
 (d) Some ran from the fields, others from the town. (**GVE 102 Note 2** p. 217)
 (e) Someone will say something.
 (f) But who is calling? Some magistrate? No-one.
 (g) Catiline, are you hesitating to go away to some country?
 (h) Verres left the house with some companion.

Page 219

Exercises

1 *ipsi*: dat. sing. m. f. n. *or* masc. pl. nom. – *calamitati, consules, conuiuio, nuntii*; *ipsa*: nom. sing. fem. *or* nom./acc. pl. neut. – *grauitas, signa, simulacra*; *ipsā*: abl. sing. fem. – *grauitate*.

2 *ipsi uoluere* (= *-erunt*) they themselves wanted; *signum ipsum* the statue itself; *ipsae clamarunt* (= *-auerunt*) the women themselves shouted; *consilio ipso* by the plan itself; *ipsi homini pepercerunt* they themselves spared the man *or* they spared the man himself (*ipsi* = dat. sing. *or* nom. pl. masc.); *ipsa laetitia* the joy itself; *obsecrarunt* (= *-auerunt*) *ipsi oraruntque* (= *-aueruntque*) they themselves begged and prayed; *noli ipsam retinere* don't keep the girl herself.

3*(a) No-one can be with/of a calm mind. (CICERO)
 (b) The wise man conquers Fortune with courage. (SENECA)
 (c) Alas, Fortune, who is a more cruel god to us than you? (HORACE)
 (*te* = ablative of comparison.)
 (d) That man enjoys riches the most who least needs riches. (SENECA)
 (*fruor* is followed by the ablative.)
 (e) Alas, how difficult it is not to betray a crime by one's expression. (OVID)
 (f) Silver is cheaper than gold, gold is cheaper than virtues. (HORACE)
 (g) An honourable death is better than a shameful life. (TACITUS)

(h)   [There is] always something new out of Africa. (PLINY)
(i)   The whole life of man is nothing other than the journey to death. (SENECA)
(j)   Nature shows different routes to different people. (SALLUST) (*or* ... one route to one man, a different one to another)

Page 219

Reading

(a)   *omnibus aliis*: comparison after *melior*.
(b)   *summā ui*: describing how.
(c)   *saxis*: instrument – 'with which'.
(d)   No ablative phrase.
(e)   *summā grauitate*: describing the praetors.
      conuiuiis: *fruor* takes the ablative.
(f)   *more Graeco*: describing how they acted.
(g)   *otio et pace* and *bello et calamitatibus*: describing how they prefer to live.
(h)   *ceteris praetoribus*: comparison after *peiorem*.
(i)   *summā ui*: *utor* takes the ablative.
(j)   *eo tempore*: time when.
      summā celeritate: describes how he came.
      multis uerbis: instrument – 'with which'.

Pages 220–1

Reading exercise / Test exercise

Omitted.

English–Latin

1(a)   *Verres Rubrio peior erat.*
 (b)   *Lampsaceni pace et otio fruebantur.*
 (c)   *Philodamus erat uir magnae grauitatis* [gen.], *Verres magnā cupiditate* [abl.].
 (d)   *coqui conuiuium sermone et laetitiā parabant.*
 (e)   *Verres et comites more Graeco bibebant.*
 (f)   *Lampsaceni ianuam pugnis caedebant et eodem tempore summā uoce clamabant.*

2   *Philodamus erat uir magnā grauitate, aliis tamen semper multo hospitalior. Rubrium et comites ad conuiuium inuitauit. omnes summā celeritate*

peruenerunt. sermone et laetitiā bibebant. subito autem Rubrius Phil-
odamum iussit filiam uocare. Philodamus autem negabat se eam uocatu-
rum esse. tumultus tum erat.

DELICIAE LATINAE: 4B

Page 221

Word exercise

Consult an English dictionary for meanings.

calamity > *calamitas* disaster; hospitable > *hospes* (stem *hospit-*) host;
clarity > *clarus* famous; turpitude > *turpis* disgusting; cupidity > *cupiditas*
lust; use > *usus* use; vim > *uis* force; negligence > *neglego* I ignore;
reception > *recipio* (stem *recept-*) I receive; gravity > *grauitas* seriousness;
sermon > *sermo* speech; convenient > *conuenio* I meet; intellect >
intellego (stem *intellect-*) I understand; oration > *oro* (stem *orat-*) I beg;
retention > *retineo* (stem *retent-*) I hold back; bibulous > *bibo* I drink;
celerity > *celeritas* speed; usufruct > *usus* use + *fruor* (stem *fruct-*) I enjoy;
concurrent > *concurro* I run together.

Page 222

Real Latin

Horace

What has the loss-causing day not diminished?
The age of our parents, worse than our grandfathers, has brought
forth
Us more wicked, soon to produce
An offspring more corrupt. (*Odes* 3.6.45ff.)

4C (i)—(ii) *(Text pp. 76–7)*

NOTES TO 4C

In these two sections, we introduce a new tense, the pluperfect
active and deponent ('x had -ed'). We pick up and explain further
the uses of *qui* 'who'. We encounter more ablative usages. And we
explain the locative case.

4c(i)

126   *qui ... erat*: 'who ... was'. In this instance, *qui* is easy to
        translate. It is nominative, because it is the subject of the
        verb *erat*.

        Lilybaei: 'at Lilybaeum'. This is the first example of the
        locative case. For other examples, see ll. 134, 135, and
        4c(ii), ll. 150, 155. See **GVE 110**.

127   *quem*: this refers to *hic homo*, masculine. *hic homo* is called
        the antecedent (remember this term) of *quem*. *quem* itself is
        accusative because it is the object of *dico*.

        nobili genere natus: 'born from a noble family'. The ablative
        used with *natus* is the first example of the ablative of origin.
        See **GVE 108 1**.

128   *quam*: this picks up *uirtutem*, feminine (i.e. *uirtutem* is the
        antecedent). *quam* is accusative because it is the object of
        cognouerant.

        cognouerant: 'they had become acquainted with'. This is the
        first pluperfect active. To recognise this tense, note the
        endings *-eram* etc. (exactly as in the imperfect of *sum*,
        which you recently learned) added on to the perfect active
        stem. Other examples in this passage are (with the stem
        and ending separated by a hyphen): *colleg-erat* (l. 129), *de-
        dux-erat* (l. 130), *fec-erat* (l. 132), *fec-erant* (l. 134), *constitu-erat*
        (ll. 139, 143).

128–9   *Verre praetore*: i.e. 'during Verres' praetorship'. This is an
        ablative of attendant circumstances (cf. **GVE 100B 2**),
        which is explained further at **GVE 109**.

129   *quae*: the antecedent is *omnia*, neuter. *quae* is accusative
        because it is the object of *collegerat*.

130   *quos*: the antecedent is *comites*, masculine. *quos* is accusative
        because it is the object of *deduxerat*.

131   *quae*: lit. 'which cups', i.e. 'and these cups'. Here *quae*
        connects the sentence (it is a 'connecting relative') with

the preceding one. It is accusative because it is the object of *fecerat*. Its antecedent is *pocula* (which happens to be repeated, for clarity). Other examples of this connecting relative are *quod* (ll. 132, 138), *quibus* (l. 139), *quas* (l. 141). See **GVE 107**.

132   *ea pocula . . . esse*: '[they reported] that these cups were . . .' As often in reported statement in Latin, the preceding verb is to be understood before one, or even a number, of following statements.

       quod: 'and this'. See note on l. 131 above. *quod* is accusative because it is the object of *audiuit*. Its antecedent is the whole of the statement of Verres' friends that Diodorus had some beautiful cups. That is why its gender is neuter. See **GVE 107**.

134   *quorum*: *quorum* is genitive because it depends on *mentionem* ('mention of which'). Its antecedent is *pocula*, neuter. See **GVE 106**.

135   *Melitae*: 'in Malta'. Another example of the locative case. See above on l. 131 (and also *Lilybaei* l. 134). See further **GVE 110**.

136   *Melitam*: 'to Malta'. Note the absence of preposition, as also with *Lilybaeum* at l. 141 below. See further **GVE 110**.

138   *quod*: see note on l. 131 above. *quod* is accusative because it is the object of *audiuit*. Its antecedent is the news that Verres had sent men to Malta to ask for the cups. That is why its gender is neuter.

       qui: the antecedent is *Diodorus*, masculine. *qui* is nominative because it is the subject of *constituerat*. See **GVE 106**.

139   *quibus*: 'and [in] this . . .', agreeing with *litteris*. See note on l. 131 above. *quibus* is ablative because it agrees with *litteris*, which is governed by the preposition *in*. Its antecedent (repeated for clarity) is *litteras*. See **GVE 107**.

140   *ausus erat*: 'had dared'. This is the first example of the
       pluperfect deponent. Note that you can tell the subject is
       Diodorus because the participle *ausus* has a masculine sin-
       gular ending.

141   *Lilybaeum*: see note on l. 136 above and **GVE 110**.

       quas: 'and this [sc. letter]'. See note on l. 131 above. The
       antecedent is *litteris*, feminine, from l. 140. *quas* is accusa-
       tive because it is the object of *perlegit* (tr. 'had read', as
       often perfect tenses after *ubi* and *ut* = 'when'). See **GVE
       107**.

142   *qui*: the antecedent is *Diodorus ipse*, masculine. *qui* is nom-
       inative because it is the subject of *constituerat*.

143   *Lilybaeo*: 'from Lilybaeum'. Note the absence of a prepo-
       sition. See further **GVE 110**.

4C(ii)

145   *quae*: 'and this'. The antecedent is 'what Diodorus had
       done about the cups', and so the connecting relative is
       neuter. It is accusative because it is the object of *audiuit*.

       non mediocri insaniā et furore: 'with ...' These could be
       construed as ablatives of manner (cf. **GVE 100B 3**), or as
       ablatives of cause 'out of / because of' (translating *se gerere*
       as 'acting, behaving'). For the latter, see **GVE 108 2**.

146   *potuerat*: 'he had [not] been able'. The other pluperfect
       active forms in this passage are: *commouerat* and *collegerat* (l.
       149), *cognouerat* (l. 156), and *concupiuerat* (l. 167).

148   *totā prouinciā*: 'over the whole province'. The ablative is
       used here of place where, as in many instances where a
       noun denoting location is used. Other examples are: *totā
       Siciliā* (lines 153, 166), and *totā Romā* (l. 158). See **GVE
       110 Note 1**.

150   *qui*: the antecedent is *Verres*, so *qui* is masculine s. It is
       nominative because it is the subject of *uolebat*. See **GVE
       107**.

152   *quem ... sciebat*: 'whom he knew to be absent'. *quem* is
      masc. sing. because its antecedent is *Diodorum*. It is accu-
      sative because it is *both* the object of *sciebat and* the subject
      of an accusative and infinitive phrase governed by *sciebat*.

156   *quos cognouerat*: *quos* is masc. pl. because its antecedent is
      hospites. It is accusative because it is the object of *cognouerat*.
      See **GVE 107**.

      quae: 'and these things'. The antecedent is 'the things
      Diodorus was saying at Rome', and so *quae* is neuter.
      quae is accusative because it is the object of *audierunt*
      (= *audiuerunt*).

157–9 *rem ... periturum esse*: this is all an indirect statement (so
      expressed by accusative and infinitive). There is only one
      introductory verb, that is [*litteras ...*] *mittebant* 'they started
      to send [letters] [saying] that ...' The subject of the first
      indirect statement is *rem* 'that the matter ...' The second
      has 'it' as its subject (note the neuter form of *perspicuum*,
      'that it was ...') and the phrase *omnia ... fieri* is in its turn
      an indirect statement introduced by *perspicuum esse* ('clear
      that everything *fieri*'). The third statement following
      directly on *litteras ... mittebant* has *eum* (i.e. Verres) as its
      subject, 'that he *insanire*'. The fourth also has Verres as
      subject ('that he ought to ...'), and so does the fifth,
      though this can only be inferred from the masc. sing. form
      of the participle *periturum* ('that he would be done for ...').

159–60 *hoc uno crimine*: 'because of ...' Ablative of cause. See **GVE
      108 2**.

160   *quas*: 'and this/these'. The antecedent is *litteras*, and so *quas*
      is fem. pl. It is accusative because it is the object of *perlegit*.

161–2 *primum annum ... habere*: another series of indirect state-
      ments only loosely introduced by *sensit* (l. 160). The first is
      best approached by translating '[he realised] that it was the
      first ...' The second can be more easily understood '[he
      realised] that he ...' In English, such passages are also often
      rendered without introductory verbs. They are easier to

spot in Latin, because the main verbs of the indirect statements are always in the infinitive form (and the subjects in
the accusative case).

162   *pudore ... metu ... timore*: 'because of ...' All three are
       ablatives of cause. See **GVE 108 2**.

164   *Verre praetore*: see note on 4C(i), ll. 128–9.

       prouinciā domoque caruit: note that *careo*, like *utor* and *fruor*,
       takes an ablative.

165   *dicam*: '... am I to say?' See note on 4A(ii), l. 31.

       hōc clarius: remember that comparative adjectives have
       neuter in *-ius* and see **GVE 100B 1** for the construction of
       hōc (remembering that the long vowel makes this an abla-
       tive form).

166   *Verre praetore*: see above on l. 164.

167   *quas*: see note on 4A(i), l. 126. The antecedent is *res*, so *quas*
       is fem. pl. It is accusative because it is the object of *con-
       cupiuerat*.

TRANSLATION OF 4C

4C(i)

Diodorus, who Maltese was, at Lilybaeum for many years was living. This man whom I am mentioning was of noble family born
and fine and popular on account of his goodness, which all the
Lilybitani acknowledged. But Verres being praetor, almost about
to lose he was everything which at home he had collected. For
[**130**] the retinue which Verres to Lilybaeum had brought Diodorus cups certain to have they announced; those cups than all
others more beautiful to be. (Which cups, as later I heard, Mentor
with supreme skill had made.) Which when Verres heard, with
desire inflamed, Diodorus to himself called and the cups, of which
mention his retinue had made, demanded. That man himself at
Lilybaeum [**135**] those cups not to have replied, but in Malta with
a relative certain to have left. Then the defendant / that man began

to send men to Malta, began to write to certain Maltese, the cups began to demand, began to order Diodorus to that relative his to send letters. Which when he heard, Diodorus, who his own things to protect had decided, to relative his a letter sent; which in [**140**] letter to write he had dared the relative to owe [ought] to deny himself the cups to have, but to assert himself them in few those days to have sent to Lilybaeum. Which when the relative read, thus he did. Meanwhile Diodorus himself, who to be absent from his home for a while had decided rather than the silver to lose, from Lilybaeum departed.

Now learn the Learning Vocabulary at *GVE* p. 225.

4c(ii)

[**145**] Which things when the defendant / that man heard, not with moderate madness and rage himself to conduct to everyone seemed; in this way he acted, because not he had been able the silver from Diodorus to steal. [With] Diodorus therefore absent he threatened, he shouted openly, he wept. Finally servants his he ordered Diodorus in the whole province to look out for; but that man by now camp had moved and the cups had collected; at that [**150**] time at Rome he was living. Verres therefore, who by some means Diodorus into the province to recall wanted, this plan devised: he decided Diodorus, whom absent to be he knew, on a false certain charge to accuse. The matter transparent was in all Sicily, Verres of silver by desire the man absent to have accused.

[**155**] Meanwhile Diodorus at Rome poorly dressed around patrons and connections whom he knew was going round, and the matter all was telling. Which things when the father and friends of Verres heard, a letter strongly worded to the defendant / that man they sent the matter transparent to be in all Rome and unpopular; [it] obvious to be all those things on account of silver to be happening; to be mad that man; to beware to owe [ought]; about to die to be as a result of this [**160**] one accusation. Which when Verres read, he realised himself foolishly to have acted; for the first year of the province for him [it] to be; himself no money at this time to have. Anger his therefore not from shame but from fear and apprehension he checked; Diodorus absent to condemn not he

dared. Diodorus meanwhile, Verres [being] praetor, almost three years from province and home stayed away.

[165] What more should I say? Nothing than this more transparent to be is able, judges. At that time, Verres [being] praetor, in all Sicily, no one was able to keep or at home to preserve those things that Verres more greatly had desired.

Now learn the Learning Vocabulary at *GVE* p. 226.

EXERCISES FOR 4C

Pages 228–9

Exercises

1 *conatus/-a/-um eram* (see ***GVE* 105**) I had tried; *excogitaueram* I had devised (see ***GVE* 104**); *uisus/-a/-um eram* I had seemed; *monueram* I had warned; *usus/-a/-um eram* I had used; *feceram* I had made; *afueram* I had been away; *collegeram* I had collected; *commoueram* I had moved.

2* you (pl.) had begged, *oraueras*; you (s.) had caught sight of, *conspicati eratis*; he had moved, *commouerant*; they had urged, *hortata erat*; I had spared, *peperceramus*; she had remembered, *recordatae erant*; we had welcomed, *receperam*; I had embraced, *amplexi eramus*; you (s.) had cut down, *cecideratis*; we had forgotten, *oblitus eram*; they had ignored, *neglexerat*; you (pl.) had advanced, *progressus eras*.

3* *constitueram*; *passus eras*; *reuocauerant*; *recordati erant*; *cognouerat*; *adepta erat*; *excogitaueramus*; *complexi eratis*; *collegeramus*; *commoueras*.

4*

Present	Future	Imperfect	Perfect	Pluperfect
reuocat	reuocabit	reuocabat	reuocauit	reuocauerat
reuocant	reuocabunt	reuocabant	reuocauerunt	reuocauerant
tenet	tenebit	tenebat	tenuit	tenuerat
tenent	tenebunt	tenebant	tenuerunt	tenuerant
arbitratur	arbitrabitur	arbitrabatur	arbitratus/ -a/-um est	arbitratus/ -a/-um erat
arbitrantur	arbitrabuntur	arbitrabantur	arbitrati/ -ae/-a/-sunt	arbitrati/ -ae/-a erant

uidetur	uidebitur	uidebatur	uisus/-a/-um est	uisus/-a/-um erat
uidentur	uidebuntur	uidebantur	uisi/-ae/-a sunt	uisi/-ae/-a erant
neglegit	negleget	neglegebat	neglexit	neglexerat
neglegunt	neglegent	neglegebant	neglexerunt	neglexerant
sentit	sentiet	sentiebat	sensit	senserat
sentiunt	sentient	sentiebant	senserunt	senserant
utitur	utetur	utebatur	usus/-a/-um est	usus/-a/-um erat
utuntur	utentur	utebantur	usi/-ae/-a sunt	usi/-ae/-a erant
patitur	patietur	patiebatur	passus/-a/-um est	passus/-a/-um erat
patiuntur	patientur	patiebantur	passi/-ae/-a sunt	passi/-ae/-a erant
fit	fiet	fiebat	factus/-a/-um est	factus/-a/-um erat
fiunt	fient	fiebant	facti/-ae/-a sunt	facti/-ae/-a erant
non uult	nolet	nolebat	noluit	noluerat
nolunt	nolent	nolebant	noluerunt	noluerant
est	erit	erat	fuit	fuerat
sunt	erunt	erant	fuerunt	fuerant
colligit	colliget	colligebat	collegit	collegerat
colligunt	colligent	colligebant	collegerunt	collegerant
constituit	constituet	constituebat	constituit	constituerat
constituunt	constituent	constituebant	constituerunt	constituerant

5   Impf., *excogito*; he had called back, *reuoco*; perf., *patior*; you (s.) had collected, *colligo*; fut., *circumeo*; pres., *commoueo*; they had read through, *perlego*; fut., *cognosco*; you (s.) had tried, *conor*; perf., *absum*; you (pl.) had been, *sum*; perf., *recipio*; they had gone out, *egredior*; perf., *ingredior*; pres., *pono*; fut., *utor*; we had killed, *caedo*.

Pages 231–2

Exercises

In the next answer the antecedent is underlined.

1*(a) Diodorus used to have small *cups*, which Mentor had made.

(b) *The letter*, which he had written, soon arrived in Sicily.

(c) He was calling back *the men* who had asserted that they were in Rome.

(d) *The thing* which you have devised is criminal.

(e) *Diodorus*, who Verres knew had certain very beautiful cups, had gone away.

(f) Diodorus had been born from a noble *family* which had never become well-known.

2(a) *quem*: He was a man whom all the women used to love.

(b) *cui*: She was a woman to whom every man was pleasing.

(c) *quam*: The young girl, whom Verres had wanted to love, was noble.

(d) *qui*: Many men, who had become the companions of Verres, were the sons of noblemen.

(e) *quae*: Mentor had made the small cups which the companions of Verres had caught sight of.

(f) *quorum*: Many men, whose greed the good citizens had thought was very great, were going to Verres.

(g) *quod*: The companions of Verres removed from the temple the statue which that man had dared to desire.

(h) *quos*: The companions, whom Verres had led away with him to Lilybaeum, had caught sight of the cups of Diodorus.

3 *poculis* (neut. pl.); *seruus* (masc. sing.); *genus* (neut. sing.); *filio* (masc. sing.); *fana* (neut. pl.).

4(a) . . . and when he had heard it . . .

(b) . . . and when he had told these things . . .

(c) . . . and when they had recalled these women . . .

(d) . . . and when they had caught sight of them . . .

(e) . . . and when he had threatened him/her . . .

Pages 234–5

Exercises

1(a) A young girl of excellent reputation.

(b) When Cicero and Antonius were consuls.

(c)   Under my leadership.
(d)   Young girls born from a noble family.
(e)   He removed the gold out of boldness and greed.
(f)   From Rome.
(g)   At home.
(h)   From Lilybaeum.
(i)   In the whole province.
(j)   In the absence of the praetors.

2(a)   *uir magnae uirtutis / uir magnā uirtute.*
(b)   *Verre praetore.*
(c)   *te duce.*
(d)   *puer genere nobili natus.*
(e)   *sic/ita cupiditate egit.*
(f)   *Romae.*
(g)   *domo.*
(h)   *Lilybaeum.*
(i)   *totā Siciliā.*
(j)   *ceteris absentibus.*

3(a)   He who has much desires more. (SENECA)
(b)   The poor man is not he who has too little but he who desires more. (SENECA)
(c)   He who begins (it) has half the deed. (HORACE)
(d)   Fortune snatches nothing away except what she has given. (SENECA)
(e)   It is sweet to remember what was hard to endure. (SENECA)
(f)   Diaulus was recently a doctor, now he's an undertaker;
      what he does as an undertaker, he had also done as a doctor. (MARTIAL)

Pages 235–6

Reading exercise / Test exercise

Omitted.

**English–Latin

1(a)   *Diodorus, qui multa pocula pulchra habebat, Lilybaeo Romam abierat.*
(b)   *Verre praetore, totā prouinciā uiri facta scelesta excogitare poterant.*
(c)   *Verres, qui genere nobili natus erat, semper cupiditate potius quam uirtute agebat.*
(d)   *comites, quos Verres secum ad prouinciam duxerat, erant scelesti.*

2   *quod ubi Verres audiuit, insaniā Diodorum absentem accusare constituit.*
totā prouinciā res clara erat. fama erat Verrem cupiditate argenti uirum
innocentem absentem accusauisse. Diodorus, qui hoc tempore Romae erat,
omnia quae audiuerat suis patronis narrauit. quod ubi pater Verris audi-
uit, litteras isti misit. quibus in litteris narrabat omnes totā urbe scire
Verrem esse scelestum. Quas [or *quod*] *ubi Verres perlegit, cupiditatem*
timore potius quam pudore repressit.

DELICIAE LATINAE: 4C

Pages 236–7

Word exercises

For meanings, consult an English dictionary.

generation > *genus* (stem *gener-*) family; literal > *littera* letter; ante-natal
> *ante* before + *natus* born; mode > *modus* way, manner; rational >
ratio (stem *ration-*) reason; primary > *primus* first; constitution > *constituo*
(stem *constitut-*) I decide; revoke > *reuoco* I call back; circuit > *circumeo*
(stem *circumit-*) I go around; circumlocution > *circum* around + *loquor*
(stem *locut-*) I speak; conservation > *conseruo* (stem *conseruat-*) I save;
commotion > *commoueo* (stem *commot-*) I disturb; collection > *colligo*
(stem *collect-*) I collect.

Mottoes

Page 238

The things which are moderate are permanent.
What is locked is safe.
I wish for what [is] above.
What he wants, he really wants.
He who envies is a lesser person.
He who touches me will regret it.
He who goes plainly [goes] safely.
Let him who stands still beware.
What God wills will happen.
I want what God wants.
What I have said, I have said.
What I do, I do strongly.
What [is] honourable [is] useful.

What I could, I have done.
What you wish to be done to you, do to another.
Hold onto what [is] yours.
What [is] true [is] safe.
What I wish will be.

Real Latin

O fortunate Rome, born in my consulship. (Cicero)
We should despair of nothing under the leadership and augury of
Teucer. (Horace, *Odes* 1.7.27)
He who hates vices also hates human beings. (Pliny)
[There was] nothing he touched which he did not enhance. (Dr
Johnson)

Unreal Latin

l. 4   'points to a Motor Bus.'

ll. 5–6   'There fills ... me a fear of the Motor Bus.'

ll. 7–8   'To the Motor Bus I shall shout / so that I may not be
            killed by the Motor Bus.'

l. 12   'O Motor Bus.'

ll. 14–16   '... Motor Buses, / and there filled the whole market-
            place / a plethora of Motor Buses.'

ll. 18–20   'surrounded by Motor Buses. / Lord, defend us /
            Against these Motor Buses.'

4 D (i)—(ii) *(Text pp. 78–9)*

NOTES TO 4D

In these two texts, the passive voice ('x is being -ed, was being -ed,
has been -ed, had been -ed', etc.) is introduced. Do not be concerned about the apparent rush of tenses here. Just be certain,
before you embark on this section, that you are thoroughly
acquainted with the deponent forms at **GVE 58, 68, 75, 77, 81, 90,
96–7, 105**.

4D(i)

168   *P. Caesetio . . . praefectis*: 'in the prefecture of . . .' The
        construction is the same as with e.g. *Verre praetore* 'in
        Verres' praetorship'. For another example, see l. 175 be-
        low. See **GVE 109**.

169   *egressae erant*: 'had gone out of'. Pluperfect deponent (from
        egredior). Once more, be warned that you need to know
        the deponent forms listed in the introductory note to this
        section before you proceed. If you did not recognise *egres-*
        sae erant, now is the time to do some revision.

173   *a classe nostrā*: here *a* means 'by . . .' (not 'from', a meaning
        you learned in 1D). This usage often indicates that there
        is a passive verb lurking, 'x was -ed by y'. So expect the
        form of sentence to proceed 'The ship by x is being / was
        being / was -ed'.

172–3   *capta est . . . inuenta est . . . abducta est*: the first examples of
        the passive voice. The nom. fem. sing. ending of the par-
        ticiples (*capta, inuenta, abducta*) shows that the subject is fem.
        sing. – here the noun *nauis*.

173   *nuntiatum est*: the nom. neut. sing. ending of the participle
        (*nuntiatum*) shows that the subject is neut. sing. – here the
        connecting relative pronoun *quod* (see **GVE 107**), 'which
        [thing] when it was announced . . .'

175   *exhiberi*: the first example of a passive infinitive. It com-
        pletes the meaning of *iussit* (l. 174).

        P. Caesetio . . . ducibus: 'under the leadership of . . .' See
        note on l. 168 above.

176   *a nautis . . . ab omnibus*: As in l. 172 above, *a/ab* here means
        'by'. Expect a passive verb after *a nautis*. In the case of *ab*
        omnibus, the verb occurs first and might be best translated
        provisionally 'there was awaited' (expecting the subject),
        rather than 'it is awaited' (as in the Running Vocabulary).

        appellitur . . . exspectatur: these are present passive forms, but
        translate them as past tenses. Latin often uses the present

tense in historical narrative, just as certain dialects/registers of English do (cf. 'So he comes home, and he says to the wife, "Where's me supper?" and she says, "It's in the dog." '). Note that the subject precedes the first verb (*nauis . . . appellitur*), but follows the second (*exspectatur . . . supplicium*). This order (A subject B verb, B verb A subject) is a rhetorical device known as chiasmus, and is one of many tricks of word order used by Latin writers to make their points forcefully and succinctly.

177   *a Verre*: again *a* means 'by' here. Expect a passive verb. This is *habiti sunt*. Note that the nom. masc. pl. participle shows that the subject is nom. masc. pl. (so *ei praedones*).

    ut: here merely qualifies *hostes* ('*as* enemies') and does not introduce its own clause.

178   *securi percussi sunt*: the participle (nom. masc. pl.) shows that the subject is still *ei praedones*. Note that *securi* is an ablative (expressing the means by which the deed was done).

    uidebantur: literally 'were seen (as)', the imperfect passive of *uideo* (for more of these forms, see 4D(ii)). But it is usually better to translate this verb in its passive forms using the English verb 'I seem'. However, the next example, *uisus est* in l. 181 must be translated 'was seen' (so you always have to keep your options open).

179   *ab eo*: again here *ab* means 'by' and looks forward to passive verbs (*abducti et . . . dati sunt*).

    abducti et . . . dati sunt: the nom. masc. pl. participles show that the subject is nom. masc. pl. (here *illi*). It is usual, where there are a number of passive verbs of this form (participle + *sum*), for the part of *sum* to occur only once (as here).

    ab eo: again *ab* means 'by', and looks forwards to a passive verb. This is *distributi sunt*. Note that the nom. masc. pl. participle shows the subject is nom. masc. pl., in this case *alii*. This *alii* looks forward, as often, to another *alii*. The first means 'some', the second 'others' (see **GVE 102 Note 2**).

180   *missi sunt*: as the participle shows (nom. masc. pl.), the subject is nom. masc. pl. (*alii*: see previous note for meaning).

181   *a nullo*: *a* means 'by'. Expect a passive verb. This is *uisus est* (see note on l. 178 for meaning). The participle ending shows that the subject is nom. masc. sing., so *archipirata* (a masc. noun of the 1st declension, like *nauta*).

    arbitrantur: this form is deponent ('they think'), as you should know from *Learning Vocabulary* 2C. The only real safeguard against mistaking deponent forms for passive (and vice versa) is to learn thoroughly the deponent verbs as you meet them. Expect an indirect statement after this verb ('that . . .').

182   *a Verre*: *a* again means 'by'. So expect a passive verb. Since you are also expecting accusative and infinitive (indirect statement), you ought to be looking for an infinitive (or infinitives). So these ought to be passive. The first comes in *datam esse*, where the acc. fem. sing. ending shows the subject of the phrase was *pecuniam* ('money to have been given by . . .'). A second indirect statement follows, with a new subject (*archipiratam*) and a passive verb (*liberatum esse*), whose participle (acc. masc. sing.) confirms that the subject is *archipiratam*.

4D(ii)

185   *securi feriebantur*: further examples of this imperfect passive form are *cognoscebantur* and *defendebantur* in l. 193, and *feriebantur* (l. 194). For *securi*, see note on 4D(i), l. 178 above.

186–7   *habita erat . . . capti erant*: these are pluperfect passive forms (as below in l. 188 are *remoti atque abducti erant*).

187   *a Verre*: again *a* means 'by'. Expect a passive verb. This comes with *remoti atque abducti erant* (see note on ll. 186–7).

The participles – nom. masc. pl. – show that the subject is *omnes*.

187–8 *aliquid*: lit. 'something', here governing the genitives *artifici* and *formae*. Translate 'some [of] x' (see **GVE 102 *aliquis* Note 3**).

191–2 *eos . . . coniunctos esse*: all this is an indirect statement, which will eventually be solved by the verb *arguebat*. Tr. 'That they . . .' Note that the second verb in the phrase is passive (*coniunctos esse*). The participle (acc. masc. pl.) shows that it still has the subject *eos*.

192–3 *a multis ciuibus Romanis . . . ab omnibus*: again *a/ab* here means 'by' and makes you expect a passive verb in each case. *cognoscebantur* resolves the first phrase, and *defendebantur* the second. For the forms, see above on l. 185.

195 *est gesta*: note that the participle (nom. fem. sing.) shows the subject to be *haec . . . res*. The usual order for the perfect passive would be *gesta est* and the normal word order for this sentiment might have been *haec res igitur gesta est*. Cicero focuses attention on *haec* and *res* by artifically separating them and also by inverting the normal order of the two elements of the verb.

196–9 *capta est . . . liberatus . . . missi . . . abducti . . . percussi . . . ablata . . . ablatum . . . auersum*: in this list, only the first verb is supplied with a part of *sum* (*capta est*). But all the other participles listed above can be inferred to have the requisite part understood (*est* for the singulars, *sunt* for the plurals). The rhetorical effect is thus crisper than if *est/sunt* had been used, and Cicero is able to build up to a climax with (1) anaphora ('repetition', here of *omnis*) with polyptoton ('varying the forms of the same word', i.e. *omnis/omne*) (2) increasing the size of the second section, while keeping some repetition (*omnis uestis ablata* followed by *omne aurum et argentum ablatum et auersum*).

TRANSLATION OF 4D

4D(i)

P. Caesetius and P. Tadius [being] prefects, ten ships half-full,
which from harbour had set out, a ship certain of pirates captured.
But what [**170**] I have said? The ship not they captured, but they
found and appropriated. It was that ship full of young men most
handsome, full of silver, full of clothing. Which ship, as I have said,
by fleet our not captured was but found and appropriated was.
Which when to Verres it was announced, although on the shore
with women certain he was lying drunk, he drew up himself
however and at once ordered everything that in [**175**] the ship was
to be displayed. P. Caesetius and P. Tadius [being] leaders, the ship
of the pirates to Syracuse by the sailors is brought to shore. There
is expected by everyone punishment. Those pirates, who old and
ugly were, by Verres as enemies were considered and with an axe
were struck; those, who handsome seemed or who craftsmen were,
by him were appropriated and to friends were given. Others by
him among his governor's retinue and son were [**180**] divided up,
others, who musicians were, to friends certain to Rome were sent.
But the pirate chief himself by no one was seen. Today, judges,
everyone thinks money to Verres secretly by the pirates to have
been given and the pirate chief to have been freed.

Now learn the Learning Vocabulary at GVE p. 241.

4D(ii)

The Syracusans, men knowledgeable and considerate, held a count
every day [**185**] of the pirates who with the axe were being struck.
But of the pirates a great number to be missing soon they realised
(for the number of them had been calculated from the number of
oars that with the ship had been captured). For by Verres everyone
who anything either of skill or looks had possessed removed and
appropriated had been. But the defendant / that man wicked, an
outcry of the people there to be about to be suspecting, in the
pirates' place [**190**] to substitute he began citizens Roman, whom
into prison previously he had thrown (them Sertorian soldiers to
have been or by their own wish with pirates linked to have been

he claimed). In this way, citizens Roman, who by many citizens Roman were recognised and by all were defended, with the axe were being struck.

[195] This therefore was achieved thing, this was the victory brilliant; Verres [being] praetor, a ship of pirates was captured, the leader of the pirates freed, musicians to Rome sent, handsome men and craftsmen to the house of Verres appropriated, in their place citizens Roman with the axe struck, all clothes removed, all gold and silver removed and stolen.

Now learn the Learning Vocabulary at *GVE* p. 242.

EXERCISES FOR 4D

Pages 247–8

Exercises

1* *captum iri* to be about to be captured; *liberatum iri* to be about to be set free; *iussum iri* to be about to be ordered; *ablatum iri* to be about to be taken away; *repertum iri* to be about to be found.

2(a) Verres said the robbers would be captured.
(b) Verres said that the Roman citizens would not be freed.
(c) Verres asserts that the cups of Diodorus will be taken away.
(d) Diodorus says that the cups will not be found by Verres.
(e) Verres said that his friends would be ordered to find the cups.
(f) I shall go to see if he is at home.
(g) Maecenas goes to play, Virgil and I to sleep.

For (f) and (g), see *GVE* **118 Note 2**.

Pages 249–50

Exercises

1   *liberor, liberaris, liberatur, liberamur, liberamini, liberantur* I am freed etc.; *adiuuabar, adiuuabaris, adiuuabatur, adiuuabamur, adiuuabamini, adiuuabantur* I was being helped etc.; *iubebor, iubeberis, iubebitur, iubebimur, iubebimini, iubebuntur* I shall be ordered etc.; *uideor, uideris, uidetur, uidemur, uidemini, uidentur* I am seen / I seem etc.; *latus eram, latus eras, latus erat, lati eramus, lati eratis, lati erant* I had been carried etc.; *caesus sum, caesus es, caesus est, caesi sumus, caesi*

estis, caesi sunt I have been killed / I was killed; *reuocari* to be called back; *confirmatus esse* to have been confirmed; *recipior, reciperis, recipitur, recipimur, recipimini, recipiuntur* I am received; *dicar, diceris, dicetur, dicemur, dicemini, dicentur* I shall be said.

2*   she followed (deponent); he is accused (passive); they were taken away (passive); he was left (passive); he is carried (passive); he speaks (deponent); he lied (deponent); he used to catch sight of (deponent); he will try (deponent); he will consider (deponent); it will be told (passive); it was announced (passive); it was seen (passive); it dared (deponent).

3   *capietur; liberari; feriebantur; ablatum erat; reuocatus esse; perlectum est.*

4*(a)   The ship was not captured by our fleet.
 (b)   The news was announced to Verres by a messenger.
 (c)   The ship was brought to Syracuse by the sailors.
 (d)   The craftsmen were taken away by Verres.
 (e)   The pirates were executed with an axe by the Romans.

5*(a)   Nothing had been said by Verres
 (b)   The ship was captured by a pirate.
 (c)   Young men are sent by Verres to Rome.
 (d)   The pirates' ship was being taken away by our men.
 (e)   My treasure will be given to the [my] friends.
 (f)   It was announced to Verres that the ship had been captured and that the pirates were being killed with an axe.

6(a)   *homines a Romanis defendebantur.*
 (b)   *numerus praedonum a te cognitus est.*
 (c)   *pecunia a Verre data est.*
 (d)   *ciues Romani a Verre securi feriuntur.*
 (e)   *nautae ab illo liberabuntur.*
 (f)   *pocula a Diodoro ablata erant.*

Page 251

Reading exercise / Test exercise

Omitted.

**English–Latin

1(a)   *nauis a Romanis inuenta est.*
 (b)   *pecunia Verri a praedonibus dabatur.*

(c) *iuuenes Romam mittuntur.*
(d) *nuntiatum erat nauem captam esse et Syracusas appelli.*
(e) *nemo praedones captum iri senserat.*
(f) *Verres Romae accusabitur.*

2   *Syracusani rationem habebant praedonum qui necati erant. quae ratio habita erat e numero remorum qui capti erant. magnus numerus praedonum deerat, quod multi a Verre liberati erant. ciues autem Romani in praedonum locum substituti sunt. Verres illos milites Sertorianos fuisse arguit. quamquam a multis Syracusanis cogniti erant securi percussi sunt.*

Page 253

Res gestae diui Augusti 'The achievements of the divine Augustus'

The achievements of the divine Augustus, by which he subjected the whole world to the power of the Roman people, and the monies which he disbursed for the republic and people of Rome.

At the age of nineteen, I raised an army on my own initiative and expense, [5] by means of which I freed the republic which had been overwhelmed by the tyranny of a political clique. The senate enrolled me into its ranks in the consulship of C Pansa and A Hirtius and gave me power. The people in the same year made me consul and triumvir.

The senate-house and the temple of Apollo, the shrine of the divine Julius, the Lupercal, the portico near [10] the Circus Flaminius, the temples on the Capitol to Jupiter Feretrius and Jupiter the Thunderer, the temple of Quirinus, the temples of Minerva and Queen Juno and Jupiter Libertas on the Aventine, the temple of the Lares at the top of the Sacred Way, the temple of the Di Penates in the Velia, the temple of Youth, the temple of the Great Mother on the Palatine [were all buildings] I built.

The Capitol and the theatre of Pompey I rebuilt without any inscription [15] of my name. Channels for water in many places, falling into disrepair through age, I restored. The Julian forum and the basilica which was between the temple of Castor and the temple of Saturn I finished.

Three times I put on a gladiatorial show and at these shows around ten thousand men took part in combat.

[20] Hunts involving African beasts in the circus or in the forum or in the amphitheatres I put on for the people twenty-six times, in which around three and a half thousand beasts were killed.

DELICIAE LATINAE: 4D

Page 255

Word exercises

For meanings, consult an English dictionary.

Class > *classis* fleet (originally, rank); decimate > *decimus* tenth; juvenile > *iuuenis* young man; prefect > *praefectus* prefect; inebriated > *ebrius* drunk; adjacent > *ad* near + *iaceo* I lie; liberate > *libero* (stem *liberat-*) I free; vest > *uestis* clothing; nefarious > *nefarius* wicked; quotidian > *cotidie* daily.

Page 256

Real Latin

Lucretius

[The nature of the Gods is] far removed and separated from our affairs;
For relieved of all pain, relieved of dangers,
Powerful of its own resources, and needful of us in no way,
It is not won over by good deeds nor is it affected by anger.

Publilius Syrus

(a)   An angry lover tells himself many lies.
(b)   The miser [is] himself the cause of his own misery.
(c)   Loving is an enjoyment for a young man, a reproach to an old.
(d)   To love and stay sane is [something] hardly granted [even] to a god.
(e)   The same person who causes [it] cures the wound of love.
(f)   It is time, not the mind, which brings an end to love.

Martial

Your seventh wife, Phileros, is now being buried on your property.
   A property yields more to no one than to you, Phileros. (10.43)

Page 257

Part of the Creed

[Christ] who for us men and for our salvation came down from heaven.

And he was made flesh of the Holy Spirit from the Virgin Mary; and he was made man. He was also crucified for us; he suffered under Pontius Pilate and was buried.

And he rose again on the third day according to the scriptures.

4 E (i)–(iii) *(Text pp. 79–82)*

NOTES TO 4E

In these three passages, you will meet two new verb forms for the first time. One is the present participle ('while -ing'). Compare **GVE 77–8**, **81**, **82**, where you learned the deponent perfect participle ('having -ed'), the future participle ('about to . . .'), and the perfect participle passive ('having been -ed'). An ablative absolute usage common with the present participle will also be met ('while x was -ing').

The other is a new form of the pluperfect and introduces the subjunctive mood. The marker for this is *cum* ('when', 'since', 'although').

You will also complete your package of nouns by adding *mare* ('sea') and others like it. We focus also on the meanings of *cuius* ('whose', 'of which') and its plural *quorum* ('whose', 'of which').

4E(i)

200   *egredientem eum*: 'him as he was leaving'. This is the first example of the present participle. Here the phrase is in the masc. acc. sing. and is the object of the verb *sequuntur* in the next line, i.e. 'they follow him as . . .' For forms, see **GVE 120** (active and deponent have the same form).

     sequuntur: tr. 'followed'. For the use of present tense to refer to past events, see note on 4D(i), l. 176 and **GVE 112**.

Note. There is another example in this passage at l. 208, *nuntiatur* ('someone announced').

202   *Cleomenem egredientem nauīsque sequentīs*: the present participles are both accusative and are object of the verb *inspiciebat*.

203   *soleatus, cum pallio purpureo*: Cicero is suggesting that Verres is not behaving like a Roman. His wearing of the *solea* ('sandals') in public would have been deemed effeminate. His purple *pallium* is Greek, and its colour is associated in antiquity with the dress code of tyrants and kings. Effeminate dress does not necessarily suggest lack of heterosexual tendencies – Verres was *muliercula quādam nixus*.

204–5 *cum classis . . . adpulsa esset*: 'when the fleet . . . had been driven [ashore]'. This is the first example of *cum* 'when' (see **GVE 124**) and of the subjunctive mood (here the tense is pluperfect: see **GVE 121–3** for forms).

205   *egentes*: the present participle is nom. masc. pl., agreeing with *nautae*. Note that *cibo* is the object of *egentes* (*egeo* takes an ablative).

207   *potans atque amans*: The present participles are nom. masc. sing., agreeing with *Cleomenes*.

208   *ebrio Cleomene, nautis cibo egentibus*: 'with Cleomenes drunk (and) the sailors lacking food'. The construction is ablative absolute (see **GVE 109** and further **GVE 120 Note 6**).

210   *Cleomene potante et ebrio*: 'with Cleomenes [still] drinking and [already] drunk'. Ablative absolute (see previous note).

210–11 *cum uidisset adeuntīs*: 'when he had spotted [them] arriving'. See note on l. 204 above for *cum* and the pluperfect subjunctive. *adeuntīs* is acc. pl. masc. and agrees with *praedones* (object of *uidisset*).

211–12 *malum erigi, praecidi ancoras imperauit . . . et iussit*: The accusative and infinitive phrases (*malum erigi* and *ancoras praecidi*) depend on *imperauit* ('he ordered that x and y'). Note the way he orders the words here (noun verb, verb noun) in an arrangement called chiasmus (see 4D(i) l. 176 note). Note also the use of two different verbs for 'ordered'. This technique is known as *uariatio* ('variation').

212–13 *cum ... aduolauisset*: 'although ... had flown'. *cum* with the subjunctive has three possible meanings, 'when', 'since' and 'although'. As with other things in Latin, you will often need to 'hold' the word until it is resolved by the context. The meaning 'although' is often pointed by a word in the main clause like *tamen* 'nevertheless' (as here).

213 *cuius*: 'of which'. The genitive sing. refers back to *nauis* (the antecedent), and grammatically relates to *celeritas* ('the speed of which [i.e. the ship] ...'), subject of *erat*. See further **GVE 126**.

214 *fugiens*: the present participle is nom. sing. fem. and agrees with *nauis*.

215 *fugientes ... sequentes*: the present participles are nom. pl. masc. and agree with *ceteri*.

216 *fugientes*: the present participle is nom. pl. fem. and agrees with *naues*.

217–8 *cum ... capta esset*: 'when ... had been captured'. See note on ll. 204–5 above.

218 *cuius*: the genitive sing. refers back to *nauis* (the antecedent), and depends on *praefectus* (subject of *erat*). See note on l. 213 above.

219 *cuius*: The genitive sing. refers to *nauis* (the antecedent), and depends on *praefectus* (subject of *occisus est*).

4E(ii)

220 *cum ... peruenisset*: 'when ... had come to ...' See note on 4E(i) ll. 204–5. For the case of *Helorum* (accusative of place to where after a verb of motion), see **GVE 110**.

221 *fluctuantem*: the present participle is acc. sing. fem. and agrees with *nauem* (object of *reliquit*).

222 *cum . . . uidissent*: 'since they had seen . . .' Here *cum* plus subjunctive means 'since'. You have already met it in the meanings 'when' and 'although'. There is often little to choose between the meanings 'when' and 'since'.

exeuntem*: the present participle is acc. sing. masc. and agrees with *imperatorem* (the object of *uidissent*).

223 *quorum*: 'whose'. The genitive is masc. pl., because the antecedent is *ipsi* (nom. masc. pl.). It depends on *naues* (subject of *erant*). See further **GVE 126**.

224 *cuius*: 'whose'. The genitive is masc. sing., because the antecedent is *dux*. It depends on *nomen*. See further **GVE 126**.

225–6 *uictum iri*: the so-called future infinitive passive (see **GVE 118**). Translate: 'that . . . would be defeated'.

226–7 *cum . . . ausus esset*: Here *cum* means 'since'. The meaning 'although' is not ruled out until you reach *incluserat se domi*.

228 *Cleomene . . . manente*: 'with Clemones staying . . .' Ablative absolute (see **GVE 109** and **120 Note 6**).

cuius*: The genitive is sing. fem., because the antecedent is *classis*. It depends on *princeps*, the complement of *erat* (subject is *Cleomenes*).

230–1 *o tempus . . . nequitiam*: these are accusatives of exclamation! See **Reference Grammar L(c)7**.

231–2 *Verrem amore, classem . . . incendio . . . conflagrantem*: the present participle, *conflagrantem* 'burning', will eventually explain the ablatives, *amore* 'because of love' and *incendio* 'because of a fire'. It agrees with *Verrem*, object of *uidere*.

232 *quarum*: this is a connecting relative (see **GVE 107**). It agrees with *rerum grauium* and depends on *nuntius* (subject of *peruenit*) – 'Of which [these] serious matters a messenger

...' For the case of *Syracusas* (accusative of place where to after verbs of motion) see **GVE 110**.

quo: 'to where'. Not the ablative of *qui* (see **GVE 106**). The signal that *quo* means 'to where' is likely to be a word or phrase indicating a place (here *in praetorium*).

235–6   *nemo* ... *nemo*: the repetition of the same word at the start of parallel clauses is a popular figure of speech called anaphora.

236   *dormientem*: the present participle agrees with *Verrem*, object of *excitare*.

238   *conflagrantīs*: the present participle agrees with *nauīs*, object of *conspicati*.

238–9 *Syracusani*: the subject is immediately followed by two indirect statements (accusative and infinitive), *magnam* ... *esse* and *mox* ... *fore*, both dependent on *intellexerunt*: 'the Syracusans realised that ...'

4E(iii)

241   *cum* ... *commorati essent*: try to work out at precisely what point you can tell that *cum* means 'when' and not 'since' or 'although'.

248   *quo*: as in the previous passage, *quo* means 'to where' (and is not the ablative of *qui*). The clue is in the phrase *ad forum* which precedes. *hic* ('here') in l. 250 clinches it.

252   *quorum*: 'of which'. The antecedent is *omnibus* (comparative ablative after *turpius*), 'than all of which *mentionem feci*'.

252–3 *huic naui piraticae ludibrio erat...*: translate the opening dative phrase as 'to ...' The subject of the first *ludibrio erat* ('was a laughing-stock') is *gloria*, of the second *nomen* and of the third *multitudo*. The predicative dative construction ('x [nom.] is [for] a Y [predicative dative] to z [dative]') was explained at **GVE 88.6**. Note the repetition of *ludibrio erat*, an example of anaphora.

TRANSLATION OF 4E

4E(i)

[200] There departs Cleomenes from the harbour. Departing him
six ships undermanned follow. Verres however, who in many days
not had been seen, then Cleomenes departing and ships following
was inspecting: which man, praetor of the people Roman, stood in
slippers, with a Greek cloak purple, on a woman certain leaning on
the shore. When the fleet on the fifth day at Pachynus at last [205]
had landed, the sailors, food lacking, the roots of palms wild to
collect they began. Cleomenes, who was thinking himself soon
another Verres to be about to be, all the days on the shore was
staying drinking and making love.

See however suddenly, drunk [being] Cleomenes, the sailors
food lacking, there is announced a ship of pirates to be in the harbour of Odyssea. Our however fleet was, [210] Cleomenes drinking and drunk, in the harbour at Pachynus. Which pirates when he
had seen approaching, the leader Cleomenes in ship his the mast to
be erected, to be cut the anchor-cables he instructed and the other
ships him to follow he ordered. When the ship of Cleomenes,
whose speed amazing was, in a short time to Helorus had flown
escaping, the rest, however, as they were able, rather more slowly
to Helorus they were sailing, [215] not the pirates' attack escaping
but their leader following. Then the ships last escaping in danger
first were; the last for/because ships first they attacked [did] the
pirates. When the first by the pirates captured had been a ship of
the Haluntines, whose prefect Phylarchus was, soon an Apollonian
ship was captured, whose prefect Anthropinus was killed.

Now learn the Learning Vocabulary at *GVE* p. 258.

4E(ii)

[220] Meanwhile Cleomenes, when to Helorus he had come,
himself onto the land from the ship he threw, and the ship tossing
about at sea he abandoned. The remaining prefect of the ships,
when their leader onto the land departing they had seen, followed;
for they themselves, whose ships slower than the ship of Cleo-

menes were, by sea in no way the pirates to escape were able. Then the pirates' leader, whose name [225] Heracleo was, who the fleet Roman so easily conquered about to be not he had thought, it to be set on fire and burned ordered. Cleomenes, since in public to be not he had dared, although night it was, had shut himself at home. Cleomenes at home remaining, the fleet of which Cleomenes leader was by pirates was burnt.

[230] O time unhappy for the province of Sicily! O situation disastrous! O the defendant's / that man's wickedness! On one and the same night, judges, to see it was permitted Verres with passion, the fleet Roman with the fire of pirates, burning. Of which matters serious a messenger to Syracuse came to the governor's residence, to where the defendant / that man from the party they had led back slightly before the women with singing and a band, but [235] (so strict was at home Verres' control) in a matter so serious no one to Verres was let in, no one dared Verres sleeping to arouse. The disaster however in a short time by everyone was known; for the ships burning seeing, the Syracusans a great disaster to have been sustained and soon danger for themselves the greatest to be about to be at once they understood. There rushed together [240] therefore from the city whole a very great crowd.

Now learn the Learning Vocabulary at *GVE* pp. 259–60.

4E(iii)

The pirates, when for one that night at Helorus they had waited, the flaming ships by now they had abandoned and to approach began [to] Syracuse. Which pirates presumably often had heard nothing to be more beautiful than the Syracusans' walls and harbours and they had decided themselves never those things about to see [245] to be except Verres [being] praetor. At once therefore without any fear into itself the harbour to penetrate they began.

Gods immortal! A pirate ship, you [being] praetor, Verres, right up to the forum of the Syracusans reached! To where never Carthaginian ships (while at sea they were very powerful), never a fleet Roman in so many Punic and [250] Sicilian wars to reach were able, here, you [being] praetor, pirates' ships roved freely about. O sight unhappy and bitter! O deed more disgusting than all of which mention I have made! To this ship piratical for a joke was the city's renown, for a joke was the people Roman's name, for a joke was our men's multitude that Syracuse inhabits.

Now learn the Learning Vocabulary at *GVE* pp. 260–1.

EXERCISES FOR 4E

Pages 262–3

Exercises

Morphology

1   *reuocans, reuocantis* calling back; *incendens, incendentis* setting fire to; *accipiens, accipientis* receiving; *sentiens, sentientis* feeling; *iubens, iubentis* ordering; *adipiscens, adipiscentis* getting; *egrediens, egredientis* going out; *fruens, fruentis* enjoying; *recordans, recordantis* remembering; *exiens, exeuntis* going out.

2*   *inspicienti: seruae, uiro* (dat. sing.), *muliere* (abl. sing.); *accedentem: principem* (acc. sing.); *nitente: seruā* (abl. sing.); *commorantum: mulierum* (gen. pl.); *conflagrantibus: moenibus, ceteris* (dat./abl. pl.); *circumiens: Cicero, mulier* (nom. sing.).

3*(a) Verres was standing on the shore, leaning on a woman.
  (b) (Lit.) The pirate replied to them asking that he had seen the ships fleeing.
       (Eng.) When they asked him, the pirate replied ...
  (c) (Lit.) The sailors being in need of food Cleomenes did nothing.
       (Eng.) Although the sailors were in need of food ...
  (d) While Verres was making love to a woman, it was announced that the ship had been captured.
  (e) You can see the ship ablaze with fire.
  (f) They caught sight of the rest following a little more slowly.
  (g) While waiting in Syracuse, the pirates saw the walls of the city.
  (h) Verres said that he had not seen the ships approaching the harbour.
  (i) No day is long for a busy man. (SENECA)
  (j) Nothing is difficult for someone in love. (CICERO)

4   *Verre absente; nautis sequentibus; populo inspiciente; nauibus conflagrantibus; Cleomene commorante; multitudine principem hortante.*

Pages 265–6

Exercises

(See **GVE 121–3**, p 263 and 264.)

1* *eguissem* (etc.); *conflagrauissem*; *commoratus essem*; *secutus essem*; *acceptus essem*; *incensus essem*; *nisus/nixus essem*; *occidissem*; *sensissem*; *liberatus essem*; *accessissem*.

2*(a) Since Cleomenes had fled, the others followed.
 (b) Since the pirates had advanced very quickly, the last ships of the Romans were the first in danger.
 (c) Although the commander had reached the shore quickly, the rest however were sailing more slowly.
 (d) When Cleomenes had reached the shore with his ship, he hid (himself) at home.
 (e) The rest also abandoned their ships since they had not been able to escape from the pirates by sea in any way.
 (f) The leader of the pirates ordered the ships to be burned[†] when they had been captured.

  [†]*incendi* = present infinitive passive – see **GVE 118**, p. 246.

3(a) *cum imperator ad litus nauigauisset.*
 (b) *cum naues incensae essent.*
 (c) *cum praedones Syracusis commorati essent.*
 (d) *cum moenia inspecta essent.*
 (e) *cum multitudo incendium conspicata esset.*
 (f) *cum nautae cibo eguissent.*

4 *eguit* indicative, perfect; *conflagrasset* subjunctive, pluperfect; *tulerat* indicative, pluperfect; *recordatus esses* subjunctive, pluperfect; *constituisse* infinitive, perfect; *excogitaueras* indicative, pluperfect; *accepissent* subjunctive, pluperfect; *captus esse* infinitive, perfect passive; *occisi essent* subjunctive, pluperfect; *conspicati sunt* indicative, perfect.

Pages 267–8

Reading exercise/Test exercise

Omitted.

** English–Latin

Note: *conflagro* means 'burn' intransitive, e.g. 'the building is burning'. *incendo* means 'burn' transitive, e.g. 'Alfred burned the cakes' and can be used in the passive, e.g. 'the ships are being burned' *naues incenduntur.*

1(a) *multitudo nauis conflagrantis conspicata est.*
 (b) *reliqui praefecti nauium Cleomenem, cum in terram exiisset, secuti sunt.*
 (c) *Cleomenes, cuius uxor in litore cum Verre erat, nauibus sequentibus e portu egressus est.*
 (d) *praefecti nauium, cum mari praedones effugere non potuissent, principem secuti e nauibus egressi sunt.*

2 *praedones nauibus incensis Syracusas accedere constituerunt. audiuerant enim portum Syracusanorum pulcherrimum esse et sciebant se numquam nisi Verre praetore eum uisuros esse. quod cum statuissent Syracusas nauigauerunt. piratica nauis Verre praetore, nostris nauibus conflagrantibus, usque ad portum Syracusanorum accessit. pro di immortales! o factum turpissimum!*

Page 268

Res gestae diui Augusti *'The achievements of the divine Augustus'*

I freed the sea from pirates. The whole of Italy of its own accord took an oath of loyalty to me, and demanded me as leader of the war in which I was victorious at Actium. The same oath was sworn by the provinces of the Gauls, the Spains, Africa, Sicily and Sardinia. Of all the provinces of the Roman people to which there were neighbouring tribes that did not [5] obey our commands, I increased the boundaries. The Gauls and the Spains, likewise Germany, I pacified. The Alps from that region which is nearest the Adriatic sea to the Tuscan sea I pacified. My fleet through the ocean from the mouth of the Rhine to the region of the east right up to the territory of the Cimbri sailed. Egypt to the empire of the Roman people I added. Very many other tribes experienced the protection of the Roman people [10] under my leadership, with whom before with the Roman people there had been no relationship involving embassies and friendship.

DELICIAE LATINAE: 4E

Page 269

Exercise

stabilis stable; *mobilis* mobile; *laudabilis* praiseworthy; *durabilis* durable; *nauigabilis* navigable.

Page 270

Word exercises

1. *lex*; *pax*; *miles*; *dux*; *caput*; *custos*; *pes*.

2. temporal; vocal; nominative; operate; littoral; principal; multitudinous.

Adapted medieval Latin

Once Saint Columba was staying for a few days in the province of the Picts and found it necessary to cross the river Ness. When he arrived at the bank, he saw some of the inhabitants of this region burying a poor little fellow whom, as the inhabitants themselves said, a water beast had bitten with its huge teeth as the fellow was swimming a little earlier in the river. The holy man hearing this ordered one of his companions to swim to the other bank and bring back to him the boat which stood there. The companion, named Lugneus Mocumin, without delay undressed and wearing only a tunic threw himself into the waters.

But the beast, which had been hiding in the depths of the river, feeling the water above it disturbed, suddenly emerging hurried with a huge roar and open mouth towards the man who was swimming in the middle of the river. Between Lugneus and the beast there was no more than the length of one pole. Then the blessed man, seeing this, while the barbarians and his brothers trembled with fear, raising his holy hand, made the sign of the cross in the air, saying to the beast 'Proceed no further; do not touch the man, but swiftly depart.' Then indeed the beast at the order of the holy man fled back swiftly in terror. The brothers with great wonder glorified God in the blessed man, and the barbarians, because of the miracle which they themselves had seen, magnified the God of the Christians.

(The original of this adapted text can be read in Keith Sidwell, *Reading Medieval Latin* (Cambridge 1995), p. 89.)

4F (i)–(ii) *(Text pp. 82–4)*

NOTES FOR 4F

In these two sections, you will meet some more tenses of the subjunctive mood (present and imperfect). These will be introduced in sentences which have the forms 'I beg you / persuade you / order you to ...', or 'it happens that / I bring it about that'. In all cases, the word introducing the clause with the subjunctive verb begins with *ut* or *ne*.

Your knowledge of the uses of the present participle will be extended, and we will give some attention to the tricky ablative of the relative pronoun (*qui*).

4F(i)

255–6　*non ad ... salutem ... sed ad ... sanguinem*: the verb *pertinet* solves these. Note the way the orator uses contrast (called antithesis) with *non ... sed ...* The *sed* phrase is longer, putting greater emphasis on the positive part of the antithesis.

256　*quā in causā*: 'in which [this] case': connecting relative in the ablative (agreeing with *in causā*). See **GVE 107** and **137.2**.

257–8　*hortor precorque ut ... detis, neue ... exspectetis*: 'I urge and beg that you should give ... and that you should not be awaiting ...' The first example of an *ut/ne* + subjunctive clause after verbs of admonition, persuasion and command. See **GVE 134** for these clauses. The subjunctives are present tense. Note the difference between present indicative *datis/exspectatis* and present subjunctive *detis/exspectetis* (only one letter, but absolutely crucial). See **GVE 127–9** for forms of the present subjunctive.

toti Siciliae: dative because *persuadebo* takes a dative object.

259   *persuadebo ut . . . sit*: 'I will persuade . . . to be . . .' Another example of the construction met at ll. 257–8 above. Here you meet for the first time the present subjunctive of *sum* (see **GVE 129 Note 2** for forms).

260   *cui nomen C. Seruilio erat*: 'whose name was C. Servilius'. Dative + *sum* is a way of saying 'x has . . .' One might expect *Seruilius*, but *Seruilio* is attracted into the same case as *cui*. This construction is explained in the note on 2A, l. 48. There is another example at l. 272 below.

263   *uisum est . . . auditum*: note that 'it' is the subject of both verbs (the neuter sing. ending of the participle shows this). *est* is understood with the second participle.

265–6   *accidit ut . . . loqueretur*: 'It happened that . . . was speaking.' This is the first example of *ut* + subjunctive introduced by the verb *accidit* (see **GVE 135**). The verb is imperfect subjunctive (for forms see **GVE 130–2**). Generally in such clauses, the subjunctive will be imperfect if the main verb is past, present if the main verb is present.

267   *imperauit ut ueniret*: '[Verres] ordered [Servilius] to come'. See note on ll. 257–8 for the construction.

267–8   *accidit ut . . . adesset*: 'It happened that [Verres] was present . . .' See note on ll. 265–6. This is the first time you have met the imperfect subjunctive of *sum* (*essem* etc.). See **GVE 130 Notes 1 and 2**.

268   *cum . . . imperasset ut adiret*: '[when] Verres had ordered [him] to come'. Note that *imperasset* is an alternative form for *imperauisset* (pluperfect subjunctive: see **GVE 121**). There is another example below at l. 270 (*affirmasset*). Note

that *adiret* is the imperfect subjunctive of *adeo* (see **GVE 130 Note 1**).

271–2 *imperauit ut ... circumsisterent ... -que ... caederent*: 'he ordered ... to stand around ... and beat ...' See note on l. 267.

 multa ... orantem: '[him] as he made many appeals' (lit. 'praying many things'). The present participle is acc. masc. sing., agreeing with *eum*.

272 *cui Sextio nomen erat*: see note on l. 260 above.

273 *clamitanti*: dative of disadvantage (see **GVE 48.1**) agreeing with a pronoun ('him') left out. See **GVE 136(b)**. Compare *iacenti* in l. 274.

274–5 *hortabatur ut ... tunderet*: 'urged ... to beat'. See note on l. 267.

274 *iacenti*: see note on *clamitanti*, l. 273 above.

275 *prope morienti*: '[him] as was nearly dying'. *morienti* is the dative object of *persuasit*. It agrees with a pronoun left out. See **GVE 136(b)**.

275–6 *persuasit ut responderet neue taceret*: 'persuaded ... to ... and not to ...' See note on ll. 257–8 above.

276 *ita ... ut ... uoluerat*: 'in such a way ... as he ...' Here the verb in the *ut* clause is indicative, not subjunctive. *ut* only means 'to' or 'that' when the verb in its clause is subjunctive. So it is very important to know the forms of both indicative and subjunctive so well that you can instantly tell the difference.

277–80 Note the word-play with *Venereus, uenustas* and *Veneris*. No wonder Verres dedicates a statue of *Cupido*, 'lust'. In mythology, Cupid is Venus' son, and Venus is the goddess who presides over sexual intercourse.

4F(ii)

282   *perfecit ut ... profugeret ... -que perueniret*: '[he] brought it about that he ... and ...' This construction is exactly the same as that with *accidit*. See above on ll. 265–6.

283   *quo*: lit. 'to where', but tr. 'and ... to there'. See **GVE 137.3** with **107**.

284–5 *se ... iturum et ... delaturum*: the accusative + infinitive phrase continues the indirect statement introduced by *loqui et queri coepit*. As always, the participles agree with the accusative subject (here *se*). The auxiliary infinitives (*esse*) are to be understood (see further **GVE 143**).

287   *accidit ut ... ueniret*: see note on ll. 265–6.

287   *quo*: 'and ... to there ...' See note on l. 283.

287–8 *imperauit ut ... deferretur...*: 'he ordered ... to be ...' See note on l. 267.

291   *ardebant (A) oculi (B), toto ex ore crudelitas (B) eminebat (A)*: chiasmus with variation in *toto ex ore*. See above on l. 176.

292–3 *imperat ut ... nudetur et deligetur et caedatur*: the English translation would use a past tense for *imperat* ('he ordered that Gavius be ...').

297–9 *accidit ut ... caederetur ... et ... audiretur*: see notes on ll. 265–6 (though here the imperfect subjunctives are passive: see **GVE 132**).

300–1 *persuasit*: as you might by now expect, this verb looks forward to a clause beginning with *ut* ('to'), with subjunctive verb (*parceret*). A second, negative, clause follows, beginning with *neue* ('and not to'), also with subjunctive verb (*caederet*). See note on ll. 257–8 above.

301–2 *perfecit ut*: see note on l. 282 above. The clause has two verbs (*caederetur* and *compararetur*), articulated by the construction *non modo ... sed etiam* 'not only ... but also'.

302   *crux! inquam*: this interjection + repetition draws audience
       attention sharply to something significant. The *crux* was a
       punishment reserved for slaves, not Roman citizens. The
       direct speech at l. 299, where the actual words of Gavius
       are reported as he supposedly spoke them, has the same
       effect.

TRANSLATION OF 4F

4F(i)

[255] The remaining case, judges, which I now conduct, not to the
allies' safety but to citizen Romans' life and blood is relevant.
Which in case I urge you, to whom I speak, I urge and pray that
attention most carefully you should give and that not reasons you
should expect. For, if you wish, very easily all Sicily I shall persuade that a witness it should be.

   [260] For in the forum at Lilybaeum a citizen Roman, to whom
the name C. Servilius was, with rods and blows before the feet of
Verres was thrown down. Surely not you can deny, Verres, you
this to have done? Dare this first to deny, if you can: by all at
Lilybaeum it was seen, by all in the whole of Sicily heard. I say a
citizen Roman, when by lictors your he had been beaten, before
eyes your [265] to have fallen. But what for reason, gods immortal!
It happened that Servilius spoke rather freely about the defendant's
/ that man's wickedness. Which to the defendant / that man when
it was announced, Servilius he ordered that to Lilybaeum he
should come (it happened that Verres at Lilybaeum was present).
Servilius therefore, when Verres had ordered that he should arrive,
to Lilybaeum came.

   [270] Which things when Servilius had strongly asserted, Verres
six lictors ordered that him they should surround and much begging with blows should beat. Finally the nearest lictor, to whom
Sextius was the name, the eyes for him shouting to beat began.
And so that man, when his eyes with blood had been filled, fell;
nevertheless, Verres Sextius urged that for him lying down [275]
the sides he should beat. With which methods at length [him]
nearly dead he persuaded that he should reply and not remain

silent. That man, when thus he had replied as Verres had wanted, half-dead was carried away and a short time later died. That however man devoted to Venus, dripping with all charm and elegance, from the property of Servilius in the temple of Venus a silver statue of Cupid he placed. Thus even the fortunes [280] of men he misused for the nocturnal vows of desires his.

Now learn the Learning Vocabulary at *GVE* p. 273.

4F(ii)

Gavius this, whom I mention, a man of Consa was. By the defendant / that man into chains at Syracuse he had been thrown, but he brought it about that secretly from the stone quarries he fled and to Messana came. To where when he had come, to speak and complain he began himself, a citizen Roman, into chains to have been thrown; himself now to Rome about to go and [285] Verres about to report. Whom into the ship embarking slaves of Verres dragged back. And so Gavius at once to the magistrate was brought. On that very day it happened that Verres came to Messana. To where when he had come, he ordered that the matter complete to himself should be reported. The slaves therefore reported Gavius, a citizen Roman, to have complained himself in Syracuse in chains to have been; whom already embarking onto [290] a ship and Verres threatening by them to have been dragged back. Verres, with villainy and rage inflamed, into the forum came; there blazed his eyes, complete from face cruelty stood out. Into the forum entering, suddenly he orders that Gavius middle in forum be stripped and bound and flogged. When that man unhappy himself a citizen Roman to be was shouting, and Lucius Raecius a knight Roman [295] [as] referee was naming, then the defendant / that man him by Sertorius into Sicily to have been sent says. Then he orders his slaves that the man they strip, bind, flog. Which things when the defendant / that man had ordered, the slaves thus did, and it happened that middle in the forum at Messana with rods was beaten a citizen Roman, judges, and no other voice of that man miserable was heard except this – 'A citizen Roman I am.' Which words [300] using, did persuade Gavius Verres, by whom so appallingly he was being beaten, that him he should spare and not flog? Not at all, judges. That man for brought it about that not only he was flogged, but even a cross (a cross! I say) for that man unhappy was prepared. Onto a cross dared Verres a man to lift who himself a citizen Roman to be was saying.

Now learn the Learning Vocabulary at *GVE* pp. 274–5.

EXERCISES FOR 4F

Page 279

Exercises

Morphology

See ***GVE* 127–33**, pp. 275–9.

1*	Verb	Pres. Subj.	Impf. Subj.
	concido	*concidam*	*conciderem*
	hortor	*horter*	*hortarer*
	morior	*moriar*	*morerer*
	sum	*sim*	*essem*
	timeo	*timeam*	*timerem*
	aufero	*auferam*	*auferrem*
	PASSIVE:	*auferar*	*auferrer*
	reuoco	*reuocem*	*reuocarem*
	PASSIVE:	*reuocer*	*reuocarer*
	nauigo	*nauigem*	*nauigarem*

2 *clamet* pres. subj; *amat* pres. indic; *dormiret* impf. subj; *auferret* impf. subj; *conspicatus esse* perf. infin. (deponent); *conati essent* pluperf. subj. (dep.); *dat.* pres. indic; *dicetur* fut. indic. (passive); *excogitat* pres. indic; *curet* pres. subj; *nescirem* impf. subj; *cupiuisse* perf. infin; *loquitur* pres. indic. (dep.); *abstulisset* pluperf. subj; *monearis* pres. subj. (pass.); *accidat* pres. subj; *aget* fut. indic; *persuadet* pres. indic; *perficias* pres. subj.

3 Indicative

Note: indicative formed first, subjunctives formed second.

Verb	Present	Imperfect	Pluperfect
ago	*agit*	*agebat*	*egerat*
PASSIVE:	*agitur*	*agebatur*	*actus erat*
perficio	*perficit*	*perficiebat*	*perfecerat*
commoror	*commoratur*	*commorabatur*	*commoratus erat*
libero	*liberat*	*liberabat*	*liberauerat*
PASSIVE:	*liberatur*	*liberabatur*	*liberatus erat*
iaceo	*iacet*	*iacebat*	*iacuerat*
sequor	*sequitur*	*sequebatur*	*secutus erat*
nolo	*non uult*	*nolebat*	*noluerat*
accidit	*accidit*	*accidebat*	*acciderat*

Subjunctive

Verb	Present	Imperfect	Pluperfect
ago	*agat*	*ageret*	*egisset*
PASSIVE:	*agatur*	*ageretur*	*actus esset*
perficio	*perficiat*	*perficeret*	*perfecisset*
commoror	*commoretur*	*commoraretur*	*commoratus esset*
libero	*liberet*	*liberaret*	*liberauisset*
PASSIVE:	*liberetur*	*liberaretur*	*liberatus esset*
iaceo	*iaceat*	*iaceret*	*iacuisset*
sequor	*sequatur*	*sequeretur*	*secutus esset*
nolo	*nolit*	*nollet*	*noluisset*
accidit	*accidat*	*accideret*	*accidisset*

Page 281

Exercises

1(a) Verres persuaded Servilius that he should go to Lilybaeum / to go to Lilybaeum.

(b) Servilius, when he came / had come to Lilybaeum, was flogged by the lictors.

(c) Verres had ordered the lictors to flog the man.

(d) Servilius, as a Roman citizen, begs Verres not to flog him nor to kill him.

(e) Just as Verres flogs Roman citizens, so I assert that he himself will be flogged by Roman citizens.

(f) Verres urges certain slaves not to spare Servilius nor to give help to him begging (when he begs for it).

2(a) *ut Lilybaeum adeat.*
(b) *ne abeatis.*
(c) *ut Seruilium caederent.*
(d) *ne taceret.*
(e) *ut mihi credas.*
(f) *ne quis fugiat neue abeatis.*

Page 282

Exercises

1(a) It happens that Servilius speaks slightly too freely about the wickedness of Verres.

(b) Verres brought it about that Servilius came to Lilybaeum.

(c) It happened that Servilius, when he had come to Lilybaeum, was flogged by the lictors.

(d) Gavius, when he was in chains at Syracuse, said that he would bring it about that he would escape and come to Messana.

(e) Verres will bring it about that Roman citizens are killed.

2*

	perficiam ut:		I shall bring it about that:
(a)	*Verres Lilybaeum adeat.*	(a)	Verres comes to Lilybaeum.
(b)	*uir a lictoribus caedatur.*	(b)	the man is flogged by the lictors.
(c)	*serui eum ad terram abiciant.*	(c)	the slaves throw him to the ground.
(d)	*uerberibus moriatur.*	(d)	he dies from the blows.
(e)	*socii Romam profugiant.*	(e)	the allies escape to Rome.

	accidit ut:		It happened that:
(a)	*Verres Lilybaeum adiret.*	(a)	Verres came to Lilybaeum.
(b)	*uir a lictoribus caederetur.*	(b)	the man was flogged by the lictors.
(c)	*serui eum ad terram abicerent.*	(c)	the slaves threw him to the ground.
(d)	*uerberibus moreretur.*	(d)	he died from the blows.
(e)	*socii Romam profugerent.*	(e)	the allies escaped to Rome.

Pages 283–4

Reading exercise / Test exercise

Omitted.

**English–Latin

Verres uirum, cui Gauio erat nomen, in uincla coniecerat. qui perfecerat ut profugeret Messanamque perueniret. affirmauit se Verrem Romae delaturum esse. Verres autem, cum hoc audiuisset, seruis suis imperauit ut uirum caperent. illi in nauem ingredientem retraxerunt et ad magistratum duxerunt. Verres cum Messanam peruenisset, imperauit ut Gauius medio in foro nudaretur et caederetur. lictores ei oranti clamitantique se esse ciuem Romanum non pepercerunt. itaque accidit ut ciuis Romanus a Verre necaretur.

Page 285

Res gestae diui Augusti *'The achievements of the divine Augustus'*

The people who killed my father I drove into exile through legal tribunals avenging their crime, and afterwards when they made war on the republic I defeated them twice in battle.

Wars by land and sea, civil and foreign, throughout the world I often waged, [5] and as victor all the citizens seeking pardon I spared. Foreign peoples which could safely be pardoned I preferred to preserve rather than exterminate. In my triumphs there were led before my chariot nine kings or sons of kings.

When from Spain and Gaul, business in those provinces having been successfully settled, to Rome I returned, in the consulship of Ti. Nero and P. Quintilius, the altar of Augustan peace [10] the senate in honour of my return decreed should be consecrated in the Campus Martius, on which the magistrates and the priests and the Vestal Virgins [the senate] ordered to make an annual sacrifice.

[The temple of] Janus Quirinus, which to be shut our ancestors wished when throughout the whole empire of the Roman people by land and sea there had been obtained, through victories, [15] peace, although, before I was born, from the foundation of the city twice only in all it is handed down to memory that it had been closed, three times under my leadership the senate decreed [it, i.e. Janus Quirinus] should be shut.

With new laws having been passed at my instigation, many practices of our ancestors, already going out of fashion in our time, I brought back, and I myself handed on practices of many things to posterity to be imitated.

DELICIAE LATINAE: 4F

Page 287

Martial

You ask me to recite to you my epigrams. No.
    You don't want to listen, Celer, but to recite [yourself]. (1.63)

Crotti

Is this love? Is this fury? Or [is it] madness of mind?
    I don't want, I want, and I don't want again, and again I want.
Is this ice? Is this fire? For my spirit equally
    Is on fire, and my soul is numbed in my cold mouth.
It is not, truthfully, love or fury, fire or ice:
    It is I myself who have stolen and snatched myself from myself.

4 G (i)–(ii) *(Text pp. 85–6)*

NOTES FOR 4G

In these two sections, we concentrate on some rather more specialised usages of the subjunctive. You will meet (straightaway) conditional clauses ('if …') with subjunctive verbs ('if x were -ing / were to …, y would be -ing / would …'). Instances where relative clauses have subjunctive verbs are also explored. You will meet *quamuis* ('although') with subjunctive. And you will come across the use of subjunctive in clauses inside indirect speech.

4G(i)

305–6 *si … adesset et si … iudicaret, … quid … posset? quid diceret?*: 'If … were present … and if … were judging, … what … would he be able…? What would he be saying?'

This is the first example of a conditional clause with sub-junctive verbs. Such conditions are unreal or unfulfilled. The imperfect subjunctive usually refers to present time (there is another example at 4G(ii), ll. 339–42). But see note on ll. 330–3 in 4G(ii) below. For full discussion, see **GVE 139**.

306–9 *si audiret ... posset...*: 'If he were hearing ... would he be able ...?' See previous note.

307–9 *percussos ... liberatum ... captam atque incensam ... actum*: understand *esse* with all these participles ('that ... was/were -ed'). See further **GVE 143**.

310 *posses ut tibi ignosceret postulare?*: note that here after *posses* you await an infinitive. But it does not arrive until after the *ut* clause. So you must hold *ut*, keeping in mind the various possibilities ('as', 'when', 'to', 'that') until the sense is re-solved. The verb *ignosceret* tells you *ut* cannot mean 'as' or 'when', because it is subjunctive, and in these meanings *ut* always takes indicative verbs. The type of *ut* + subjunctive met here is not resolved until you meet the infinitive you have been expecting after *posses*. *postulare* tells you that *ut* must mean 'to' (indirect command: see **GVE 134**).

312 *ab eo qui praetor esset*: lit. 'by him who was a praetor', i.e. 'by the sort of man who was a praetor'. For this use of subjunctive verbs in *qui* clauses, see **GVE 140.1**. There are further examples at ll. 313–14 (*eum qui ... diceret* 'the sort of man who said ...'), and at 331–2 (in 4G(ii): *eum qui ... non daret* 'the sort of person who did not give ...').

315–16 *quod ... quaereret*: 'because he was asking for ...' For this use of the subjunctive (inside a clause within indirect speech), see **GVE 142**.

317–18 *hoc ... hic ... hōc ... uno*: note the repetition at the beginning of each colon (= section of a sentence) of different forms of the same word (anaphora with polyptoton). This is a favourite device for producing emphasis.

319–21 *si ... ducaris, quid clames ... ? si ... dicas, nonne putes ... ?*: 'If you were to be led, what would you cry ... ? If you were to say, would you not think ... ?' The first example of an unreal/unfulfilled condition with present subjunctive verb. In such clauses, the present subjunctive always refers to the future ('if ... were to,... would ...'). See **GVE 139**. There is a further example at ll. 324–7 (*si tollas ..., si tollas ..., si constituas ..., ... praecludas* 'if you were to remove ..., if you were to remove ..., if you were to decide ..., you would shut off ...').

322 *assecuturum*: understand *esse* with this participle ('that you would gain ...'). See further **GVE 143**. There is a further example at l. 324 (*futuram* 'that ... would be ...').

324–7 *si...*: see note on ll. 319–21 above.

326–7 *iam omnīs..., iam omnia..., iam omnīs..., iam omnem*: note the use of anaphora with *iam* and anaphora with polyptoton with *omnis* (for these terms, see note on ll. 317–18 above). Cicero is to be envisaged banging the rostrum with each repetition. Note how he also keeps a certain balance in the length of the phrases.

4G(ii)

328–9 *cum* looks forward to *nominaret*. Note that in l. 329 *ut* simply qualifies *cognitorem* (so means 'as').

329–33 *si ... cognosceret, ... remitteres; si ignoraret, ... si uideretur, ... constitueres, et ... tolleres*: 'If he had recognised, you would have remitted; if he had been unacquainted with [him] ... if it had seemed right, you would have decided ... and you would have lifted ...' Here the imperfect subjunctive refers not to the present, but to the past. See further **GVE 139 Note 3**.

332 *eum qui ... daret*: see note on l. 312 in 4G(i) above.

334 See the note at **GVE p. 290** (with the wrong line reference in some editions). An example with *dicam* expressed occurs at l. 338 (*quid dicam ...* 'what am I to say [about] ...'). See further **GVE 152 Note 1**.

336–7 *facinus ... scelus ... parricidium*: repetition is not the only way to produce emphasis. Here each colon increases in weight through the gradation of vocabulary: *scelus* is worse than the more neutral *facinus*, and *parricidium* ('killing one's father') is the worst outrage of them all.

338–9 *uerbo ... potest*: note the way Cicero uses the word-order to place the due emphases here. First he expostulates that there is no suitable word (*uerbo satis digno*), then he brings in the scale of criminality involved (*tam nefaria res*), resolves the opening ablative phrase with *appellari*, and ends with the crushing impossibility involved in the search for the right term (*nullo modo potest*). Latin writers, both in prose and in verse, like to make full use of the versatility of word-order the case-system allows them. See further **Reference Grammar W** (*GVE* pp. 546–7).

339–42 *si ... uellem, ... commouerentur*: 'If I were wanting ..., ... would be moved.' See note on ll. 305–6 in 4G(i).

Note once more the use here of anaphora (of *si non*) and the forceful antithesis between various groups to whom he might be speaking and the final group, *bestias*.

TRANSLATION OF 4G

4G(i)

[305] If the father himself of Verres now were present and if now he were judging, by the gods immortal, what to do would he be able? What would he be saying? If he were hearing by you citizens Roman with the axe having been struck, by you a pirate chief having been liberated, on account of your carelessness a fleet Roman having been captured and burned, by you finally Gavius onto a cross having been raised, would you be able from him pardon to seek, would you be able that you [310] he should forgive to beg?

O name sweet of liberty! O law famous of our state! Did it come about that a citizen Roman in a province of the people Roman by him who praetor was in the forum with rods was flogged? What? On to a cross you to raise dared him who himself a citizen Roman to be was saying? But, one may object, Gavius a spy to have been [315] you say and to have shouted himself a citizen Roman to be because a delay to his death he was seeking. This you, Verres, say, this you acknowledge, that man to have shouted himself a citizen Roman to be. This I cling to, here I stick, judges, with this I am content one [thing], I pass over and omit the rest. A citizen Roman himself to be he was saying. If you, Verres, among the Persians or in furthest India to death [320] were to be led, what else would you shout except you a citizen to be Roman? If a citizen you to be Roman were to say, surely you would think you either escape or delay to death about to gain? Men humble, from undistinguished station born, sail, go to those places which never before they have seen, thinking themselves safe to be about to be and this thing for themselves for a protection about to be. If you were to remove this hope, if you were to remove this protection [325] for citizens Roman, if you were to decide nothing to be of help in this utterance 'Citizen Roman I am', then all provinces, then all kingdoms, then all free states, then all the circle of the lands from citizens Roman you would shut off.

4G(ii)

What? When Gavius Lucius Raecius the knight Roman who then in Sicily was as referee was naming, why a letter to him did you not send? If [330] Raecius had recognised the man, something from the ultimate penalty you would have remitted; if he had not known [him], then, if thus to you it had seemed right, a new law you would have established and him who a referee not he gave, although a citizen Roman he was, onto a cross you would have lifted.

But what I more about Gavius? Not only to Gavius then you were hateful, [335] Verres, but also to the name, stock, law of the people Roman an enemy; not to that man, but to the cause common of freedom hostile you were. For a crime it is to bind a citizen Roman, villainy to beat, almost parricide to kill: what should I say on to a cross to raise? By a word enough worthy so criminal a thing to be called in no way it is possible. If these things not to citizens Roman, if not to [340] any friends of our state, if not to men, but to beasts to complain of and denounce I were wishing, nevertheless everything dumb and inanimate would be moved...

EXERCISES FOR 4G

Pages 292–3

Exercises

Morphology/syntax

1(a)   If Verres' father were here, he would judge his son to be an enemy of our state.
       If Verres' father had been here, he would have judged his son to be an enemy of our state.

(b)   If we were to pardon Verres, we should be stupid.

(c)   If Verres were to demand my cups, I should send a letter to him without delay.

(d)   Even animals if they heard these things would be moved.
       Even animals if they had heard these things would have been moved.

(e)   Unless you kept on shouting that you were a Roman citizen, you would be killed.

(f)   If you had this protection, even the enemy would spare you.
       If you had had this protection, even the enemy would have spared you.

(g)   If there were foresight, there would be no evil. (GELLIUS)

(h)   Wine prepares the mind (gets you in the mood) for lovemaking, unless you were to have too much. (OVID)

2*(a)   *si ciuis Romanus essem.*

(b)   *si praesidium postulet.*

(c)   *si mora non esset.*

(d)   *si amici commoueantur.*

(e)   *si praesidium postularemus.*

(f)   *si clamitem.*

(g)   *uelim dicere.*

(h)   *uellem rogare.*

(i)   *postularem/postulauissem.*

(j)   *commouear.*

Pages 295–7

Reading exercise / Test exercise

Omitted.

English–Latin**

Quamquam Gauius Raecium cognitorem nominauerat [cum ... nomi-nauisset], litteras non misisti. uelim, Verres, te hoc mihi dicere. cur moratus es? cur statim litteras non misisti? nonne Gauius 'si litteras ad Raecium mittas' inquit 'me ciuem Romanum esse dicat. si adesset, me quem accuses innocentem esse affirmaret.' sed tu, Verres, summā Gauio neglegentiā crucem parauisti. si bestiis hanc rem narrarem hae etiam commouerentur.

Page 297

Res gestae diui Augusti *'The achievements of the divine Augustus'*

In my sixth and seventh consulships, after I had extinguished civil wars, and with the consent of all had taken charge of everything, the republic from my power to the judgement of the senate and the people of Rome I transferred. For this service of mine by a decree of the senate I was named Augustus and with laurel the door-posts [5] of my house were wreathed publicly and a civic crown above my door was fixed and a golden shield placed in the Julian senate house, which, that to me the senate and people of Rome gave [it] for the sake of my courage, clemency, justice and piety, was witnessed by the inscription on that shield. After that time, in authority I stood above everyone, but I had no more power [10] than the rest who were colleagues of mine in each magistracy.

When I was performing my thirteenth consulship, the senate and the equestrian order and the whole people of Rome gave me the title 'Father of my fatherland', and this, in the porch of my house that it should be inscribed, and in the Julian senate house, and in the Augustan forum, beneath the chariot which had been put there in my honour by a decree of the senate, [they all] re-solved. As I write this, [15] I am seventy-six years old.

Section Five
The conspiracy of Catiline in Rome 64–62

5A *(Text pp. 98–100)*

NOTES FOR 5A

The translation now reverts to normal English word-order.

In this section, since **GVE** already gives notes on new grammar, only a general note is given at the beginning of each sub-section telling you what new grammar to expect. References to the original are included at the end of each passage.

Note on Sallust's style

Sallust's language is very different from Cicero's. Cicero writes long sentences, with much use of anaphora (repetition), with much amplification, all building up to tremendous climaxes. Sallust tends to write more concisely.

- He often omits *esse* ('to be'), e.g. 5A(ii), l. 33: *libido sic accensa* ('her lust [was] so inflamed') and l. 34: *uerum ingenium eius haud absurdum* ('But her intellect [was] not absurd').
- He uses the historic infinitive, e.g. 5A(i), ll. 19–21: *sed in dies plura agitare, arma . . . parare, pecuniam portare* ('But day by day he stirred up many things, got arms ready, carried money . . .').
- He goes to the heart of the matter without lengthy Ciceronian background explanations e.g. 5A(i), ll. 5–6: *erat ei cum Fuluia muliere nobili stupri uetus consuetudo* ('He had with Fulvia a long-standing sexual relationship') – the behaviour was reprehensible (*stuprum* always reflects dis-

honour on the persons who perform the action and the illicitness of the action itself); it was habitual (*consuetudo*); and it had been going on a long time (*uetus*).

In these three passages, you will meet:

(a) *ut* + subjunctive meaning 'that', giving the result of an action. These clauses are easy to spot because they will be flagged by markers meaning 'to such an extent', 'so', 'so great', 'of such a kind' (*adeo, tam, tantus, talis*). See further *GVE* 144.

(b) *ut* + subjunctive meaning 'in order that / to' and indicating purpose. See further *GVE* 145.

(c) The historic infinitive. See *GVE* 146.

(d) The ablative of respect, indicating the point in which someone or something is x (e.g. 'learned in ...', 'fortunate in ...'). See *GVE* 147.

The grammar section also reviews the various ways in which *ut* and *qui* are used and gives pointers to help resolve their meanings as you read (pp. 310–11).

TRANSLATION OF 5A

5A(i)

But in that conspiracy was Q. Curius, born in a not ignoble position, so devoted to his lusts that the censors removed him from the senate. In this man there was such great vanity that he could not keep quiet about what he had heard; such great arrogance that he himself never concealed his own crimes; such great temerity that he always said and did whatever he wanted. He had with Fulvia, a noble woman [5], a long-standing sexual relationship. But Curius became so poor that he was less pleasing to her. Suddenly he began to boast so much as to promise the seas and mountains to Fulvia. And he became so arrogant and wild that sometimes he threatened her with death if she did not accede to his every demand. But Fulvia, learning the reason for Curius' arrogance, considered the matter so dangerous to the state that [10] everything which she had heard about the conspiracy of Catiline she told to many people.

Those things as told by Fulvia were primarily responsible for the consulship being entrusted to M. Tullius Cicero. For previously the majority of the nobility had been so envious that they were unwilling to entrust the consulship to a new man. For they argued 'The consulship would be sullied if a new man however outstanding were to obtain it.' But when [15] the danger came, envy and arrogance were put behind them. Therefore, after the elections were held, M. Tullius and C. Antonius were declared consuls; it was this event that in the first instance had alarmed the conspirators. None the less Catiline's madness did not diminish but day by day he stirred up more trouble, he got ready weapons in strategic locations throughout Italy, and he conveyed money to Faesulae to a person called Manlius [20].

Now learn the Learning Vocabulary at GVE pp. 300–1.

5A(ii)

At that time, Catiline is said to have gathered to himself a very large number of men, and also a few women, who at first had sustained their enormous expenditure by prostitution, but later, when they were not able to make a living in this way because of their age, they had fallen into massive debt. Therefore they had joined Catiline to free themselves from debt [25], and Catiline happily welcomed them into the conspiracy in order to stir up the city slaves through them and burn the city. Their husbands he thought he would either bring over to his side or kill.

But among them was Sempronia, who had committed many crimes with a daring that was frequently male. This woman was fortunate enough in her birth and beauty, but especially in her husband and [30] children; learned in Greek and Latin literature, she was more learned in singing and dancing than a respectable married lady needs to be. But to her everything was always dearer than honour and chastity; her lust was so intense that she more often propositioned men than was propositioned by them. But her intellect was not foolish; she could write poetry, make a joke, use words which were chaste or gentle [35] or forward. In a word, there was much wit and much charm in her.

Now learn the Learning Vocabulary at GVE p. 302.

5A(iii)

Although these things had been prepared, Catiline still sought the consulship for the following year. Nor meanwhile was he inactive, but in every way he set traps for Cicero. But Cicero, in order to evade these traps, had ensured through Fulvia that Q. Curius should reveal to him Catiline's plans. Therefore [40] Catiline, after the day of the elections had come and he had been defeated, decided to make war. Therefore in order to have allies in different parts of Italy, he placed C. Manlius at Faesulae and others in other places throughout Italy. Meanwhile at Rome he did many things at the same time; he organised an ambush on the consuls, he prepared fires, he laid siege to strategic locations with armed men, he went around with a weapon and [45] he urged his associates always to be on their guard and at the ready; night and day he hustled and stayed awake, and he was not exhausted by the lack of sleep or by hard work. Finally, when he had made no progress, he summoned the leaders of the conspiracy at night and said 'I have sent Manlius ahead to the army and likewise others to other strategic locations to begin the war. I would myself now be setting off for the army, were Cicero not still [50] alive, but I want Cicero to be killed first, so that he does not hinder my plans.' When he had said this, although the rest of the conspirators were terrified, C. Cornelius, a Roman knight, promised his help and he and L. Vargunteius, a senator, decided a little later that night to enter Cicero's house with armed men in order to take him by surprise and kill him. Curius, when he realised that such great [55] danger threatened the consul, quickly told Cicero through Fulvia of the plot which was in train. Therefore in order that Cicero should not be killed, they were kept from the door, and so had undertaken this great crime to no purpose.

Now learn the Learning Vocabulary at *GVE* p. 304.

EXERCISES FOR 5A

Page 306

Exercise

1(a)   There was such great madness in Catiline that day by day he stirred up more trouble.

(b)   There is such great danger that Fulvia wishes to tell the consul everything.

(c)   Sempronia was so learned in Latin literature that she composed poetry.

(d)   So great a conspiracy was fabricated that the consulship was not entrusted to a noble man.

(e)   Catiline is so inflamed with rage that he sets an ambush against the consuls, he often encourages his associates, he himself goes around with a weapon, [and] he never sleeps.

2**(a)   *tanta . . . ut consulatus nouo homini mandaretur.*
  (b)   *tam docta ut uersus faciat.*
  (c)   *adeo inflammatus . . . ut homines armatos opportunis locis per Italiam collocaret.*
  (d)   *tam . . . ut senatu moueretur.*
  (e)   *tantum facinus, ut nemo dormire possit.*

Pages 307–8

Exercises

1(a)   Several women joined Catiline in order to free themselves from debt.

(b)   Catiline sent Manlius to the army to prepare for war.

(c)   Cornelius and Vargunteius are going to Cicero to kill him.

(d)   The guards of Cicero's house kept Cornelius and Vargunteius from the door so that the consul might not be killed.

(e)   Fulvia told the consul everything she had heard so that he might escape great danger.

(f)   Aelius wrote speeches for others to speak.

(g)   Nothing can be put so stupidly that it may not be said by one of the philosophers.

2**(a)   *ut pecuniam rogaret.*
  (b)   *qui Ciceronem interficerent.*
  (c)   *ut illa sibi crederet.*
  (d)   *ne interficiatur.*
  (e)   *ne a coniuratoribus petatur.*

Page 309, top

(a)   The nobles did not want to entrust [prolative] the consulship to Catiline.

(b)   Fulvia had said to many people that Catiline was preparing [acc. and inf.] a conspiracy.

(c)   Catiline day by day stirred up [historic] more trouble, put [historic] arms in place, and sent [historic] money to Manlius.
(d)   Catiline says that he is not conspiring [acc. and inf.].
(e)   Sempronia writes [historic] poetry and employs [historic] chaste vocabulary.
(f)   Cicero forbade Cornelius and Vargunteius to enter [prolative] his house.

Page 309, foot

(a)   Sempronia, born of a noble family [true ablative], was learned in Latin literature [respect].
(b)   A man called [respect] Curius was Fulvia's lover at that time [temporal].
(c)   You were wrong not in the whole matter [respect] but in the timing [respect].
(d)   That night [temporal] Cornelius and Vargunteius were kept from Cicero's door [true ablative].
(e)   Catiline, although he was fortunate in family and looks [respect], was nevertheless a man of very little wisdom [description].

Pages 310–11

Exercise

(a)   Them that they should be armed he encouraged [*ut*, indirect command, solved by *hortabatur*].
(b)   Sempronia is so clever that she composes poetry very easily [*ut*, result, solved by *tam*].
(c)   As I shall order, so shall you do [*ut*, 'as', solved by indicative and *ita*].
(d)   The insults of these men the wise man takes as jokes [*ut*, 'as', because it does not control a clause].
(e)   Cicero ensured that he was not killed [*efficio ut*].
(f)   In order that the associates of Catiline should not kill the consul, Fulvia told the whole story to [her] friends [*ne*, purpose, because *narrauit* is not a verb of command].
(g)   How fortunate Sempronia is [*ut* controls the main clause]!

Page 311

Exercise

(a)   Catiline is sending his associates into many parts of Italy to burn the city [*qui*, purpose, solved by subjunctive *incendant*].

(b) Sempronia, who was always propositioning men, was a respectable Roman lady [*quae* solved by indicative *petebat*].

(c) The people of Clusium sent ambassadors to seek help from the senate [*qui*, purpose, solved by subjunctive *peterent*].

(d) Many people thought that a conspiracy was the way to free themselves from debt [*quā*, purpose, solved by subjunctive *possent*].

(e) Some women also joined the conspiracy who had fallen into very great debt [*quae*, relative, solved by indicative *conciderant*].

(f) No one can be fortunate who is an enemy of the state [*qui*, consecutive, solved by subjunctive *sit* and *nemo*].

(g) I love you because you are so brave [*qui*, causal, solved by subjunctive *sis* and context].

Page 312

Reading exercise / Test exercise

Omitted.

**English–Latin

Catilina, quamquam coniurationem parauerat, nihilominus consulatum iterum petebat. interea, sociis persuadere conabatur ut Ciceronem adgrederentur. Cicero autem consilium ceperat ut periculum fugeret. per Fuluiam et Curium perfecerat ut Catilinae consilia audiret.

iterum nobiles adeo timebant ut consulatum Catilinae non mandarent. tum bellum gerere constituit. socios in diuersis partibus Italiae collocauit. interea, Romae consuli insidias parare, cum telo esse, socios ut fortes essent hortari.

Page 317

Exercise

(a) since you have come to the Carthaginian city.

(b) a huge temple to Juno.

(c) he sees the Trojan battles in sequence.

(d) and wars already spread by rumour throughout the whole city.

(e) this reputation will bring some redemption for you.

(f) he feeds his mind on an illusory scene.

(g) and he turns aside his fiery horses.

(h) it gives them pleasure to go to the Greek camp as well and to see the abandoned places.

(i) he runs down from the top of the citadel.
(j) through the friendly silences of the quiet moon.

Page 320

Exercise

mīrātur mōl[em] Aeneās, māgālia quondam,
mīrātur portās strepitumqu[e] et strāta uiārum.   5
īnstant ārdentēs Tyriī: pars dūcere mūrōs
mōlīrīqu[e] arc[em] et manibus subuoluere saxa.
pars optāre locum tect[o] et conclūdere sulcō;
iūra magistrātūsque legunt sānctumque senātum.
hīc portūs ali[i]effodiunt; hīc alta theātrīs   10
fundāmenta locant ali[ī], immānīsque columnās
rūpibus excīdunt, scaenīs decor[a] apta futūrīs;
....

feruet opus redolentque thymō fraglantia mella.

Page 321

Virgil's Aeneid

They hastened along their way meanwhile, where the path
                                                         pointed,
and were already climbing the hill which in its great bulk over the
                                                               city
looms and looks down over the facing citadels.
Aeneas is amazed at the size, once huts,
[5] is amazed at the gates and the hustle and bustle and the paving
                                                    of the streets.
The Carthaginians eagerly press on: some of them build walls
and work at the citadel and roll rocks uphill by hand.
Others choose a place for a house and mark it out with a furrow;
they choose laws and magistrates and a revered senate.
[10] Here some are digging harbours; here deep

foundations for theatres others are placing, and huge columns
from the rocks they quarry, ornaments fit for productions to come;
....

The work seethes and the fragrant honey smells of thyme.
[20] 'O lucky men, whose walls already rise!'
Aeneas spoke and looked up at the roofs of the city.

5 B *(Text pp. 102–4)*

NOTES FOR 5B

In these three passages, you will meet three constructions which
develop syntax you already know:

(a)   *fore ut* + passive subjunctive, meaning 'that it will turn out
      that x will/would be done'. See further **GVE 149**. (Com-
      pare the future infinitive passive (e.g. *amatum iri* 'that there
      will be a movement towards loving', *i.e.* 'that x will/would
      be loved') which you have already met.)
(b)   *quo* + subjunctive to indicate purpose (used with compar-
      ative forms). See further **GVE 148**.
(c)   The ablative absolute using noun + perfect participle pas-
      sive ('with x having been -ed'). See further **GVE 150–1**.

TRANSLATION OF 5B

5B(i)

During the same period, at Rome Lentulus, just as Catiline had
ordered, was inciting whomever he believed to be ready for revolution, either through his own or others' efforts [60]. So he gave to
someone called P. Umbrenus the job of seeking out the ambassadors of the Allobroges and persuading them into a war alliance. For
Lentulus knew that the Allobroges were both publicly and individually overwhelmed by debt and that the Gallic race is by nature
warlike. Therefore he thought that [= it would happen that] they
would easily be drawn into such a plan. Umbrenus, because he had
done business in Gaul [65], was known to the majority of the

leaders of the states and knew them; and so without delay, as soon as he had spotted the ambassadors in the forum, he asked them a few things about the position of the state and its unfortunate plight. After he saw that they were complaining about the greed of the magistrates, accusing the senate of being no help [= of the fact that there was nothing of help in it] and awaiting death as the cure for their misfortunes, he said 'Yet I will show you a way, if only you are willing to be men [**70**], by which to escape all these great problems of yours.' When he had said this, the Allobroges, drawn into the greatest expectations, began to beg Umbrenus to take pity on them; there was nothing so difficult that they would not do it, in order to free their state from debt. He led them into a house which was near the forum. In addition he summoned Gabinius, in order that there should be greater authority [**75**] in his speech and so that he might persuade them more easily. In Gabinius' presence, he revealed the conspiracy, named his confederates, and many innocent people besides, in order that the spirits of the ambassadors should be raised higher. He persuaded them to promise their help, and when they had promised their help, he sent them home.

Now learn the Learning Vocabulary at GVE pp. 324–5.

5B(ii)

But the Allobroges, inasmuch as they had not yet decided to join the conspiracy [**80**], considered the matter for a long time. On the one side were their debt, their enthusiasm for war, and the great rewards that the prospect of victory held out [= in the hope of victory]; but on the other were the greater resources of the Roman state, percentage politics [= safe plans], and sure rewards in place of uncertain expectations. As they turned these things over, in the end the fortune of the republic won the day. And so to Q. Fabius Sanga, the patron of their state, they revealed everything, as they had learned it. Cicero [**85**], learning the plan through Sanga, told the ambassadors of the Allobroges to make a vigorous pretence of enthusiasm for the conspiracy, to approach the rest, to make fine promises, and do everything they could to make the conspirators as out in the open as possible.

Now learn the Learning Vocabulary at GVE pp. 325–6.

5B(iii)

But at Rome Lentulus, with the rest who were leaders of the conspiracy, after gathering (as it seemed) great forces, had decided that, when Catiline [90] had come nearer with his army, L. Bestia, holding a meeting, would complain about the actions of Cicero; they had decided that, when that meeting had taken place, the rest of the membership of the conspiracy would carry out their tasks. These tasks they had decided to share out in the following way: Statilius and Gabinius would with a large band of men set fire to twelve strategic locations in the city simultaneously, in order that an easier approach [95] to the consul might be made; Cethegus would lay siege to Cicero's door and violently attack him when the door had been broken down; sons of households, the great majority of whom were from the nobility, would kill their parents; finally that, when the city was on fire, Cicero dead, and everyone unnerved by the slaughter and fire, they would charge out to Catiline [100].

Now learn the Learning Vocabulary at GVE p. 327.

EXERCISES FOR 5B

Page 328

Exercise

(a) Catiline told his associates that there would be fire and slaughter in the city.
(b) Umbrenus summoned Gabinius, in order to persuade the Allobroges more easily by his words.
(c) The Allobroges, inasmuch as they thought the prizes of war would be great, considered the matter for a long time.
(d) But the ambassadors finally realised that they would be very easily defeated by the resources of the Roman state.
(e) Therefore the ambassadors of the Allobroges told Cicero everything, in order to bring to their state greater help.

Pages 330–2

Exercises

1   *dimissus*, having been sent away; *requisitus*, having been sought out; *oppressus*, having been crushed; *apertus*, having been opened;

simulatus having been feigned; *consideratus*, having been considered; *fractus*, having been broken; *obsessus*, having been besieged, *existimatus*, having been thought; *sollicitatus*, having been bothered.

2*   Having been joined (pass.); having complained (dep.); having set out (dep.); having been prevented (pass.); having gained (dep.); having spoken (dep.); having striven (dep.); having been summoned (pass.); having been stopped (pass.); having been placed (pass.); having addressed (dep.); having died (dep.); having been thrown away (pass.); having been driven (pass); having been completed (pass.).

Note: we no longer give the Latin words in this sort of exercise.

3(a)   with the conspiracy having been prepared.
 (b)   with these things having been told.
 (c)   with the soldiers having been summoned.
 (d)   with the army having been placed.
 (e)   with the signal having been given.
 (f)   with enthusiasm having been feigned.
 (g)   with the enemy having been crushed.
 (h)   when they had considered the prizes.
 (i)   now that their parents were dead.
 (j)   after sending away a few.

4*(a)   Catiline having left the city [when...], Lentulus sought new allies.
 (b)   With the ambassadors of the Allobroges remaining at Rome [while...], Umbrenus was summoned by an associate.
 (c)   Umbrenus revealed the conspiracy, after summoning Gabinius to give greater authority to his speech.
 (d)   With the plan revealed, and his associates named [although...], Umbrenus nevertheless was not able to persuade the Allobroges to become conspirators.
 (e)   Cicero, with the plan known [because/after...], wanted to have the conspirators as out in the open as possible.
 (f)   Things well done but badly spoken I consider badly done.
 (g)   Nothing is thought up and finished at once.

***English—Latin*

1(a)   *omni spe sublatā.*
 (b)   *militibus dimissis.*

(c) *sociis requisitis.*
(d) *rebus consideratis.*
(e) *praemio dato.*
(f) *urbe obsessā.*

2 *Umbrenus Allobrogum legatos e foro domum cuiusdam duxit. deinde*
Gabinium, uirum magnā auctoritate, uocauit, quo celerius eis persuaderet.
Gabinio uocato, Umbrenus legatis persuasit ut operam pollicerentur. sed
nondum se coniurationi adiungere constituerant, quippe qui arbitrarentur
fore ut opibus ciuitatis Romanae uincerentur. postremo rem omnem Sangae
aperuerunt. Cicero, consilio per Sangam cognito, Allobrogibus praecepit ut
studium simularent, quo facilius coniuratores caperet.

Virgil's Aeneid

We opened up the walls and revealed the buildings of the city.
Everyone got ready for the work and under the feet
they placed slippings of wheels, and ropes of tow upon the neck
they stretch; the deadly device scales the walls
[5] pregnant with arms. Boys and unwed girls around it
sing sacred songs and rejoice in touching the rope with their
                                                          hands;
it comes up and slips threateningly into the middle of the city.
O fatherland, O Ilium dwelling of the gods, and famous in war
walls of the Trojans! Four times on the very threshold of the gate
[10] it stopped and four times from its belly the arms let out a
                                                          sound;
but we pressed on, mindless and blinded by madness,
and lodged the ill-omened monster on our sacred citadel.

5 C *(Text pp. 104–7)*

NOTES FOR 5C

In these three sections, the focus is upon three areas:

(a) The subjunctive to express orders, wishes, possibility. See
     further **GVE 152–3**.
(b) Impersonal verbs (i.e. verbs which only have a third person
     singular). See further **GVE 154–5**.

(c)   The future perfect tense ('I shall have . . .', 'I shall have been -ed'). See further **GVE 156–8**.

For good measure, we throw in here some more numerals (see **GVE 159**).

TRANSLATION OF 5C

5c(i)

But the Allobroges, on the instructions of Cicero, through Gabinius met up with the rest of the conspirators. From Lentulus, Cethegus, Statilius and also Cassius they demanded an oath, to bring sealed [= which they were to bring] to their citizens; otherwise they would not easily be persuaded [= it would not easily turn out that] into so great a business. The rest, suspecting nothing, gave the oath, Cassius promised that he would come there shortly, and set off from the city a little before the ambassadors [105]. When this oath had been given, Lentulus sent the Allobroges off to Catiline with one T. Volturcius, so that they might cement their alliance with Catiline before continuing homewards. Lentulus himself gave Volturcius a letter for Catiline, a copy of which is written below [110]:

'I urge you to consider the danger you are in. You should understand that you are a man. You should consider your plans. You should seek help from everyone, even from the lowest.'

To this he added commands verbally:

'You have been judged a public enemy by the senate. Why then do you reject the slaves? You should take in the slaves. In the city the things you ordered have been made ready. Now that these things have been made ready, you should set out [115]. Do not delay coming nearer in person.'

Now learn the Learning Vocabulary at GVE pp. 334–5.

5c(ii)

When these things had been done in this way, after agreeing on a night for the departure of the Allobroges, Cicero, having been informed of everything by the ambassadors, ordered the praetors to capture the retinues of the Allobroges by means of an ambush at the Mulvian bridge. Without delay, they went to the bridge. The praetors, military men, put in place their troops without any noise [120] just as they had been ordered and staked out the bridge in hiding. After the ambassadors had arrived at that place with Volturcius and a shouting arose from both sides at once, the Gauls, quickly realising the plan, without delay handed themselves over to the praetors; Volturcius at first encouraged the rest and defended himself from the massed ranks with a sword. Then, when he had been deserted by the ambassadors, timidly and despairing of his life [125], he handed himself over to the praetors as though to his enemies.

Now learn the Learning Vocabulary at *GVE* p. 336.

5c(iii)

When these things had been done, everything was quickly reported to Cicero by messengers. But he was overwhelmed by great anxiety and joy simultaneously. For he was happy in the knowledge, now that the conspiracy was out in the open, that the state had been rescued from danger; furthermore, however, he was anxious because such important citizens had been arrested. Therefore he spoke to himself as follows [130]:

'It is on citizens who have committed a very great crime that we are about to pass judgement when we [shall] have summoned them into the senate. It will fall to me to give my opinion. I want them to be punished. For if they were to be spared by us, it would be a considerable disgrace to the republic. If they are not [shall not have been] punished, I think that [it will come about that] the state will be seriously [135] harmed. But if I demand [shall have demanded] the supreme punishment and Roman citizens [shall] die at the command of a consul, their punishment will be a burden on me. Nevertheless, it is fitting for me to place the republic before my own safety. If I give [shall have given] this opinion, and criminal men are killed [shall have been killed], at least I shall have saved the republic from such great dangers as these. This is my decision. It is fitting for me to show myself resolute in this opinion [140]. Nor do I think that [it will come about that] I will ever regret this steadfastness.'

So Cicero, once his mind was made up, ordered Lentulus and the rest of the conspirators to be summoned before him. They came without delay. Because Lentulus was a praetor, the consul himself led him into the senate holding him by the hand; the rest [145] he ordered to come into the temple of Concord under guard. There he summoned the senate, and brought in Volturcius with the Allobroges. He told Flaccus the praetor to bring to the same place the letter which he had received from the ambassadors.

Now learn the Learning Vocabulary at *GVE* pp. 337–8.

EXERCISES FOR 5C

Page 339

Exercises

1(a) Please go away.
 (b) Let us delay.
 (c) Let us stay.
 (d) Let him not complain.
 (e) Let them not ask for a reward.
 (f) Let us not die in vain.
 (g) Let him come.
 (h) Let us go away.
 (i) What was I to say?
 (j) What am I to say?
 (k) What was he to do?

2*(a) Let us die and rush into the midst of the arms.
 (b) Let us live, my Lesbia, and let us love.
 (c) Let us not wish for difficulties.
 (d) Please be careful, my Tiro.
 (e) Let us make man in our image and likeness and let him rule the fishes of the sea.
 (f) And God said 'Let there be light' and there was light.
 (g) God also said 'Let there be a firmament in the midst of the waters and let it divide the waters from the waters.'
 (h) Be sensible, strain wines and cut back hope to a short distance.
 (i) What is she to do? Should she fight? A woman who fights will be

defeated. Should she shout? But in his right hand was a sword to prevent her.

(j)   When I saw this, what should I have done, judges?

Page 341

Exercise

(a)   I would have wanted you to have invited me to dinner.
(b)   Would you think / would you have thought it could ever happen that words would fail me?
(c)   Would that the Roman people had one neck.

Pages 342–3

Exercises

1(a)   It is fitting for me to give this opinion.
 (b)   You ought to have gone away.
 (c)   The ambassadors voted to pretend enthusiasm for the conspiracy.
 (d)   Lentulus will repent of that oath.
 (e)   Everyone may have hope.
 (f)   The same things do not please everyone.

2*(a)   *me studii coniurationis paenitet.*
 (b)   *Catilinae placuit Romā abire.*
 (c)   *tibi licet queri.*
 (d)   *uos oportet uos consuli tradere.*
 (e)   *uirum decet in proelio mori.*

Page 344

Exercise

1(a)   They run together.
 (b)   Battle went on for a long time.
 (c)   They came to the forum.
 (d)   There is a movement to arms.
 (e)   You were not believed.
 (f)   We will not spare our efforts.
 (g)   The state will be harmed by the conspirators.
 (h)   We were ordered to go into battle.
 (i)   Food, sleep, sex – this is the circle we run round.

2*(a)   *pugnatur.*
  (b)   *concursum est.*
  (c)   *tibi non parcetur.*
  (d)   *a Cicerone Catilinae non creditum est.*
  (e)   *Lentulo praeceptum erat.*

Pages 346–7

Exercise

1   [Just 1ˢᵗ person singular given] *cunctatus ero; tradidero; occupauero, occupatus ero; eripuero; praebuero; commisero, commissus ero; exortus ero; fuero.*

See **GVE 156–8**, pp. 344–6.

2*   He shall have moved, *mouerint;* you shall have been in, *infueris;* she will have been prepared, *paratae erunt;* they shall have been summoned, *conuocatus erit;* they shall have thought, *putauerit;* you will have tried, *conati eritis;* we shall have hindered, *impediuero;* I shall have lived, *uixerimus;* those things shall have arisen, *exortum erit;* they shall have been able, *potuerit.*

3*   *uixero; agressus erit; putauerint; requisita erit; uisum erit; tradideritis; occupati erunt; puniueris.*

4   Pluperfect; they shall have encouraged; pluperfect; you will have been punished; pluperfect subjunctive; she will have been rescued; perfect; you will have arisen; perfect; pluperfect; I shall have harmed; he will have considered; perfect; pluperfect subjunctive; she will have shown; I will have complained; perfect; perfect; they shall have feigned; perfect; we shall have approached; pluperfect subjunctive; he will have brought about; pluperfect.

5*(a)   If we have not [shall not have] told the consuls that the Romans are in danger, the conspirators will seize the state.
  (b)   When the consul has punished [shall have punished] the wicked citizens, he will tell everyone that the republic is safe.
  (c)   If I order [shall have ordered] the conspirators to go into the temple of Concord, they will not delay.
  (d)   In a few days those men will have been killed.
  (e)   When the conspirators [shall] have been killed, their punishment will lie heavy on Cicero.
  (f)   If the consul does not decide [shall not have decided] that [it will

come about that] the conspirators are executed, the state will be in great danger.

(g)   The wise man will not be harmed by poverty, nor by pain.

Page 348

**English–Latin

Ciceronem ingens cura occupauit. sic igitur secum locutus est: 'te sentias rem publicam a periculo seruauisse. ne cuncteris summum supplicium a coniuratoribus postulare. si a te eis parsum erit, rei publicae nocebitur. si ciues Romani iussu consulis interfecti erunt, hoc supplicium oneri tibi erit. nihilominus te oportet audacem esse. puto fore ut te huius audaciae non paeniteat. nam rem publicam seruaueris.'

Page 349

Virgil's Aeneid

Saying this, to the very altar
he dragged him trembling and slipping in the copious blood of his
son,
[10] and he wrapped his hair in his left hand, and with his right
he pulled out and buried in his side right up to the hilt a gleaming
sword.
This was the end of the destiny of Priam, this death
took him by fate as he saw the burning of Troy and the fall
of Pergamum, [Priam] over so many peoples and lands once the
proud
[15] ruler of Asia. He lies on the beach, a great torso,
the head ripped from his shoulders, a body without a name.

DELICIAE LATINAE: 5C

Page 350

Life of Aurelian

We've beheaded a thousand, a thousand, a thousand [men].
One man! We've beheaded a thousand.
Let the man who killed a thousand drink a thousand [cups].
No one has as much wine as Aurelian has spilt blood.

The Vulgate: the creation of heaven and earth

In the beginning God created heaven and earth. But the earth was empty and void and there was darkness on the face of the deep, and the spirit of God moved over the waters. And God said, 'Let there be light!', and there was light. And God saw that the light was good: and he divided the light from the darkness. And he called the light 'Day' and the darkness 'Night': and evening and morning was done, the first day.

God also said, 'Let there be a firmament in the middle of the waters: and let it divide the waters from the waters.' And God made the firmament and divided the waters which were beneath the firmament from those which were above the firmament. And so it was done. And God called the firmament 'Sky': and evening and morning was done, the second day.

But God said, 'Let the waters which are beneath the sky be gathered together into one place and let there appear dry land'. And so it was done. And God called the dry land 'Earth'. And he called the gatherings of waters 'Seas'. And God saw that it was good. And he said, 'Let the earth bring forth vegetation which is green and produces seed, and fruit-bearing trees which bear fruit according to their kind, and let its seed [lit. whose seed] be in itself over the ground.' And so it was done. And the earth brought forth green vegetation, which produced seed according to its kind, and trees which bore fruit, and each of which had a sowing according to its species. And God saw that it was good. And evening and morning was finished, the third day.

But God said, 'Let there be lights in the sky's firmament, and let them divide the day and the night, and let them be for signs and seasons, days and years: let them shine in the firmament of the heaven and illuminate the earth.' And so it was done. And God made two great lights: the greater light to be in charge of the day: and the lesser light to be in charge of the night: and [he made] the stars. And he placed them in the firmament of the heaven to shine upon the earth and be in charge of day and night, and to divide light and darkness. And God saw that it was good. And evening and morning was finished, the fourth day.

God also said, 'Let the waters produce crawling creatures with [lit. of] living spirit and flying creatures over the earth beneath the firmament of the heaven.' And God created huge sea-monsters, and every living and moving animal which the waters had brought forth according to their kinds, and every flying creature according to its type. And God saw that it was good. And he blessed them, saying, 'Increase and multiply and fill the waters of the sea: and let the birds multiply above the earth.' And evening and morning was completed, the fifth day.

God also said, 'Let the earth bring forth living animals in their own kind, beasts of burden and reptiles and beasts of the earth according to their types.' And so it was done. And God made the beasts of the earth according to their types, and beasts of burden and every reptile of the earth in its own way. And God saw that it was good. And he said, 'Let us make man in our image and likeness, and let him be lord over the fish of the sea and the birds of the sky and the beasts and the whole earth, and every reptile which moves upon the earth.' And God created man in his own image: in the image of God created He him, male and female He created them, and God blessed them and said, 'Increase and multiply and fill the earth and bring it under your control and rule over the fishes of the sea and the birds of the sky and all the creatures which move upon the earth.' And God said, 'Lo! I have given to you every plant which produces seed on the earth and all the trees which have in themselves the ability to sow their own kind, so that they might be [used] as food for you: and [I have given these also] to all the animals of the earth, and every bird of the sky, and all that move upon the earth and in which there is a living soul, so that they may have [them] to eat.' And so it was done. And God saw all the things that he had made, and they were very good. And evening and morning were finished, the sixth day.

Therefore the heavens and the earth were completed and all their decoration. And God finished by the seventh day his work which he had done: and he rested on the seventh day from all the work that he had effected. And he blessed the seventh day and sanctified it because on it he had ceased from all the work which God had created to do. (Genesis 1.1–2.3)

5D *(Text pp. 109–11)*

NOTE ON CICERO'S STYLE

If concision is the hallmark of Sallust's style, fullness (*copia*) is the main characteristic of Cicero's. His sentences are on the whole longer and more complex (the term most often heard is periodic). He makes much use of antithesis (contrast). For example, in 5D(i), ll. 149–50, we read: *non atrocitate animi moueor ... sed singulari quādam humanitate ac misericordiā* ('It is not by fierceness that I am moved..., but by a unique sort of humanity and pity'). And the first leg of the contrast (*atrocitate animi*) is briefer than the second (*singulari ... misericordiā*). He uses word-play. For example, at 5D(i), 150–1, he says: *uideor enim mihi uidere ...* ('I seem [am seen] to myself to see ...'). He is fond of the rhetorical question. For instance, at 5D(i), 149–50, he asks: *quis enim est me mitior?* ('For who is milder than I?'). He uses anaphora (repetition) freely. For example, at 5D(i), ll. 164–6, he rams home his point with *qui nos, qui coniuges, qui liberos nostros..., qui singulas ... domos* ('who us, who wives, who our children..., who our individual houses ...'). And the sentence begins punchily (*qui nos*), but gradually opens out, first with a slightly longer word (*coniuges*), then with a phrase (*liberos nostros*) followed by the verbs governing the three objects (*trucidare uoluerunt* 'they wished to butcher'), then with a pair of much longer *qui* clauses with varied subordinate structures within them. Anacoluthon (lack of connecting words like *et*) also hammers home the message, e.g. 170–2 .

Cicero's style is public and forensic. He spells out everything with a wave of the hand and a thump of the fist. Sallust's is private and philosophical, inviting the individual reader to linger over the phrases. Both writers wish to make moral points.

NOTES FOR 5D

There are only two new grammatical departures in these four passages:

(a)   The passive verbal adjective meaning 'to be -ed', which is called the gerundive. See further **GVE 160–1**.

(b)   *Ne* and *ut* + subjunctive verbs with verbs of fearing ('I am afraid that/lest'). See further **GVE 162**.

TRANSLATION OF 5D

5D(i)

In this case, I am not influenced by harshness of outlook – for who is gentler than I? – but by a special humanity and compassion. For I seem [150] to myself to see this city, the light of the world and the focus of all races, suddenly collapsing because of one conflagration. Before my eyes there remains the appearance and madness of Cethegus, revelling in your slaughter, of Lentulus as king, and of Catiline arriving with his army. When I set these things before my mind's eye, it is then I shudder at the tears of mothers of the household, then at the panic of girls and boys [155], then at the ill-treatment of Vestal Virgins, and, because these things seem to me really pitiful and pitiable, it is for that reason that I shall show myself stern and determined against those who have wished to bring these things to pass. For I ask you, if any father of the household, when his children have been killed by his slave, or his wife murdered, or his house set on fire, did not exact the bitterest penalty from his slaves [160], would he seem to be merciful and compassionate or most inhumane and cruel? To me indeed he would seem to be savage and made of iron, if he did not lighten his own pain with the pain of the guilty party. It is in this way that we will be regarded as compassionate, if we are [= shall have been] most determined in the case of these men who have wished to butcher us, our wives and our children, who have tried to destroy the homes of each of us and [165] this entire civic dwelling-place; but if we wish [= shall have wished] to be rather indulgent, we shall be regarded as excessively cruel.

For Lentulus gave us to Cethegus to be killed, and the rest of the citizens to Gabinius to be murdered; the city he gave to Cassius to be burned, the whole of Italy to Catiline to be laid waste and torn apart. Lentulus summoned Gauls to subvert [170] the foundations of the state, incited slaves to set the city on fire, and summoned Catiline to lead an army against the city. What is more to be feared than this crime? What less to be ignored than this act of villainy?

Now learn the Learning Vocabulary at *GVE* p. 355.

5D(ii)

Since this is the case, do not be afraid that you may seem to have been too severe in dealing with so appalling a crime as this. You should be much more afraid that [**175**] we may seem to have been cruel to our fatherland by remitting the penalty. This, I say, is more to be dreaded than that we should seem to have been too harsh against our bitterest enemies. But I hear, conscript fathers, the voices of those who seem to be afraid that I may not have enough protection to put your decisions into practice. Everything has been taken care of, prepared, and decided, conscript fathers, with my greatest care [**180**] and diligence and also with the greatest willingness of the Roman people to preserve our supreme power and maintain our common fortunes. All men of every rank are here, of every tribe and finally of every age-group; the forum is packed, so are the temples around the forum, and all the approaches to this temple and area [**185**].

Now learn the Learning Vocabulary at *GVE* p. 356.

5D(iii)

This is the only case in which everyone has the same opinions. For who is there who does not accede to defending the safety of our fatherland and preserving its dignity with passion and commitment? What knight is there, whom this case does not bring to support the harmony of the state? What *tribunus aerarius* is there who does not acquiesce in an equal desire to defend the republic? Who finally is there to whom [**190**] these temples, the sight of the city, the possession of liberty are not both most dear and most sweet and agreeable? There is no slave who does not shudder at the boldness of the citizens, who does not desire this state to remain intact, who is not prepared to defend the safety of the republic as much as he dares and can.

Now learn the Learning Vocabulary at *GVE* p. 357.

5D(iv)

Since this is the case, conscript fathers, the support of the Roman people does not [195] desert you; you must take care not to appear to desert the Roman people. You have a consul ready and willing not to protect his own life but to see to your safety. All ranks agree in mind, will and voice to preserve the republic. Our shared fatherland, besieged by the firebrands and armaments of an impious conspiracy, holds out her hands to you in supplication, to you [200] she entrusts herself, to you she entrusts the life of all her citizens, to you she entrusts the altars of the household gods, to you she entrusts that everlasting flame of Vesta, to you she entrusts the temples of all the gods. Moreover, today you must make judgement about your lives, about the life of your wives and children, and about the fortunes of everyone. You have a leader who has you in mind, but forgets himself. You have all ranks [205], all men, the whole people of Rome, with one and the same attitude. Think on! An empire rooted in such toil, a freedom established by such courage, fortunes increased by such divine benevolence, one night almost destroyed. Today we must see to it that never hereafter could this be brought about by our own citizens. No indeed, you must see to it that [210] never hereafter can this thought even be contemplated by citizens.

Now learn the Learning Vocabulary at *GVE* pp. 358–9.

EXERCISES FOR 5D

Pages 361–2

Exercise

1* *arcessendus* to be summoned; *delendus* to be destroyed; *augendus* to be increased; *proponendus* to be set before; *necandus* to be killed; *dormiendum* it must be slept; *commorandum* it must be delayed; *uerendus* to be feared; *progrediendum* it must be advanced.

2(a) I must take care.
 (b) To destroy the city.
 (c) For the sake of doing the work.

(d)   The general handed over the suppliant to the soldiers to be killed.

(e)   To defend the citadel.

(f)   We had to advance.

(g)   Cicero sees to the safety of the citizens.

(h)   To stretch out the hands.

(i)   For the sake of killing the leader.

(j)   You will have to go.

(k)   Cicero will hand over the conspirators to the guards to be looked after.

(l)   To destroy the altars.

(m)   For the sake of summoning Catiline.

(n)   To preserve the will.

(o)   Lentulus assigned everything to Catiline to be destroyed.

(p)   Carthage must be destroyed.

(q)   The citadel had to be captured.

(r)   Grief is not to be increased.

(s)   Punishment will have to be levied.

(t)   Suppliants must not be handed over.

(u)   You must spare the citizens.

(v)   The citizens were not to be harmed by me.

(w)   All must die.

(x)   Nothing is to be done without reason.

(y)   One must pray that [his] mind is healthy in a healthy body.

(z)   One must speak to no one but to one about to listen.

3*(a)   *mihi abeundum est.*

(b)   *Ciceroni prouidendum erit.*

(c)   *ad concordiam conseruandam.*

(d)   *supplicii sumendi causā/gratiā.*

(e)   *ad ciues arcessendos.*

(f)   *nobis progrediendum erat.*

(g)   *patria nostra conseruanda est.*

(h)   *coniuratores puniendi sunt.*

(i)   *patriae nostrae a nobis nocendum non est.*

(j)   *nulli coniuratori a Cicerone parcendum est.*

Pages 363–4

Exercises

1(a)   I am afraid the city will be set on fire.

(b)   We must take care that the enemy do not enter the city.

(c) There is a danger that a captured suppliant will be killed.
(d) Cicero was afraid that he might not seem to be severe enough.
(e) All ranks were afraid that the impious enemy might capture the city.
(f) There was anxiety that the Vestal Virgins might be distressed.
(g) I am afraid to tell you all this.
(h) Many citizens were afraid that the consul was not angry enough.
(i) Before old age I saw to it that I lived well, in old age that I may die well. However, dying well is dying willingly.

2*(a) *uereor ne fugam ciuium nostrorum uideam.*
  (b) *omnes loqui timebant.*
  (c) *Cicero metuit ut senatus satis seuerus esset.*
  (d) *supplex hostes non timet.*
  (e) *est cura ne pueri interficiantur.*
  (f) *erat periculum ne urbs deleretur.*

Reading exercise / Test exercise

Omitted. This passage is translated in S. A. Handford, *Caesar: The Conquest of Gaul* (Penguin).

**English–Latin

1(a) *supplex manūs tendit ad eos qui misericordes sint.*
  (b) *Lentulus is est quem omnes timeant.*
  (c) *is est qui facinora scelesta committat.*
  (d) *nemo est qui concordiam ordinum omnium non cupiat.*
  (e) *uereor eum qui semper queratur.*

2   *uobis prouidendum est, o patres conscripti, ne populo Romano desitis. ego ad salutem rei publicae defendendam consul paratus sum. omnes ordines consentiunt. seruus est nemo qui ad rem publicam defendendam paratus non sit. patria ipsa manūs supplices uobis tendit. patria uobis defendenda est. omnes timent ne coniuratores alii libertatem nostram deleant. uobis prouidendum est ne hoc umquam posthac fieri possit.*

Pages 365–7

Virgil's Aeneid

Alas, blind intellects of seers! What use are vows to the mad woman, what use are shrines? A soft flame eats away at her marrow

meanwhile, and the silent wound lives in her heart.
Unhappy Dido burns, and wanders through the whole city
          raging, . . .
[10] Now she brings Aeneas with her through the middle of her
          city walls
and shows him the wealth of Sidon and the city she has built,
she begins to speak and stops in the middle of a word;
now as the day slips away she seeks the same feasts,
and again madly demands to hear of the toils at Ilium
[15] and hangs again on the lips of the speaker. . .
Absent she hears and sees him absent,
[20] or in her lap she holds Ascanius, captivated by the likeness to
          his father,
to see if she can beguile her unspeakable passion.
The towers begun do not continue rising, the youth do not train
          in arms,
nor build harbours or ramparts for times of war
secure; the building works interrupted hang idle, as do threatening
[25] great walls and cranes towering up to the sky. . .
With such words she pleaded, and such tears did her most unhappy
sister report back and forth. But he is moved by no
tears nor is he amenable to hearing any words;
the fates stand in the way and the god blocks up the man's ears,
          otherwise ready to yield. . .
No differently is the hero pounded this way and that by her
          persistent words,
and feels the anguish in his great heart;
his mind remains unmoved, [and] his tears roll down in vain.
Then indeed unhappy Dido, terrified by her fate,
[40] begs for death.

Page 368

Res gestae diui Augusti '*The achievements of the divine
Augustus*'

In the consulship of M. Vinicius and Q. Lucretius, and afterwards
in the consulship of P. Lentulus and Cn. Lentulus and for the third
time in the consulship of Paullus Fabius Maximus and Q. Tubero,

although the senate and Roman people agreed that I should be
appointed sole guardian of laws and morals with executive power,
I nevertheless [5] accepted no magistracy contrary to the ancient
custom handed down to us.

5 E *(Text pp. 112–14)*

NOTES FOR 5E

Two points:

(a) Further developments in the use of the perfect participle
     passive ('having been -ed'). See **GVE 163**. A summary of
     participles can be found at **GVE 164**.
(b) *Dum* 'while', 'until', 'provided that', *priusquam/antequam*
     'before', *utpote qui* 'inasmuch as'). See further **GVE 165–6**.

TRANSLATION OF 5E

5E(i)

After the senate agreed with Cato's opinion, Cicero, fearing that
there might be a revolution that night, ordered the triumvirs to
prepare everything which was needed for the execution. While the
triumvirs on his orders were making these preparations, the consul
stationed guards. After the guards had been stationed, he himself
led Lentulus down into [215] the prison. The rest entered the
prison led down by the praetors. There is in the prison a place
called the Tullianum, sunk about twelve feet beneath the ground,
the appearance of which is terrifying, because it has been made
disgusting by neglect, darkness and stench. After being sent down
into that place Lentulus waited there until the executioners who
had been given their orders should garotte him; this [220] eventually they did. Thus that patrician from the illustrious family of the
Cornelii, who had had consular power at Rome, met with a death
worthy of his character and actions. In the same manner, punishment was levied on Cethegus, Statilius and Gabinius.

Now learn the Learning Vocabulary at GVE p. 370.

5E(ii)

While these things were going on at Rome, Catiline drew up two legions out of the whole force which he himself [225] had led and Manlius had had. But out of the whole force, only around a quarter were equipped with military weapons, the rest carried hunting spears or lances or sharpened stakes. But after Antonius began to approach with his army, Catiline, disturbed by the danger, started making his way through the mountains. At one time he moved his camp towards the city, at another towards Gaul [230], but he did not give the enemy the opportunity to fight a battle. He was hoping within a short time to have great forces, provided that his allies at Rome succeeded with their plans. Meanwhile he rejected slaves, fearing that people might think he had shared the cause of citizens with runaways. But after the message had reached the camp that at Rome the conspiracy had been revealed and that Lentulus and the rest of the conspirators [235] had been executed, the majority of those who had joined Catiline for the sake of plunder deserted him. The rest Catiline formed into a column and led over rough mountain terrain by forced marches into the territory of Pistoria, with the intention of escaping unnoticed to transalpine Gaul. But Q. Metellus Celer, sent by the senate, was waiting with three legions in the territory of Picenum [240] for Catiline to move his camp into Gaul. For from the difficulty of the situation, he judged that it would turn out that Catiline would flee into transalpine Gaul before he could be cut off by the Roman legions.

Therefore Metellus, when he had learned of his route from deserters, quickly moved camp and took up position at the very foot of the mountains, where Catiline [245] had to descend as he hurried into Gaul. But Antonius was not far away either since he was following on more level ground. But Catiline, after he saw that he was hemmed in by mountains and enemy troops and that things in the city had gone against him and that there was no hope either of flight or successful defence, decided in these circumstances to test his luck in war and to fight with Antonius as soon as possible [250].

Now learn the Learning Vocabulary at *GVE* p. 371.

EXERCISES FOR 5E

Page 373

Exercises

1   Having delayed (dep.); having been cooked (pass.); having died (dep.); having used (dep.); having been given (pass.); having been helped (pass.); having been aroused (pass.); having been brought (pass.); having been done (pass.); having been recognised (pass.); having tried (dep.); having followed (dep.); having been understood (pass.); having spoken (dep.); having arisen (dep.); having been promised (pass.); having been taken (pass.); having been broken (pass.); having been moved (pass.).

2(a)   Lentulus, seeing the darkness, nevertheless said that he did not fear death.

(b)   The rest followed the guards who had been stationed by the consuls.

(c)   The consul, after much internal debate, had decided to punish them.

(d)   Celer, sent by the senate, was in the territory of Picenum.

(e)   Catiline saw the column drawn up by the consul.

(f)   There was no escape for Catiline, who was cut off by mountains and enemy forces.

3*(a)   *militem captum custodes interfecerunt.*

(b)   *ad agmen uisum Catilina festinauit.*

(c)   *Cicero custodibus dispositis praecepit.*

(d)   *facies agminis instructi duce digna non erat.*

(e)   *milites Catilinae progressi sunt, armis captis usi.*

Page 375

Exercises

1(a)   While the senate was considering the matter, Catiline was drawing up his legions.

(b)   Catiline was waiting until his associates should complete their plans at Rome.

(c)   Before Catiline should go into Gaul, he was awaiting new forces from the city.

(d)   While Catiline stayed near Pistoria, at Rome the conspirators surrendered to Cicero.

(e)   The consul is happy provided the republic is safe.
(f)   All the women love you because you are so handsome.

2*(a)   *dum ea Romae geruntur, Catilina militibus locutus est.*
  (b)   *'manebo' inquit 'dum amici nostri adueniant.'*
  (c)   *'dum salui sint, consilia nostra perfici possunt.'*
  (d)   *'me oportet res quasdam Lentulo narrare, antequam ad Galliam proficiscar.'*
  (e)   *sed dum Catilina loquebatur, consul bellum parabat.*

Page 376

Reading exercise / Test exercise

This is a difficult test exercise. We provide some notes:

1–2   *quem . . . aiebant:* 'Whom they said, as he was *proficiscentem*, was *retractum* [sc. *esse* understood].'

2–3   *se indicaturum* (sc. *esse*): 'that he would give information'.

3   *iussus:* 'ordered'; this picks up *is*, looks forward to *edicere*.

5   *se missum* (*esse*): understand 'he said that'.

6–7   *ne eum terrerent:* 'that the capture . . . should not terrify him'.

7   *properaret:* '[by that much the more] he should hasten'.

8–9   *quo reficeret:* 'in order that he might . . .'

   . . . et illi facilius eriperentur: 'in order that they might be more easily . . .'

This passage is translated in S. A. Handford, *Sallust: The Jugurthine War; the Conspiracy of Catiline* (Penguin).

***English–Latin*

dum Romae hoc supplicium de Lentulo sumitur, Catilina copias instruxit. manebat dum milites a sociis mitterentur. sed postquam nuntiatum est Lentulum mortuum et coniurationem patefactam, iter per montes facere. consul Antonius, a senatu missus qui / eo consilio ut eum in proelio uin-ceret, sequebatur. Metellus quoque castra ab agro Piceno mouit ut Catilinae obsisteret ad Galliam Transalpinam properanti. Catilina, postquam se montibus et copiis hostium clausum esse uidit, proelium quam primum cum Antonio committere constituit, quo spem maiorem militibus daret.

Page 377

Virgil's Aeneid

But Caesar, riding in triple triumph through the Roman
walls, consecrated an immortal vow to the gods of Italy,
three hundred huge shrines throughout the whole city.
The streets resounded with joy, revels and applause;
[5] in all the temples there was a chorus of mothers, in all [temples]
altars;
in front of the altars slaughtered bullocks strewed the earth.
He himself sitting on the white threshold of gleaming Phoebus
reviewed the gifts of the peoples and fitted them to his proud
portals; in marched in long line the conquered tribes,
[10] as diverse in tongue as in the fashion of their clothing and
weapons.

DELICIAE LATINAE: 5E

Page 378

Martial

The book which you are reciting, O Fidentinus, is mine.
    But when you recite it badly, it begins to be yours. (1.38)

You recite nothing, Mamercus, and yet do you wish to appear a
poet?
    Let whatever you want be [so], provided you recite nothing.
(2.88)

Page 379

Vulgate: the birth of Christ

And it happened in those days there came forth an edict from
Caesar Augustus that all the world should be registered. This census
was first performed by Quirinius, governor of Syria; and everyone
went to make their returns to their own cities. And Joseph too

went up from Galilee from the town of Nazareth to Judaea to the city of David, which is called Bethlehem, for the reason, that he was of the house and family of David, to be registered along with his betrothed wife Mary, who was pregnant. And it happened that when they were there, the days were fulfilled that she should give birth. And she brought forth her first-born son and wrapped him in swaddling-clothes and laid him in a manger, because there was no room for them in the inn.

And there were shepherds in that region staying awake and keeping guard by night over their flocks. And behold, an angel of the Lord stood near them and the brightness of God shone around them and they were afraid with a great fear, and the angel said to them, 'Do not be afraid; for lo, I give you good news of a great joy, that shall be for all people; because today is born for you a Saviour who is Christ the Lord, in the city of David. And this is a sign for you: you shall find the infant wrapped in swaddling-bands and placed in a manger.' And suddenly there was with the angel a multitude of the heavenly host, praising God and saying:

'Glory to God in the highest,
  and on earth peace to men of good will.' (Luke 2.1–14)

5 F *(Text pp. 114–16)*

NOTES FOR 5F

There are four main areas of grammar in these two passages:

(a) The perfect subjunctive (*GVE* **167–9, 170–1**.)

(b) Indirect questions ('Catiline explains why he has called the troops together'). See *GVE* **172** (you have already met indirect statements – 'Catiline says that he called the troops together').

(c) Past unreal conditions with pluperfect subjunctive verbs ('If I had ..., x would have ...'). You have already met such conditions with present/imperfect subjunctive verbs ('If I were to ..., x would ...', 'If I were -ing ..., x would be -ing'). See *GVE* **173** (and compare **139.3**).

(d) The new conjunctions *quominus* ('in order that the less ...')

and *quin* ('how not?') with the subjunctive, in expressions
of doubt and prevention. See further **GVE 174**.

TRANSLATION OF 5F

5F(i)

So, calling an assembly, he made a speech like this.

'I know, soldiers, that words do not supply courage nor is an
army made brave instead of cowardly by a commander's speech.
But I shall tell you why I have summoned you and why I am
making a speech. This is why I have called you, to give you some
small pieces of advice and at the same time to reveal the reason for
my tactics. You are at any rate aware, soldiers, of [255] Lentulus'
cowardice. Therefore you know not only how cowardly Lentulus
has been but also how much danger this cowardice has brought to
us. Now indeed, you all know and understand how things stand
with us. For you see not only how many enemies have followed
us, but also what great armies, one from the city, the other from
Gaul, stand in our way. The shortage of grain prevents us from
[260] staying in this region. Wherever we decide to go, there is no
doubt that we must clear the way by the sword. Since you know
this, I advise you to be of brave and ready spirit, and when you
enter battle that you remember what great hope you have placed
in this battle. You must remember that we carry in our right hands
our wealth, our honour, our glory and besides our freedom and
our native land. If [265] we win, there is no doubt that everything
will be secure for us. If we yield through fear, those same things
will be against us. Besides, soldiers, it is not the same necessity that
hangs over us as them. For we are fighting for our native land, our
freedom and our lives, but they for the power of the few. There is
none of you who does not know that our cause is just. Therefore
attack more boldly, remembering [270] your former courage.'

Now learn the Learning Vocabulary at GVE p. 381.

5F(ii)

'The majority of you, if you had not become members of the
conspiracy, would have spent your lives in exile accompanied by

the highest dishonour. Some of you would have been able to live at Rome; but if you had remained there after losing your property, you could have expected nothing but someone else's wealth; you would have done this had not it seemed vile and intolerable to you [275]. You decided instead to follow me. If you wish to succeed, you have need of boldness. For to expect to find safety in flight is really madness.

'When I consider you, soldiers, a great hope of victory takes hold of me. For if you had been cowardly associates, I would never have formed this plan. Your attitude, your age, your courage stop me from despairing and so besides does necessity [280] which makes even the cowardly brave. For fear would often have conquered soldiers, had not necessity forced them to fight. But even if fortune begrudges your courage, beware of losing your lives unavenged, or of being butchered after capture like sheep! Nothing stops you from leaving a bloody and mournful victory to your enemies, if you fight like men! [285]

'You know why I have called you together. After you have entered battle, I shall know whether I have spoken in vain or not.'

Now learn the Learning Vocabulary at *GVE* p. 382.

EXERCISES FOR 5F

Page 384

Exercise

1* *disposuerim, dispositus sim; cohortatus sim; peruenerim; occupauerim; puniuerim, punitus sim; mouerim; usus sim; confecerim; ueritus sim; sumpserim, sumptus sim.*

See *GVE* **167–9** pp. 382–4.

2   Perf. ind.; perf. subj.; fut. perf. ind.; plup. ind.; plup. subj.; fut. perf. ind.; perf. subj.; perf. ind.; perf. subj.; plup. subj.; perf. subj., *or* fut. perf. ind.; perf. subj., *or* fut. perf. ind.; fut. perf. ind.; perf. subj.; perf. ind.; fut. perf. ind.; perf. subj.; perf. subj.; fut. perf. ind.; perf. subj.

Page 385

Exercises

1(a) Do not ask ...
 (b) Fear no battle-line, no battle.
 (c) Do not yield to the enemy.
 (d) Begrudge no one.
 (e) Do not resist.
 (f) Who may have said / may say this to you?

2*(a) *ne audax fuerīs.*
 (b) *ne hoc consilium aperuerīs.*
 (c) *ne te tradiderīs.*
 (d) *ne rei publicae nocuerīs.*
 (e) *ne consulem interfecerīs.*
 (f) *affirmauerit aliquis.*

Pages 386–7

Exercises

1(a) Everyone asks whether Catiline has taken on slaves.
 (b) The consul does not know whether Catiline is going to go towards Rome or Gaul.
 (c) Metellus knew which direction Catiline was going to go in.
 (d) No one knows how many soldiers Manlius had.
 (e) I do not know how much booty Catiline has acquired.
 (f) The citizens ask whether the consul has decided to punish the conspirators.
 (g) Who asked whether Lentulus was cowardly or not?
 (h) Sallust tells us what the Tullianum looked like.
 (i) We all know how many legions Catiline has drawn up.
 (j) The consuls asked whether the forces of Catiline were going to be large.
 (k) I would like to know whether Catiline or the consul is going to win.
 (l) I asked whether Catiline himself had led his soldiers into battle or not.

2(a) You write that you wish to know what is the situation with the republic.

(b) What needs to be done must be learned from the person who is doing it.

(c) We shall consider what he has done, what he is doing and what he is going to do.

(d) Whether I live or die, there is no fear in me.

(e) There is nothing more difficult than to see what is right and proper.

3*(a) *uelim uobis dicere cur conuocati sitis.*

(b) *omnes scitis quam ignauus Lentulus fuerit.*

(c) *ne mihi dixerīs quot hostes nos persequantur.*

(d) *uos hortor ut meminerītis* [or *recordemini*] *quantam spem in hoc proelio posuerītis.*

(e) *rogauerit aliquis cur pugnemus.*

Page 388

1(a) If Lentulus had not been a coward, the republic would have been in great danger.

(b) If the conspirators had had wealth, they would never have joined Catiline.

(c) The soldiers of Catiline would have tried to flee, if necessity had not forced them to fight.

(d) Catiline would have won if fortune had not begrudged him.

(e) If Catiline had had enough grain, he would have decided to stay in the mountains.

2*(a) *uos omnes aetatem in exsilio egissetis, nisi ego hoc consilium cepissem.*

(b) *si Lentulus fortis fuisset, periculum nostrum tantum nunc non esset.*

(c) *si diuitias habuissetis, nunc mecum pugnaretis.*

(d) *Catilina in exsilium abiisset, si ignauiam Lentuli prouidisset.*

(e) *nisi Catilina orationem habuisset, milites eius non sensissent quantum periculum esset.*

Page 390

Exercises

1(a) I am prevented from telling you what Catiline said.

(b) Age does not stop us from continuing the study of other things, and in particular of agriculture.

(c) There is no doubt that Catiline was a conspirator.

(d) You can never prevent me from speaking.

(e) There is no doubt that Fortune begrudged Catiline.
(f) Who would doubt that riches are to be found in virtue?
(g) No one is so old that he does not think that he can live a year [more].
(h) It is not possible for life to be lived happily unless it is lived [i.e. one lives] virtuously.

2*(a) *nihil te impedit quominus dicas.*
 (b) *non dubium est quin hoc uerum sit.*
 (c) *Catilina impeditus est ne a montibus abiret.*
 (d) *necessitudine teneor quominus ceterum exercitum sequar.*
 (e) *nullum dubium erat quin Catilina pugnare cogeretur.*

Reading exercise / Test exercise

Omitted. This passage is translated in S. A. Handford, *Caesar: The Conquest of Gaul* (Penguin).

**English–Latin

'*uidere potestis, milites, quo in periculo res nostrae sint. duo exercitūs nos impediunt ne sine proelio ab his montibus abeamus. nisi Lentulo nixi essemus, iam effugissemus. nunc autem pugnandum est pro patriā, pro libertate, pro uitā. ne ignaui fuerītis. si uicerimus, nullum dubium est quin salus nostra sit. si metu cesserimus, nihil nos impediet quominus trucidemur.*'

Page 392

Virgil's Aeneid

          ... He stood fierce in arms
did Aeneas, rolling his eyes, and checked his right hand;
and now more and more as he delayed, the speech
began to persuade him, when there came into view at the top of
          his [Turnus'] shoulder
[5] the unlucky sword-belt and with its well-known studs there
          shone forth the baldric
of young Pallas, whom, when he had been overcome by a wound,
          Turnus
had laid low and was now sporting it on his shoulders, the insignia
          of his enemy.

He, after he had drunk in with his eyes the reminder of his savage
                                                                grief
and the spoils, consumed with the spirit of vengeance and in anger
[10] terrible: 'Dressed as you are in the spoils of my people,
are you to be snatched from here from me? It is Pallas by this
                                                    wound, it is Pallas
who sacrifices you, and exacts the penalty from your villainous
                                                                blood.'
Saying this, he buried his sword in the breast he faced
hotly; but his [Turnus'] limbs collapsed with the chill
[15] and his life, with a groan, fled complaining down to the
                                                            shadows.

DELICIAE LATINAE: 5F

Page 393

Martial

Why, you ask, Fabullus, does Themison not have
  A wife? He has a sister. (12.20)

Do you ask where you are to keep fish in summer time?
  Keep them in your bathhouse, Caecilianus. (2.78)

5 G   *(Text pp. 116–18)*

NOTES FOR 5G

These three passages present the following four new features:

(a)   The gerund, a noun based on a verb, '-ing', e.g. 'Running
      is good for you' (it has the same form as the gerundive, but
      only neuter singular case-endings). See **GVE 175**.
(b)   Pronoun/adjectives *quisque* ('each'), *quisquam* ('anyone'),
      and *uterque* ('each of two'). See **GVE 176–7**.
(c)   Neuter nouns like *cornu* ('wing of an army', 'horn'). See
      GVE 178.
(d)   Comparative clauses ('just as ...', 'contrary to the way ...',
      'as many ... as', 'as though ...'). See **GVE 179**.

TRANSLATION OF 5G

5G(i)

When he had said this, Catiline waited briefly, ordered the signal to be given and led the army in battle order down onto the plain. Then, removing everyone's horses, so that, danger made equal, the soldiers might have greater courage, he himself on foot [290] drew up the army in accordance with the terrain and his forces. He placed eight cohorts in front, and the standards of the rest he placed in reserve. From them he took the centurions and the pick of the armed soldiers into the front rank. When he had done this, he put Manlius in charge of the right wing and a person from Faesulae in charge of the left [295].

But on the other side, C. Antonius, ill with gout, handed the army over to the officer M. Petreius. He placed the veteran cohorts in front, and behind them the rest of the army in reserve. He himself, going round on horseback, called each and every man by name and gave him encouragement; he asked them to remember that they were fighting against unarmed bandits for their children, their altars and their hearths. As a military professional [300], since he had been in the army for more than thirty years, he knew each soldier and his brave deeds. So by going round and naming each and every one, he fired the spirits of the soldiers. When he had gone round all of them, the soldiers were ready for fighting, for killing and for dying [305].

Now learn the Learning Vocabulary at *GVE* pp. 394–5.

5G(ii)

But when after all the reconnoitring had finished, Petreius gave the signal on the trumpet, he ordered the cohorts to advance little by little. The enemy army did the same. When they had got to a position from which the light-armed soldiers could join battle, each army broke into a run with a very great clamour, standards set for attack. They did not bother with heavy javelins, and the battle was fought with swords. The veterans, remembering their former courage [310], pressed fiercely at close quarters. The enemy without fear resisted them. Fighting continued with extreme violence. Meanwhile Catiline was occupied in the front line with his light-armed soldiers, helped those in trouble, called up fresh men in place of the wounded, anticipated everything, fought a great deal himself, and often struck the enemy; he was performing at the same time the jobs of an energetic soldier and a good general. When Petreius saw that Catiline against his expectations [315] was fighting with great force, he led the praetorian cohort into the middle of the enemy, and having thrown them into confusion, and as different people resisted in different places, killed them. Then he attacked the rest from both flanks. Manlius and the man from Faesulae fell fighting in the front rank. Catiline, after he saw that his troops had been routed and that he was left with only a few men, remembering his birth and former position, ran into the thick [320] of the enemy and there, as he fought, was run through.

Now learn the Learning Vocabulary at GVE p. 396.

5G(iii)

But when the battle was over, then indeed you could see how much boldness and how much resolution there had been in Catiline's army. For almost every place that an individual had taken up in battle while he was alive was covered with his body in death. Nor had anybody died except with a wound in the front. Catiline however was found far from his own men [325] among the corpses of the enemy, still breathing a little and retaining in his expression the ferocity of spirit he had had when he was alive. Finally, from the whole force, neither in the battle nor in the flight, was any free-born citizen taken prisoner [330].

But neither had the army of the Roman people gained a happy or bloodless victory. For all the most energetic soldiers had either died in battle or had left the field seriously wounded. However, many people who had come out from the camp to look or to take spoils, as they turned over the bodies of the enemy, found some a friend, others a guest or a near relative. There were likewise those who recognised their enemies. Thus diversely through the whole army happiness [335], sadness, grief and joy were experienced.

Now learn the Learning Vocabulary at GVE p. 397.

EXERCISES FOR 5G

Pages 399–400

Exercise

1*   *exoriundum* rising up; *dormiendum* sleeping; *petendum* seeking;
        noscendum getting to know; *fugiendum* escaping; *commorandum*
        delaying; *tenendum* holding; *eundum* going.

For declension, see **GVE 175** p. 398.

2(a)   For using.
 (b)   For the sake of going.
 (c)   By departing.
 (d)   For the sake of resisting.
 (e)   For wounding.
 (f)   By seeing.
 (g)   For the sake of rolling.

3*(a) *ad uulnerandum / uulnerandi causā.*
 (b)   *commorandi causā / ad commorandum.*
 (c)   *tenendo.*
 (d)   *oriundi gratiā.*
 (e)   *ad succurrendum / succurrendi causā.*
 (f)   *petendi.*
 (g)   *faciendo/gerundo/gerendo.*

4(a)   To wound the soldiers (gerundive).
 (b)   I must go (gerundive).
 (c)   For the purpose of advancing (gerund).
 (d)   By naming the soldiers (gerundive).
 (e)   By resisting bravely (gerund).
 (f)   To turn over the bodies (gerundive).
 (g)   The fit had to help the injured (gerundive).
 (h)   The consul handed the conspirators over to the praetors to be
        punished (gerundive).
 (i)   For the sake of departing (gerund).
 (j)   To draw up the army (gerundive).
 (k)   The mind of man is nourished by learning and thinking
        (gerund).
 (l)   Nothing is so difficult that it cannot be discovered by enquiry
        (gerund).

Pages 401–2

Exercises

1(a)   All the worst men support the conspiracy.
 (b)   All the most stupid men can understand these things.
 (c)   Nor did anyone dare to say this.
 (d)   And he forbids everyone to kill anyone.
 (e)   In every art all the best qualities are extremely rare.
 (f)   The remedies of each of the two types of fortune.
 (g)   You seem to me to be going to do both things.
 (h)   Either no one or, if anyone, *he* was a wise man.
 (i)   Everyone was speaking to the people on his own behalf.
 (j)   Nor does anyone from so great a column dare to approach the man.

2*(a)   *optimus quisque hostibus suis resistit.*
 (b)   *nec quemquam uulneratum in proelium imperator misit.*
 (c)   *milites hortabatur utriusque exercitus imperator.*
 (d)   *non potest quicquam boni dicere.*
 (e)   *Petreius unum quemque hortabatur.*
 (f)   *facta cuiusque narrando milites hortabatur.*

Pages 403–4

Exercises

1(a)   Catiline acted differently from the way Petreius had expected.
 (b)   Gabinius was as cowardly as Lentulus.
 (c)   Manlius acted exactly as he had been ordered.
 (d)   Things happened opposite to what Petreius had expected.
 (e)   He is talking as though he were a fool.

2*(a)   Nothing is so to be feared by a man as envy.
 (b)   Nothing is so deceptive as human life, nothing so dangerous.
 (c)   There are as many opinions as there are humans.
 (d)   The majority of people want to have the sort of friend they themselves cannot be.
 (e)   Babies lie as though they were completely devoid of life.

3*(a)   *hic uir tam bonus est quam ille.*
 (b)   *filius meus contra ac uolo agit.*
 (c)   *tu talis es qualis pater tuus.*
 (d)   *aliter ac ei imperatum est agit.*

(e)   *perinde ac praeceperis sic agam.*
(f)   *ambulabat quasi uulneratus esset.*

Reading exercise / Test exercise

Omitted. *De senectute* can be found translated in M. Grant, *Cicero: Selected Works* (Penguin); *Fasti* can be found in J. G. Frazer, *Ovid: Fasti* (Loeb series, Heinemann–Harvard, 1931).

Page 407

English–Latin

confecto proelio, multa cadauera cerneres illic. uideri poterat etiam quanta audacia Catilinae et exercitui infuisset. quem locum quisque pugnando ceperat, eo conciderat. nec quisquam fugerat. Catilina, qui in medios hostes celeriter moriendi causā incurrerat, longe a suis repertus est. quam uultūs ferociam uiuus habebat etiam retinebat. sed Romanis uictoria laeta non erat. nam optimus quisque aut mortuus erat aut grauiter uulneratus. ii qui spoliandi gratiā processerant cadauera uoluentes non solum hostes sed etiam amicos cognatosque reperiebant. ita illā nocte in castris agitabantur et laetitia et luctus.

DELICIAE LATINAE: 5G

Page 407

Martial

Why do I not send you my books, Pontilianus?
  In case, Pontilianus, you send me *yours*. (7.3)

Page 408

Tomorrow, you keep saying, Postumus, it's tomorrow that you'll
                                                      start living.
  Tell me, Postumus, when is that 'tomorrow' of yours coming?
How far off is that 'tomorrow' of yours? Where is it? Or where
                                          ought we to look for it?
  Can it be hiding among the Parthians and Armenians?
Already that 'tomorrow' of yours is as old as Priam or Nestor.
  Tell me, how much can that 'tomorrow' of yours be bought
                                                          for?

You will live tomorrow: it's already too late, Postumus, to start
living today.
The wise man, Postumus, is he who lived *yesterday*. (5.58)

On the tombs of seven husbands the infamous Chloe has inscribed:
'She did [them: i.e. the murders; but it also means 'she made it',
i.e. the tomb].' What could be franker? (9.15)

The Vulgate: the wise judgement of Solomon

Then there came two prostitutes to the king, and they stood in his
presence. One of them said, 'I beg you, my Lord; this woman and I
were living in one house and I gave birth in it in the bedroom.
The third day after I gave birth, she also gave birth; and we were
together, and no one else was with us in the house, except the two
of us. But this woman's son died during the night, since she
crushed it while she slept. And getting up in the silence of the dead
of the night, she took my son from my side, your maidservant,
while I slept and placed him in her bosom: her son, who was dead,
she placed in my bosom. And when I had arisen early to give my
son milk, he appeared dead; but looking more closely in broad
daylight, I realised that it was not mine, the one I had given birth
to.'
   The other woman replied, 'It is not the way you say, but your
son is dead, and mine is alive.' In reply, the other said, 'You are
lying; since my son is alive, and your son is dead.' And in this way
they squabbled in front of the king.
   Then the king said, 'Bring me a sword.' And when they had
brought a sword into the king's presence, he said, 'Divide the living
infant into two parts and give half to one and half to the other.'
   The woman whose son was alive said to the king (for her heart
was moved for her son), 'I beg you, Lord, give her the living child,
and do not kill him.' In reply she [the other woman] said, 'Let
neither she nor I have him: but let him be killed.' The king replied
and said, 'Give to this woman the living child, and let it not be
killed: for this is his mother.' And so all Israel heard the judgement
which the king had made and they feared the king, seeing that the
wisdom of God was in him for making judgements. (1 Kings
3.16ff = Vulgate III Kings 3.16ff.)

Section Six
Poetry and politics:
Caesar to Augustus

6 A *High life and society (Text pp. 119–25)*

GENERAL NOTE

Everything you read from now on is unadapted. Notes on grammar, and difficult expressions and background information, follow each Running Vocabulary. There are grammar sections and exercises on metre. We have produced selected answers to these exercises below.

As far as literary interpretation and stylistics is concerned, instead of giving selective commentary as on earlier sections, we give here short bibliographies.

General

Peter Jones, *Classics in Translation*, Duckworth 1998.
Peter Jones, *An Intelligent Person's Guide to Classics*, Duckworth 1999.
J. Henderson and M. Beard, *Classics: A Very Short Introduction*, Oxford University Press 1995.
S. Hornblower and A. Spawforth (eds.), *The Oxford Classical Dictionary* (third edition), Oxford University Press 1996.

Section 6A: Catullus

Daniel H. Garrison, *The Student's Catullus* (Oklahoma Series in Classical Culture No. 5), Norman University of Oklahoma Press 1989.

K. Quinn, *Catullus: The Poems*, London 1970 (revised edn 1973).
Guy Lee, *The Poems of Catullus*, Oxford University Press 1990.

TRANSLATION OF 6A

6A(i)

You will dine well, my Fabullus, at my house
in a few days, gods willing,
if you bring with you a good, big
dinner, not forgetting a pretty girl,
[5] wine, wit and all the giggles.
As I say, if you bring this, my charmer,
you will dine well; for your Catullus'
little purse is full of cobwebs.
But in return you will get unmixed passion,
[10] or whatever is sweeter or classier:
for I shall give you a perfume which my girl
was given by Venuses and Cupids,
and when you smell it, you will ask the gods
to make you all, Fabullus, nose.

Now learn the Learning Vocabulary at *GVE* p. 411.

6A(ii)

Marrucinus Asinius, your left hand
you do not use agreeably: over jokes and wine
you lift the linen of the rather negligent.
Do you think this is witty? You're wrong, idiot:
[5] it's ever such a cheap and tasteless trick.
You don't believe me? Believe Pollio,
your brother, who even if it cost him a million,
would like to reform your larceny: for he's
a lad stuffed full of charm and wit.
[10] And so it's either three hundred insulting verses
you can expect or you can return my linen,
which does not bother me in terms of its value,
but is a souvenir of a good old pal of mine.
For they were Spanish towels from Saetabis

[15] that were sent to me as a gift by Fabullus
and Veranius: I've got to love these towels
as much as my little Veranius and Fabullus.

Now learn the Learning Vocabulary at *GVE* p. 412.

6A(iii)

Yesterday, Licinius, at leisure
we played around a lot on my writing-tablets,
writing gay verse, as we'd agreed:
as each of us wrote short poems,
[5] we played around in different metres,
capping each other over our jokes and wine.
And from there I went away, by your charm
so inflamed, Licinius, and by your wit,
that food did not help me, poor thing,
[10] nor did sleep close my eyes in rest,
but overwhelmed by passion on the whole bed
I tossed about, longing to see the day,
so that I could talk to you and be together with you.
But when my limbs exhausted with my efforts
[15] lay half-dead on my little bed,
this was the poem I wrote for you, my dear boy,
so that you could understand from it my anguish.
Now take care not to be contemptuous, and as for my prayers,
please take care not to throw them back in my face, apple of my
                                                                eye,
[20] in case Nemesis demands poetic justice from you.
She's a violent goddess: take care not to cross her.

Now learn the Learning Vocabulary at *GVE* p. 413.

6A(iv)

Let us live, my Lesbia, and let us love,
and as for the rumours spread by joyless old men,
let's rate them all at precisely one penny.
Suns can set and return:
[5] for us when once our brief light is set,
we must sleep through one unending night.

Give me a thousand kisses, then a hundred,
then another thousand, then a second hundred,
then another thousand without a break, then a hundred,
[10] then, when we've racked up many thousands,
we'll make a shambles of the abacus's account, so we don't know
nor can any begrudger cast the evil eye on us,
knowing as he will the size of the kiss-account.

Now learn the Learning Vocabulary at *GVE* p. 414.

6A(v)

You ask, how many osculations for me
from you, Lesbia, would be enough and more.
As many as the grains of Libyan sand
that lie in silphium-bearing Cyrene
[5] between the oracle of sweltering Jupiter
and ancient Battus' sacred tomb;
or as many as the stars, in the silence of the night,
that see the secret love affairs of men:
to kiss you so many times
[10] is enough and more for crazed Catullus,
a number of kisses which snoopers could not count
nor an evil tongue bewitch.

Now learn the Learning Vocabulary at *GVE* p. 415.

6A(vi)

Poor Catullus, you should stop making a fool of yourself,
and what you see is dead and gone consider lost.
There shone once for you bright rays of sun,
when you used to follow wherever the girl led,
[5] loved by me as no woman will be loved.
Then, when those many amusing things occurred
that you wanted and the girl did not refuse,
truly the rays of sun shone bright for you.
Now she no longer wants all this: you too, powerless as you are,
refuse it,
[10] and do not pursue one who is in flight, do not live in misery,
but stubborn of heart, hang on, be firm.

Farewell, girl. Now Catullus is firm,
he won't seek out or ask for you, when you don't want him.
But you will be sorry, when you are not asked for at all.
[15] Bitch, that's your lot – what life remains for you?
Who will approach you now? Who will think you pretty?
Whom will you now love? Whose girl will you be called?
Whom will you be kissing? Whose lips will you be biting?
But you, Catullus, be stubborn and be firm.

Now learn the Learning Vocabulary at *GVE* pp. 416–17.

6A(vii)

Furius and Aurelius, colleagues of Catullus,
whether he finds a passage to furthest India,
where by the far-resounding eastern waves
   the shore is pounded,
[5] or to the Hyrcanians or the effeminate Arabs,
or to the Sagae or the Parthians with their arrows,
or to the plains that the seven-mouthed
   Nile discolours,
or crosses the lofty Alps,
[10] touring great Caesar's monuments,
the ghastly river Rhine in Gaul, and furthest Britain,
[you colleagues] ready to try all this with him
(whatever the will of the gods shall bring)
[15] give a short message to my girl,
   not pleasant words.
Let her live and fare well with her gigolos,
three hundred of whom she holds in one embrace,
never with real love, but time and again,
   [20] bursting everyone's balls;
let her not count on my love as she did before,
which thanks to her has fallen like, on a meadow's
edge, a flower, after by a passing
   plough it has been touched.

Now learn the Learning Vocabulary at *GVE* pp. 418–19.

EXERCISES FOR 6A*

Page 419

Text, pp. 119–20 (hendecasyllables)

cēnābis bene, mī Fabull[e] apud mē
paucīs, sī tibi dī fauent, diēbus,
sī tēc[um] attuleris bon[am] atque magnam
cēnam, nōn sine candidā puellā
et uīnō [e]t sal[e] et omnibus cachinnīs.   5
haec sī, [i]nqu[am], attuleris, uenuste noster,
cēnābis bene; nam tuī Catullī
plēnus sacculus est arāneārum.
sed contrā [a]ccipiēs merōs amōrēs
seu quid suāuius ēlegantiusu[e] est: 10
n[am] unguentum dabo, quod meae| puellae
dōnārunt Venerēs Cupīdinēsque,
quod tū c[um] olfaciēs, deōs|rogābis,
tōt[um] ut tē faciant, Fabulle, nāsum.

Page 420

Text, p. 124 (Scazon)

miser Catulle, dēsinās ineptīre,
et quod uidēs perīsse perditum dūcās.
fulsēre quondam candidī |tibī sōlēs,
cūm uēntitābās quō puella dūcēbat
amāta nōbīs quant[um] amābitur nūlla.   5

ib[i] illa multa cum iocōsa fīēbant,

quae tū uolēbās nec puella nōlēbat,

fulsēre uērē candidī tibī sōlēs.

nunc i[am] illa nōn uolt: tū quoqu[e] inpotēns nōlī,

nec quae fugit sectāre, nec miser uīue,   10

sed obstinātā mente perfer, obdūrā.

ualē, puella. iam Catullus obdūrat,

nec tē requīret nec rogābit inuītam.

at tū dolēbis, cum rogāberis nūlla.

scelesta, uae tē, quae tibī manet uīta?   15

quis nunc t[e] adībit? cuī uidēberis bella?

quem nunc amābis? cuius esse dīcēris?

quem bāsiābis? cuī labella mordēbis?

at tū, Catulle, dēstinātus obdūrā.

Page 421

Text, *pp. 124–5 (Sapphics)*

Fūr[i] et Aurēlī, comitēs Catullī,

sīu[e] in extrēmōs penetrābit Indōs,

lītus ut longē resonant[e] Eōā

    tunditur undā,

sīu[e] in Hyrcānōs Arabasue mollīs,   5

seu Sagās sagittiferōsue Parthōs,

sīue quae septemgeminus colōrat

    aequora Nīlus,

sīue trāns altās gradiētur Alpēs,

Caesaris uīsēns monimenta magnī,   10

Gallicum Rhēn[um] horribil[e] aequor ulti-

    mōsque Britannōs,

omni[a] haec, quaecumque feret uoluntās

caelitum, temptāre simul parātī,

pauca nūntiāte meae puellae   15

    nōn bona dicta.

cum suīs uīuat ualeatque moechīs,

quōs simul complexa tenet trecentōs,

nūll[um] amāns uērē, sed identid[em] omni[um]

    īlia rumpēns;   20

nec meum respectet, ut ant[e], amōrem,

quī [i]llius culpā cecidit uelut prāt[i]

ultimī flōs, praetereunte postquam

    tāctus arātr[o] est.

6B   49: Cicero, Caelius and the approach of civil war
(Text pp. 126–34)

READING FOR 6B: CICERO AND CAELIUS

D. R. Shackleton Bailey, *Cicero's Letters to His Friends*, Harmondsworth (Penguin) 1978 (Volume I).

TRANSLATION OF 6B

6b(i)

Caelius says good health to Cicero.
Rome, 703 from the city's foundation.

As I left, I promised that I would inform you most conscientiously
about everything happening in Rome. I have taken so much
trouble over this that I am afraid that the effort I have put in may
seem too long-winded; nevertheless, I know how inquisitive you

are and how pleased all ex-pats are to find out even the smallest detail of [5] what is going on at home. However in this case I beg you not to condemn me for uppishness in the performance of this duty; for I have delegated this task to someone else, not that it's not a very agreeable occupation for me to put some effort into remembering you, but the actual roll which I have sent you excuses me easily enough, I think. I don't know who would have the leisure not only to put these things on paper but to take any notice of them at all; [10] for here are all of the decrees of the senate, edicts, stories and gossip. If this collection by chance does not please you, let me know so that I don't bore you and cause myself vast expense at the same time. For, if anything rather more important happens in public affairs which these journeymen are not qualified to follow up, I will write a careful account for you of how it happened, what view was taken of it, [15] and what people think the consequences will be. As things stand, there's nothing much in the wind at the moment.

Now learn the Learning Vocabulary at *GVE* p. 422.

6B(ii)

If you ran into Pompey, as you wanted to, make sure you write to tell me how he seemed to you and what he said to you and the disposition he revealed (for he usually thinks one thing and says another). As for Caesar, the gossip about him is rife and not [20] pretty, but it's only rumour-mongers who arrive here. One says that Caesar has lost his cavalry (this, I think, is certainly false); another says that the seventh legion has taken a drubbing, and that he himself is cut off from the rest of the army and is being besieged by the Bellovaci; up to now nothing is certain, but neither are these uncertainties a matter of public discussion but [25] are told only as open secrets among a few of your acquaintances.

Now learn the Learning Vocabulary at *GVE* p. 423.

6B(iii)

Marcus Cicero proconsul says good health to Marcus Caelius.

Come off it – do you think this was what I told you to do, to write down for me the gladiatorial matches, the adjourned court-appearances and all the things that no one would dare tell me when I am at Rome? I am not even interested in you writing to me [30] the daily events of the greatest importance to the state, unless they are going to have something to do with me personally; others will write about them, many will tell me, and even rumour itself will waft much of this in my direction. That's the reason that it's not the past or present I'm expecting from you but, as befits a man who can see a long way ahead, the future, so that when I have observed the ground-plan of the state from your pen, [35] I can know what sort of building is under construction.

I have spent a few days with Pompey discussing nothing else but the state; these things cannot be written down, nor should they be. Be assured of this alone, that Pompey is an outstanding citizen, mentally and strategically prepared for all the state's contingencies. So give yourself to [40] the man; he will warmly welcome you, believe me. Pompey's view about who individual good and bad citizens are is the same as ours is accustomed to be.

Now learn the Learning Vocabulary at GVE p. 424.

6B(iv)

Caelius to Cicero good health.

In almost every letter I have written to you about the panthers. It will be a disgrace on you if Patiscus has sent ten panthers to Curio and you don't send many times more; these very beasts Curio has given to me as a gift, plus another ten from Africa. If only you can remember and send for beasts from Cibyra and also [45] send a letter to Pamphilia (they say that more panthers are captured there), you will achieve what you want. I'm putting all the more effort into this at the present, because I think I'm going to have to make all the arrangements without the help of my colleague [in office]. Please give yourself this instruction. In this business all you have to do is say the word, that is, give an order and an instruction. For, as soon as they are captured, you have got people to feed and transport them; I think that I'll [50] also send some other people there too, if your letter to me raises my hopes.

Now learn the Learning Vocabulary at GVE p. 425.

6B(v)

Marcus Cicero general says good health to Marcus Caelius, curule aedile.

The panther business is being diligently pursued on my orders by those who usually hunt them. But there is an astonishing shortage of panthers, and those which there are are said to be complaining bitterly that no one in my province is threatened with capture except them. And so the panthers are said to have decided to leave our province for Caria. **[55]** None the less, we're working hard on the problem, particularly Patiscus. You will have what there is; but obviously I don't know what that amounts to.

I'd like you to write to me as carefully as possible about the whole political situation. For I shall consider my most reliable information what I get from you.

Now learn the Learning Vocabulary at *GVE* p. 426.

6B(vi)

Caelius to Cicero good health.

On the subject of high politics, I've often written to you that I don't see peace lasting a year, **[60]** and the nearer that conflict comes (and it inevitably will come) the more obvious the danger appears. This is going to be the subject of the dispute between those in power. Pompey has decided not to allow Caesar to be elected to a second consulship unless he hands over his army and his provinces; but Caesar is persuaded that he cannot be secure if **[65]** he leaves his army. The condition he makes is that both should hand over their armies. In this way that love affair of theirs and their odious intercourse have not issued in clandestine back-biting but have erupted into war. I can't hit upon the strategy to pursue; and I don't doubt that you'll have the same trouble making this decision.

In this dispute I can see that Pompey is going to have the senate and the jurors **[70]** with him, while everyone who lives in fear or with bad hopes for the future will flock to Caesar's side; his army does not bear comparison. All in all, there is enough time to take stock of the forces of each man and choose one's side.

To sum up, you ask what I think will happen. If one or the other of them does not go to the Parthian war, I see great divisions looming [75] which will be judged by violence and the sword; both men are prepared, mentally and materially. If this could happen without danger to you, Lady Luck is rehearsing a block-busting, fun-filled spectacular.

Now learn the Learning Vocabulary at GVE p. 428.

6B(vii)

Caelius to Cicero good health.

Upset by your letter, in which you showed that you have nothing but negative thoughts, I am writing to you at once.

[80] I beg and beseech you, by your fortunes, Cicero, and by your children, not to make any irrevocable decisions about your well-being and safety. For I call gods and men and our friendship to witness that I told you beforehand and gave you a warning that was not equivocal but straight down the line, after meeting Caesar and finding out what his feelings would be when he had won. If [85] you think that Caesar will adopt the same tactics in letting his enemies go and offering terms, you are wrong. His words and attitudes are nothing but fierce and unyielding. He left the senate in a rage, and was clearly infuriated by these vetoes; there will be no place, I tell you, for any mediation.

If I can't persuade you completely, at least wait until [90] we know how we are doing in Spain; I can tell you that when Caesar comes it will be ours. What hope your side will have when Spain is lost, I have no idea; moreover, what your strategy is in going over to the side of the hopeless I swear escapes me completely.

What you conveyed to me without actually saying it, Caesar had heard and as soon as he had said 'Hullo' to me, he told me what he had heard about you. I said I [95] wasn't aware of that, but nevertheless I asked him to send a letter to you in terms best calculated to persuade you to stay put. He's taking me with him to Spain; for if he hadn't been doing that, I would have come running to you, wherever you might be, before returning to Rome and in person would have asked you to do this and would have held you back with all my might.

[100] Again and again, Cicero, think before you utterly destroy yourself and all your family, and despite your full understanding of the present and future dive into a situation from which you can see that there is no escape. But if either the words of the optimates worry you or you cannot bear the insolence and vanity of certain parties, I think you should choose some town not involved in the war while these things are resolved; [105] they will soon be settled. If you do this, I will judge you to have acted wisely, and you will not upset Caesar.

Now learn the Learning Vocabulary at *GVE* p. 429.

6B(viii)

Marcus Cicero general says good health to Marcus Caelius.

I would like you to believe this, that I look for nothing from this unhappy situation except for people at some time or other to realise that I wanted nothing more than peace, and when that was impossible, that I shunned nothing so much as civil war. I [110] do not think that I shall ever regret this resolve of mine. For I remember in this connection that my old friend Q. Hortensius used to boast that he had never been involved in civil war. But the praise I shall gain will be more glorious than this, because in his case it was put down to cowardice, and I don't think that could possibly be thought about me.

Nor am I frightened by the considerations which you most loyally and [115] affectionately set before me to scare me. For there is no anguish which does not seem to hang over everyone in this world-wide chaos. I would have been only too willing to sacrifice my private and domestic convenience to save the state from this.

So I am not waiting for the outcome in Spain nor [120] am I making any clever calculations. If the state survives, there will undoubtedly be a place for me in it; but if it doesn't, you yourself, I think, will arrive in the same lonely places as those in which you will hear that I have settled. But this is perhaps a gloomy prophecy and there will be a better outcome to all of this. For I can remember the despair of those who were old men during my youth. Perhaps I am imitating them now, and falling into the vice of old age. [125] I would wish it to be so; however...

This will be my final word: I shall not stir things up or act rashly. However, I beg you, wherever I end up, to look after me and my children in the way our friendship and your loyalty shall demand.

Now learn the Learning Vocabulary at GVE p. 431.

6C *The end of the civil war: the battle of Pharsalus*
(Text pp. 135–41)

READING FOR 6C: CAESAR'S *CIVIL WAR*

John Marshall Carter, *Julius Caesar: The Civil War, Book III*, Warminster (Aris & Phillips) 1993
Jane F. Mitchell, *Caesar: The Civil War*, Harmondsworth (Penguin) 1967

TRANSLATION OF 6C

6c(i)

When he was encouraging his army for battle in the normal military way, he mentioned particularly that he could use his soldiers as witnesses to the enthusiasm with which he had sought peace; he had never spilt the blood of his soldiers idly, nor had he wished to deprive the state of either of the two armies. When he had finished this speech, [5] on the request of his soldiers, burning with desire for battle, he gave the signal on the trumpet.

In Caesar's army there was a recalled veteran named Crastinus, a man of outstanding courage. When the signal had been given he said 'Follow me, and give your general the service you have promised. This is the last and final battle; when it is done, [10] he will recover his position and we our liberty.' At the same time, looking at Caesar, he said 'Commander, today I will make you thank me, whether I live or die.' When he had said this, he was the first to run forward from the right wing, with many soldiers following.

Now learn the Learning Vocabulary at GVE p. 432.

6c(ii)

Between the two lines of battle there was enough space left [15] for both sides to charge. But Pompey had told his men to wait for Caesar's attack and not to move from their position and to let Caesar's battle-line be extended; for in this way he hoped that it would turn out that the first charge and impact of the soldiers would be broken and their line stretched. At the same time, with their approach-run doubled, Caesar's soldiers would be out of breath and overcome with exhaustion. This, in [20] my opinion, was irrational. For there is a certain eagerness and alacrity which everyone has by nature, which is fired up by the desire for battle. Commanders ought not to repress but to encourage it.

But when the signal was given and our soldiers had charged with their javelins at the ready and [25] had noticed that Pompey's men were not charging, being experienced and trained by previous conflicts, they checked their advance of their own accord and stopped almost in the middle of the space so as not to approach with their energy drained, and leaving a small interval and then resuming their advance they threw their heavy javelins and quickly, as they had been ordered by [30] Caesar, drew their swords. But the soldiers of Pompey were quite up to this. They picked up the weapons which had been hurled and withstood the legions' charge; they kept their formation, threw their javelins and drew their swords. At the same time the whole body of cavalry on Pompey's left wing advanced as they had been ordered, and the whole mass of archers poured forward. [35] Our cavalry did not withstand their attack but little by little, pushed from its position, withdrew, and because of this Pompey's cavalry began to press more keenly and to deploy themselves in squadrons and to start surrounding our battle-line on the open flank. When Caesar noticed this, he gave the signal to the fourth battle-line.

They quickly advanced and with their standards set for battle put such force into [40] charging Pompey's cavalry that none of them held their ground and turning tail to a man not only abandoned their position but immediately retreated and made in flight for the highest mountains. When they were out of the way, all the archers and slingers were killed, since they had been left unarmed and without any protection. In the same attack, the cohorts surrounded the left wing while the Pompeians were still fighting in the battle-line and [45] resisting, and attacked them from the rear. At the same time, Caesar ordered the third line to advance; the Pompeians could not withstand their attack and all turned their backs in flight.

Now learn the Learning Vocabulary at GVE p. 433.

6c(iii)

After Caesar took possession of the camp he urged his soldiers not to let slip the opportunity of finishing off the business because they were taken up with plundering. When they had agreed, [50] he began to build a fortification around the hill. Because the hill was without water, the Pompeians had no confidence in their position, so left it and everyone began to retreat towards Larisa on the mountain ridges. Caesar, observing their intentions, divided his troops and ordered some of the legions to remain in Pompey's camp, sent some back to his own camp, and taking four legions with him by a more convenient route [55] began to intercept the Pompeians and after advancing six miles drew up his battle-line. When they realised this, the Pompeians took up position on a certain hill. A river ran round the bottom of this hill. Caesar encouraged his troops, even though they were exhausted by the whole day's unceasing efforts and night was already coming on, and still cut the river off from the hill with a fortification to prevent the Pompeians from being able to get water by night. [60] When the fortification was finished, the Pompeians sent ambassadors and began to negotiate surrender. A few senators who had joined them sought safety at night by escaping.

Now learn the Learning Vocabulary at GVE pp. 434–5.

6c(iv)

At dawn Caesar ordered all those who had taken up position on the hill to come down to the plain from the higher places and to throw down their arms. [65] When they had done this without demur, and with hands outstretched had thrown themselves to the ground and weeping had begged him to save them, he consoled

them and told them to get up and after saying a few words to them
about his clemency, to make them less afraid, he spared them all
and told his own soldiers that none of them should be mistreated
or have any of their property confiscated. When due care had been
given to this matter, he ordered **[70]** the other legions to join him
from the camp and the ones he had brought with him to go off
duty in turn and to go back to the camp. On the same day, he
reached Larisa.

Now learn the Learning Vocabulary at *GVE* p. 435.

6D *Four Roman poets (Text pp. 142–53)*

READING FOR 6D

6D(i): Lucretius

C. D. N. Costa, Lucretius, *De Rerum Natura*, Book v, Oxford
University Press 1984
R. E. Latham, *Lucretius on the Nature of the Universe*, Harmonds-
worth (Penguin) 1951

6D(ii): Virgil

R. D. Williams, *The Aeneid of Virgil, Books 1–6*, London 1972
David West, *Virgil: The Aeneid*, Harmondsworth (Penguin) 1990

6D(iii): Horace

K. Quinn, *Horace: The Odes*, London 1980
D. A. West, *The Complete Odes and Epodes*, Oxford 1997.

6D(iv): Ovid

Guy Lee, *Ovid's Amores*, London 1968

TRANSLATION OF 6D

6D(i) Titus Lucretius Carus

Besides, they could see that the workings of the heavens and
the different seasons of the year came round in fixed order
nor were they able to work out for what reasons this happened.

Therefore, they made a refuge for themselves by handing over
everything to the gods
[5] and making everything controlled at their command.
They located the dwellings and haunts of the gods in the sky,
because the night and moon seemed to roll along through the sky,
moon, day, and night and night's stern standards,
and night-wandering torches of the heavens, flying flames,
[10] clouds, sun, showers, snow, winds, lightning, hail,
and swift growls and great murmurings of [divine] threats.

    O unhappy human race, when such deeds to the gods
it assigned and added bitter fits of anger!
What lamentations they themselves engendered for themselves,
and what traumas for us,
[15] and what tears [they engendered] for our descendants.
Nor is there any respect for the gods in being often seen with
covered head
to turn towards the [sacred] stone and to approach all the altars,
nor in bowing down prostrate on the earth and holding out the
palms of the hands
before the temples of the gods nor in sprinkling altars with copious
blood
[20] of four-footed beasts nor in stringing together vow upon vow,
but rather in being able to observe everything with tranquil mind.

Now learn the Learning Vocabulary at *GVE* p. 438.

6D(ii) Publius Vergilius Maro

They walked in darkness under the lonely night through the
shadow
and through the empty halls of Dis and the desolate kingdoms:
as in a flickering moon under sinister light
people walk in the woods, when the sky is hidden in shadow
[5] by Jupiter, and black night has drained the colour from the
world.

....

From here is the road that leads to the waters of Tartarean
Acheron.

Here a whirlpool thick with mud and a vast vortex
[30] boils, and belches all its sand into Cocytus.
The terrifying ferryman guards these waters and rivers,
Charon, in awful filth, on whose chin enormous amounts of
white hair lie untrimmed, his eyes stand out with flame,
a filthy cloak hangs by a knot from his shoulders.
[35] He in person punts the raft with a pole, and tends to the sails
and conveys the corpses in his rust-coloured skiff,
already getting on in years, but a god's old age is youthful and
green.
To this point the whole crowd was rushing, streaming towards the
banks,
mothers and husbands and bodies, deprived of life,
[40] of great-hearted heroes, boys and unmarried girls,
and youths placed on pyres before their parents' eyes:
as many as, in the woods in the first frost of autumn,
the leaves which fall slipping from the trees, or as many as the birds
which flock
to land from the deep sea, when the cold year
[45] chases them off across the sea and sends them to sunny lands.
They stood begging to be the first to cross,
and stretched forth their hands in longing for the further bank.
But the grim sailor takes now these, now those,
but others, moved well away, he keeps from the sandy shore.
....

[50] 'Others will beat bronze to breathe more softly
(I truly believe this), and will draw faces that live from marble,
they will plead causes better, and as for the wanderings of the
heaven
they will trace them with a rod and predict the risings of the
stars:
You, Roman, remember you must rule the peoples in your empire
[55] (these will be your arts), you must impose a pattern upon
peace,
and you must spare the defeated and war down the proud.'

Now learn the Learning Vocabulary at *GVE* p. 441.

6D(iii) Quintus Horatius Flaccus

The snows have dispersed, the grass is now returning to the fields
    and to the trees their leaves;
the earth is making its accustomed changes, and, as they go down,
    rivers flow between their banks;
[5] the Grace with the nymphs and her twin sisters dares
    to lead the dances naked.
You should not hope for immortality, warns the year and
    the hour which snatches off the nourishing day:
the frosts are mitigated by the west winds, summer tramples on
                                                    spring,
    [10] destined to die as soon as
apple-bearing autumn pours out its fruits, and soon
    sluggish winter comes running back.
But the swift moons make good the losses in the sky:
    we, when we drop down
[15] where father Aeneas, where rich Tullus and Ancus [went],
    dust and shadow are we.
Who knows whether to today's sum will be added tomorrow's
    time by the gods above?
Your heir's grasping hands will be cheated of everything
    [20] that you have given to your own dear self.
Once you are dead and on you has Minos
    passed his splendid judgements,
neither, Torquatus, will your pedigree, nor your eloquence nor
                                                     your
    piety bring you back;
[25] for Diana does not free from the infernal shadows
    chaste Hippolytus,
nor is Theseus strong enough to break Lethe's
    bonds for dear Perithous.

Now learn the Learning Vocabulary at GVE p. 443.

6D(iv) Publius Ovidius Naso

It was sweltering, and the day had passed noon;
    I placed my limbs to rest them in the middle of the bed.

One of the shutters was open, the other closed,
  giving the sort of light you usually find in woods,
[5] the sort of twilight that glimmers as Phoebus flees,
  or when the night has gone but day has not yet dawned.
This is the sort of lighting to give modest girls,
  under which shy chastity may hope to find a hiding-place.
Look! Corinna comes, covered in an unbelted tunic,
  [10] with her parted hair falling over her white neck,
just as, they say, beautiful Semiramis entered her bedroom
  and Lais, loved by many men.
I ripped off her tunic; being thin, it made little difference,
  but she still fought to be covered by the tunic;
[15] since she was fighting as one who did not wish to win, she
  was conquered without trouble by her own betrayal.
When she stood before my eyes with her clothing laid aside,
  on her whole body there was no blemish anywhere:
what shoulders, what arms I saw and touched!
  [20] Her beautiful breasts, how ready for squeezing!
How flat her stomach was beneath her well-formed bosom!
  What big hips! How youthful a thigh!
Why should I detail everything? Everything I saw was
                                                    praiseworthy,
  and I pressed her close to my own body, naked.
[25] Who does not know the rest? We both lay back exhausted.
  May my afternoons often turn out like this!

Now learn the Learning Vocabulary at *GVE* p. 446.